THE OFFICE OF INDIAN AFFAIRS, 1824-1880: HISTORICAL SKETCHES

THE LIBRARY OF AMERICAN INDIAN AFFAIRS

Titles Published or in Preparation:

The Decisions of the Indian Claims Commission (microfiche)

Index to the Decisions of the Indian Claims Commission

The Expert Testimony Before the Indian Claims Commission (microfiche)

Index to the Expert Testimony Before the Indian Claims Commission

Annual Reports of the Lake Mohonk Conferences of Friends of the Indian (microfiche)

Index to the Annual Reports of the Lake Mohonk Conferences of Friends of the Indian, Introduction by Dr. Larry E. Burgess, Dr. Laurence Hauptman

The Office of Indian Affairs: 1824-1880: Historical Sketches, by Edward E. Hill

American Indian Oral History Collection (audio tape), Dr. Joseph E. Cash, General Editor

Editorial Advisory Board

Dr. Robert Athearn, Professor of History, University of Colorado

Vine Deloria, Jr., author, attorney and member Standing Rock Sioux

Dr. William Sturtevant, Curator, Department of Anthropology, National Museum of Natural History, Smithsonian Institution

THE OFFICE OF INDIAN AFFAIRS,

1824—1880:

HISTORICAL SKETCHES

BY EDWARD E. HILL
Assistant Director of General Archives Division
National Archives and Records Service
General Services Administration

CLEARWATER PUBLISHING COMPANY, INC.

New York, New York

Library of Congress Cataloging in Publication Data

Hill, Edward E
  The Office of Indian Affairs, 1824-1880.

  Edition for 1967 published under title: Historical
sketches for jurisdictional and subject headings used
for the letters received by the Office of Indian
Affairs, 1824-80.
  1. United States. Bureau of Indian Affairs.
2. Indians of North America—Government relations—
1789-1869. 3. Indians of North America—Government
relations—1869-1934. I. Title.
E93.H64 1973   353.008′4′84   73-16321
ISBN 0-88354-105-X

CLEARWATER PUBLISHING COMPANY, INC.
792 Columbus Avenue, New York, New York 10025

Manufactured in the United States of America

FOREWORD

The historical sketches contained in this book were originally prepared to enable researchers to locate correspondence contained in Microcopy 234, *Letters Received by the Office of Indian Affairs, 1824-1880,* a microfilm publication of the National Archives and Records Service. The sketches provide brief histories of the field units of the Office of Indian Affairs for that period. Individual sketches are distributed by the Archives in pamphlet form to purchasers of selected rolls of microfilm from among the 962 rolls in the complete collection.

Taken together, the sketches comprise an important reference tool, yet until now the entire compilation has been available only in a very limited number of looseleaf copies within the National Archives. The present volume is the first complete edition of the sketches in a convenient form.

The introductory material and most of the sketches were prepared for the Archives by Edward E. Hill, who was also responsible for final revision. Sketches were contributed by Carmelita S. Ryan, Evans Walker, Richard Allen and Paula J. Butts. The Tribal and Jurisdictional Indexes were also prepared for the Archives, but their formats have been significantly revised for the sake of readability. In addition, reel numbers have been added to the Jurisdictional Index and page numbers have been added to both indexes. Several other editorial and stylistic changes have also been made with the reader and researcher in mind, and the Introduction has been heavily edited.

The publisher is indebted to Dr. Herman J. Viola, formerly of the National Archives and presently with the Smithsonian Institution, for suggesting publication of this book.

TABLE OF CONTENTS

*Dates indicate years of filing of correspondence.

INTRODUCTION

The Bureau of Indian Affairs* was established within the War Department on March 11, 1824 by order of the Secretary of War, John C. Calhoun (H. Doc. 146, 1st Sess., 19th Cong., p. 6) and operated informally within the War Department from 1824 until 1832. In 1832 Congress authorized the appointment of a Commissioner of Indian Affairs, reporting to the Secretary of War, to direct and manage all matters arising out of relations with the Indians (4 Stat. 564). In 1849 the Office of Indian Affairs, as the Commissioner's Office was then generally designated, was transferred from the War Department to the new Department of the Interior (9 Stat. 395) where it remains.

During the years 1824-80 the general correspondence of the Bureau was kept in files of letters received and in copybooks of letters sent. The letters received are arranged by names of field units of the Bureau—superintendencies and agencies—and a few subject headings. They have been reproduced by the National Archives and Records Service as Microcopy 234. The historical sketches contained in this book were prepared by the National Archives as an aid to users of the microfilm. The sketches provide brief histories of the major field units of the Bureau, including information concerning dates of establishment and discontinuance, tribal and geographical areas of responsibility, locations of headquarters, related units and names and dates of appointment of superintendents and agents.

There were two principal types of field jurisdictions—*superintendencies* and *agencies*. Superintendents had general responsibility for Indian affairs in a geographic area (usually a territory but often a larger area). Their duties included supervising relations among the Indian tribes within their jurisdiction and between these tribes and persons having business with them, and supervising the conduct and accounts of agents responsible for the affairs of one or more tribes. Until the 1870's most agents were responsible to a superintendent, but some reported directly to the Bureau of Indian Affairs in Washington. In the earlier years agents were virtually diplomatic representatives of the United States. They attempted to preserve or restore peace and often to induce the Indians to cede their land and move to areas less threatened by White encroachment. They also

---

*Although "Office of Indian Affairs" was the name commonly used until 1947, the term "Bureau" is used throughout to conform to current usage.

distributed money and goods as required by treaties and carried out other treaty provisions. Gradually, as the Indians were confined on reservations, the agents became more concerned with educating and "civilizing" them.

The system of superintendencies and agencies was already well established by 1824. (From 1789 until 1824 the administration of Indian affairs had been under the direct supervision of the Secretary of War, with the exception of the Government-operated system of factories for trade with the Indians, which from 1806 to 1822 was administered by a Superintendent of Indian Trade who was responsible to the Secretary.) It was a common practice for the governor of a territory to serve *ex officio* as Superintendent of Indian Affairs, particularly in the newly organized territories. A full-time superintendent was appointed for superintendencies located in unorganized areas or in states and those places where the duties of a superintendent were particularly arduous. Superintendents and agents were appointed by the President with the advice and consent of the Senate. The number of superintendencies and agencies was restricted by Congress. Particularly significant was an act of June 30, 1834 (4 Stat. 735), which specifically authorized certain superintendencies and agencies. The President was permitted to discontinue or to transfer agencies but was given no authority to establish additional agencies. An act of February 27, 1851 (9 Stat. 574), increased the number of agencies, taking into account the greatly expanded area of the country after the Mexican War and the settlement with Great Britain of the Oregon boundary.

The restrictions on the number of agencies were evaded, in a sense, by establishing subagencies, which could be done without Congressional approval when conditions demanded. Before 1834 subagents were normally assistants to a full agent. Later most subagents became, in effect, regular agents, though usually assigned to less important agencies and receiving less salary. Additional agencies were also established by the creation of "special agencies." Often special agents were appointed to carry out some special assignment, but in other cases they were simply regular agents appointed in addition to the authorized quota. Superintendents, particularly those in newly organized areas, often appointed special and acting agents of various kinds, sometimes without official authority to do so.

The Bureau employed other kinds of agents besides those in charge of agencies. "Purchasing" and "distributing" agents were concerned, respectively, with obtaining goods and with distributing either goods or money to the Indians. "Emigration" agents assisted in the removal of Indians from one area to another. "Enrolling" agents were appointed to prepare rolls of the Indians for annuity disbursements, land allotments or other purposes. There were also treaty commissioners, inspectors and special agents for specific missions (such as the investigation of the conduct of regular field employees or the settlement of claims).

Superintendents and agents in newly established jurisdictions were allowed a good deal of latitude. The assignment of agents, for instance, was often left to the discretion of the superintendent, and agents were permitted to select sites for agency headquarters, subject to approval. Many agents had no permanent headquarters and spent much of their time traveling. Gradually, as the Indians were settled on reservations, the agencies tended to become more fixed in location, better communications were established, and the superintendents and agents lost much of their independence of action. In 1869 most of the civilian agents were suspended and replaced by Army officers. In the following year most of the Army officers were relieved, and civilians were again appointed. It was always a common practice, however, to detail Army personnel to duty with the Indian Service when there were unusual disturbances or when civilian agents were unavailable. (In the lists of superintendents and agents in the accompanying sketches military ranks are indicated only for officers on active duty detailed to the Indian Service.) During the 1870's religious denominations were allowed to nominate persons to serve as agents.

Supervision of a number of agencies by one superintendency was discontinued during the 1870's, and by 1878 the last superintendency had been abolished. Thereafter all agents reported to the Bureau of Indian Affairs in Washington. Inspectors and special agents, however, were sometimes given some supervisory authority over agents.

THE FILES

To a large extent the records reproduced in Microcopy 234 consist of communications received from superintendents, agents, and other field officials of the Bureau. These communications relate to the general situation of the Indians, their population, education, health and medical care, and their agriculture and subsistence. They cover such matters of administrative concern as emigration, land allotments, annuity payments, depredations, claims, complaints, traders, buildings, supplies, employees and accounts. There are also instructions, requests, decisions, authorizations and other communications from the Secretary of the Interior and, before 1849, from the Secretary of War. Correspondence from the War Department after 1849 consists largely of copies of military reports. The Commissioner of the General Land Office often wrote concerning reservations and matters affecting the public domain. From the Second Auditor and other Treasury officials there is much correspondence concerning accounts and other financial matters. The President, members of Congress, and other officials made inquiries and transmitted other letters. There are vouchers, accounts and communications from merchants, manufacturers, shippers, bankers and other persons and firms having commerical relations with the Bureau. There are complaints, claims, requests, inquiries and other communications from Indians, attorneys and private citizens. There are applications for office and many other letters from persons with some interest in Indians or the activities of the Bureau.

Incoming correspondence was controlled by registers. The information concerning a letter that was entered in the register was usually also written on the back of the letter or on a covering sheet to form an "endorsement." The correspondence is arranged alphabetically by name of jurisdiction or by subject heading. The letters filed under the name of a jurisdiction relate to the affairs of that jurisdiction or the Indians assigned to it and include letters from other persons beside the agent or superintendent. A letter received from the agent of one agency may be filed under the name of another agency if it is primarily concerned with the affairs of the second agency.

Although a file heading was established for each superintendency, the Bureau did not establish a separate file heading for every agency. When there was no heading for an agency, the letters received were filed under the name of the superintendency responsible for the agency. This was the usual practice for the newer superintendencies and agencies in the Far West. For most of the agencies assigned to the older superintendencies, such as St. Louis, Michigan and Western, separate file headings were established. Theoretically in these cases letters relating specifically to an agency were filed under the name of that agency, and the superintendency heading was reserved for letters of more general concern. This distinction was not always possible, in practice, however, and letters concerning any agency may be found in either the superintendency file or the agency file.

Records were filed under the names of agencies both before they had been established and after they had been discontinued. For instance, records relating to settlement of the affairs of Indians who were moved to the jurisdiction of a new agency often continued to be filed under the name of the old agency. The name of a superintendency that was the same as that of a state or territory was often continued in use as a file heading for correspondence relating to the agencies in the state or territory after the superintendency itself had been discontinued. In one case, in 1876, a *Nebraska* heading was established, although there was not then nor had there ever been a Nebraska Superintendency.

Letters received before 1836 were originally filed in registry order with no jurisdictional breakdown, and were rearranged in the Bureau about 1910 by carrying the 1836 headings backward whether or not those headings reflected the actual field organization of the Bureau.

In a very few cases the file heading was a tribal designation rather than the name of an agency. Most of the "artificial jurisdiction" files set up in 1910 have been dismantled and the records interfiled with those for the jurisdictions to which they actually belong. Such artificial subheadings as "Treaty," "Exploration" and "Claim" have also been eliminated in an effort to restore the original headings. For certain jurisdictions, however, the Bureau filed many letters relating to Indian emigration and to land reserves in separate files designated "Emigration" and "Reserves," which follow the other correspondence. Not all letters relating to these subjects were filed separately, so it is also necessary to consult the main body of correspondence relating to a jurisdiction for full coverage of such subjects.

SUBJECT HEADINGS

In addition to the headings for jurisdictions there are five subject headings: *"Annuity Goods," "Centennial," "Schools," "Stocks"* and *"Miscellaneous."* Annuity goods such as blankets, clothing and agricultural equipment were furnished to the Indians in accordance with the terms of treaties, and their procurement and transportation could not be related to specific jurisdictions. *"Centennial"* relates to Indian exhibits at the U.S. International Exhibition at Philadelphia in 1876 and has only a brief chronological span. *"Stocks"* relates to securities of various types and to funds in which Indian monies were held in trust. Much additional information relating to the first four of these subjects may be found in the correspondence relating to the individual jurisdictions.

In the *"Miscellaneous"* category are letters relating to no special jurisdiction but to a multitude of subjects such as the service as a whole; general policy in the purchases of goods; appointments; the administration of the central office; medals for Indian chiefs; persons captured by the Indians; Indians in places were the Bureau had no field representatives or over whom the Federal Government had no jurisdiction; and many matters affecting several jurisdictions. In theory, at least, letters filed under *"Miscellaneous"* could not appropriately be placed in any other category. The *"Miscellaneous"* category is not one to be ignored as containing only odds and ends; in it are documents that are of very great importance because of their concern with policy and their broad application.

Within each heading the letters are arranged by year and then alphabetically by initial letter of surname or, for certain officials, under letters indicating their offices. Letters from the Secretary of the Interior, for example, were alphabetized under "I," from the Secretary of War under "W" or "S," from the President under "P" and from the Second Auditor under "A" or "S." Early correspondence from these officials, on the other hand, was often alphabetized by their surnames. Correspondence from agents and superintendents was usually filed under the name of the individual. The major exception is correspondence from territorial governors serving as *ex officio* superintendents which was usually filed according to the name of the territory. Letters from the governor of Wisconsin Territory, for example, were filed under "W." For a very brief period (April to December, 1877) correspondence from agents and superintendents was registered according to the name of the jurisdiction. Letters from Indian groups were usually filed under the initial letter of the name of the tribe, and letters from business firms under a letter indicating the name of the company. The letters "I" and "J" are combined.

Within each letter of the alphabet, letters were arranged by date of letter, until 1836. After 1836, when the use of file numbers began, they were arranged by file numbers that were assigned as they were registered. The letters in each alphabetical section of the register were numbered sequentially. Thus, the letters received from persons whose surname began with "A" were designated "A1," 'A2," etc. There was no regard for the jurisdictions involved when these numbers were assigned. The letters were then coded for filing, and "A1" may have been designated for filing under "St. Louis" and "A2" under "Winnebago."

The period during which a series of numbers was continued varied. Sometimes several years went by before a new series beginning with "1" was started for each letter of the alphabet. In 1859, 1872 and 1873, because the numbers were started over in the middle of the year, there are two sets of numbers and, in 1873, some duplicate numbers. An attempt was made to arrange the records for these years with the earlier series of numbers for each letter of the alphabet ahead of the later sets, that is, to keep them in the same order in which they were registered. Since letters were registered when they were received, a letter written at the end of one year may have been registered and filed with the correspondence for the following year.

There are among the records some letters that were not registered, and many letters that were registered are no longer with the records. Some of the letters removed are noted in the registers, and cross-references to some are to be found in the files, but for many there is no indication of their disposition. Beginning in 1834 the referral of letters outside of the Bureau was usually noted in the register.

Some letters removed from the main series of letters received were filed with various special series of records established in the Bureau. These include the Special Files—each file relating to some particular subject that usually involved an investigation (reproduced in Microcopy 574); Special Cases, mainly concerned with disputes over land; Ratified Treaty File; Unratified Treaty File; Executive Order File; Inspectors' File; Irregularly Shaped Papers; and papers retained for some special reason in one of the divisions. Some have been placed with related papers in later correspondence series. Cross-references were usually, but by no means always, left with the records to indicate these removals and the new location. The cross-references have been microfilmed with the records.

Other letters have been lost or destroyed over the years in different ways. For many years the Bureau sent original documents to the Government Printing Office, and some were either not returned or were destroyed as no longer needed. This is especially true of annual reports received from superintendents and agents and regularly printed as supplements to the Commissioners' annual reports. Original papers were often sent to Congressional committees from which they were sometimes sent to the Government Printing Office for printing as parts of printed Congressional documents. Very rarely were these originals returned to the Bureau files. Originals instead of copies were often sent to the Courts when requested and presumably were filed with their case records. One notable series of such case records, which contains many original documents of interest, is the Indian Depredation series among the records of the U.S. Court of Claims.

Before the National Archives was established, the Bureau, finding in its files letters signed by famous statesmen such as Andrew Jackson or Samuel Houston, would sometimes extract the letters and send them to the Library of Congress for preservation, sometimes leaving in the file a record of the transfer and sometimes not. Other letters have in years long past found their way through unknown channels into private possession. Some turn up occasionally in catalogs of autograph sales and some, fortunately, have now passed into the manuscript collections of historical and research libraries. Often the user of the film will not be aware of missing items unless he carefully checks against the registers of letters received. When the missing items were enclosures, they were not registered at all.

Maps, enclosed with letters, because of their size and special use, were usually removed from the files and maintained separately. These maps are now kept separately in the National Archives Building and are described in National Archives Special List 13, *List of Cartographic Records of the Bureau of Indian Affairs.* Maps mentioned in letters as enclosures but not found with the letters are likely to be among these records. Those maps that are still with the correspondence have been microfilmed.

The records have been microfilmed in the order established by the Bureau, which is the order in which they are kept in the National Archives. Usually the endorsement of a letter is filmed before the letter itself. Enclosures are filmed chronologically, numerically, or in some other simple order following the letter. Enclosures may or may not have file numbers. Some have several file numbers including those of other agencies that may have handled them. Ordinarily everything appearing between one endorsement and the next is regarded as part of the same document.

The *Registers of Letters Received*, which constitute an alphabetical and chronological control of the letters themselves, have also been microfilmed as Microfilm Publication 18. Transcripts of the outgoing letters of the Bureau, which complement the incoming letters, are in bound volumes with indexes of addressees. The letters were recorded in a single chronological series until 1869, after which they were recorded under broad subjects, such as "land" and "finance." These letterbooks have been microfilmed as Microfilm Publication 21. The letters received during the period 1881-1907 are arranged chronologically without any jurisdictional breakdown. They are available for use in the National Archives.

A careful distinction must be made between records of the central office of the Bureau and records of the various field offices. The letters reproduced in Microcopy 234 are all records that were received and maintained in Washington. Each superintendency usually maintained comparable series of records, which to some extent duplicate the central office records. Therefore, when a particular letter that passed between the central office and a field office is missing from the records of either, a copy of it may be among the records of the other office.

Some of the records of the Bureau's field offices for the years 1824-80 are now in the National Archives Building. Others are in the regional Federal

Archives and Records Centers. Still others are scattered in various manuscript depositories throughout the country. Some of the records of field offices that are now in the National Archives Building are available in other microfilm publications—*Cherokee Agency in Tennessee, 1801-35* (Microcopy 208); *Michigan Superintendency, 1814-51* (Microcopy 1); *Oregon Superintendency, 1848-73* (Microcopy 2); and *Washington Superintendency, 1853-74* (Microcopy 5).

The records reproduced in Microcopy 234 and the other series of records in the National Archives Building mentioned above are part of Record Group 75, Records of the Bureau of Indian Affairs. There are related records in Record Group 107, Records of the Office of the Secretary of War and in Record Group 48, Records of the Office of the Secretary of the Interior. Additional information about these and other related publications is contained in "The American Indian," a select catalog of National Archives Microfilm Publications available from the National Archives, Washington, D.C. 20408.

ALASKA AGENCY
1873-1874

The Alaska Agency was established on April 5, 1873 with the appointment of Frederick S. Hall as special agent. He was instructed to suppress illegal manufacturing of liquor and to stop the sale of liquor to the natives of Alaska. Although the headquarters of the agency was at St. Michaels, the agent spent much time traveling.

On November 8, 1873, the Alaska Agency was abolished after the First Comptroller of the Treasury decided that authorization did not exist for the use of Bureau funds in Alaska. Hall, however, who did not receive word of this decision until May 25, 1874, remained on duty through the winter.

Primary responsibility for the Alaskan natives was held by the Army until 1877. From that date until 1879, when the Navy took charge, the only Government official in Alaska was a collector of customs. A civil government was established in 1884. The following year a General Agent for Education, responsible to the Office of Education, was appointed to supervise the education of Alaskan children; gradually responsibility for Alaskan natives generally was assumed by the Office of Education in the Interior Department.

ANNUITY GOODS
1856-1878

Annuity goods such as blankets and agricultural tools, were distributed to Indian tribes in conformance with the provisions of treaties. Letters received filed under the heading "Annuity Goods" concern for the most part the procurement of these goods by the Bureau. Correspondence concerning the actual distribution to the Indians was usually filed with the correspondence relating to the respective agencies and superintendencies. For the period before 1856 similar correspondence concerning annuity goods was filed under "Miscellaneous." No similar records concerning annuity goods for the years 1879 and 1880 have been found.

APALACHICOLA SUBAGENCY
1826-1842

The Apalachicola Subagency, which was responsible for the Seminole Indians living along the Apalachicola River in Florida, was established under the Florida Superintendency on January 10, 1826, with John Phagan as subagent.

Phagan was transferred to another post in 1830, but no one replaced him at the subagency until 1833. The subagency was abolished on June 30, 1834, in anticipation of the removal of the Indians to the Indian Territory. Representatives of the Bureau of Indian Affairs, mainly disbursing officers, continued to be assigned to the Apalachicola region, however, until 1839. Thereafter, Indian affairs in that area were handled by the Army.

With the exception of a few letters concerning Indian lands on the Apalachicola received during 1841 and 1842 and filed under "Apalachicola Reserves," correspondence relating to the Apalachicola Indians in Florida after 1835 was filed under the heading "Florida." Those Indians from the Apalachicola who had been removed were merged with other Seminole groups. After the "Florida" classification was discontinued in 1850, correspondence concerning Apalachicola Indians was filed under "Seminole."

SUBAGENTS

Name	Date of Appointment
John Phagan	Jan. 10, 1826
William S. Pope	Apr. 9, 1833

ARIZONA SUPERINTENDENCY 1863-1880

The Arizona Superintendency was established in 1863 with the organization of the Territory of Arizona. Arizona previously had been part of New Mexico Territory. Although it was customary for the Governor to act as *ex officio* superintendent for at least several years after a Territory was established, in Arizona the superintendent was always a separate official. Headquarters for the superintendency was established originally at La Paz, but in 1869 it was moved to Arizona City.

Between 1863 and 1865 the superintendent established a number of agencies for various tribes including the following permanent agencies: Gila River (for Pima, Papago, Maricopa and Tame Apache Indians), Papago, Colorado River (for Yavapai, Walapai, Havasupai, Mojave, Yuma, scattered Apache and other small tribes) and Moqui Pueblo. Between 1871 and 1876 the several Apache agencies included the Rio Verde, Camp Apache, Camp Grant, Chiricahua and San Carlos. By 1876 all of these had been consolidated into the San Carlos Agency. The Navajo Agency, although located most of the time at Fort Defiance, Arizona, was throughout this period considered an agency of New Mexico.

After the Arizona Superintendency was abolished in 1873, agents reported directly to the Bureau of Indian Affairs in Washington. Until the change of filing systems in 1881, however, incoming correspondence relating to the separate agencies in Arizona was still filed under the heading "Arizona" instead of under the names of the individual agencies.

See also New Mexico, California, Utah, and Colorado Superintendencies and Pima Agency. There are also field records of the Arizona Superintendency and the Moqui Pueblo Agency among the records of the Bureau of Indian Affairs in the National Archives. *

GILA RIVER (PIMA) AGENCY

In 1864 an agency was established for the Papago Indians. The following year the Pima, Maricopa and "Tame" Apache were added to its jurisdiction and it was called the Pima, Papago and Maricopa Agency. In 1869 it was located at Sacaton, Pinal County, on the Gila River Reservation and thereafter it was called

---

*References to "the National Archives" are to the National Archives Building in Washington, D.C. The official name of the archives branch of the General Services Administration is "The National Archives and Records Service."

the Gila River Agency. After 1875 the agency was known as the Pima Agency. Between 1871 and 1876 the Papago Indians were under a separate agency. The Pima Agency continued to operate beyond 1880. There is correspondence concerning an earlier special agency for the Pima and Maricopa Indians which is filed under "Pima." *See also the Tucson Agency of the New Mexico Superintendency.*

PAPAGO AGENCY

The Papago Agency was located at Tucson from 1871 to 1876. Before and after this period the Papago Indians were assigned to the Gila River (Pima) Agency.

COLORADO RIVER AGENCY

This agency, established in 1864 to handle Indian affairs in the Colorado River region, had its headquarters on the Colorado River Reservation near Parker, Arizona. There were many tribes in the area, including the Yavapai, Walapai, Havasupai, Yuma and Mojave. The agency continued to operate beyond 1880.

MOQUI PUEBLO AGENCY

The agency for the Moqui Pueblo (now called Hopi) Indians was established in 1869 at Fort Wingate, Arizona. In 1871 the agency was moved to Fort Defiance, and in 1874 it was moved again about 75 miles west to the Moqui Reservation. From October, 1876 until December, 1877, while there was no agent assigned to the Moqui Pueblo Agency, its business was assigned to the Navajo agent. The Moqui Pueblo Agency was consolidated with the Navajo Agency for the years 1883-99, after which it again became independent.

APACHE AGENCIES

The Apache Indians were located principally in the southeastern quarter of Arizona. The Camp Grant Agency, established in 1871, was abolished in 1873 at the time the Indians were moved to San Carlos. The Rio Verde Agency existed from 1872 to 1875, when these Indians also were moved to San Carlos. In 1872 the Chiricahua Agency was established to take charge of the Indians led by Cochise. It was located successively at several places in the southeastern corner of the Territory. In 1876, when the Chiricahua were moved to San Carlos with the other Apache, the agency was abolished. The White Mountain Reservation was established in 1872 with two divisions—one under the control of the Camp Apache Agency and one under the control of the San Carlos Agency. In 1875 the San Carlos Agency assumed control over both divisions, and by 1876 it was in charge of all the Apache Indians in Arizona. Apache Indians from New Mexico were also moved to San Carlos.

SPECIAL COMMISSIONERS

Vincent Colyer, Secretary of the Board of Indian Commissioners, visited Arizona in 1871 in an attempt to make peace with the warring Apache Indians. The following year Gen. Oliver O. Howard was sent as a special commissioner to pacify the Apache in accordance with President Grant's peace policy.

SUPERINTENDENTS

Name	Date of Appointment
George D. Poston	Mar. 13, 1863
George W. Leihy	Mar. 3, 1865
George W. Dent	Aug. 9, 1866
Bvt. Col. George W. Andrews	July 7, 1869
Herman Bendell	Jan. 12, 1871
John A. Tonner	Mar. 26, 1873

AGENTS

Gila River (Pima) Agency

Name	Date of Appointment
M. O. Davidson (special)	Began service as Papago agent, Feb. 24, 1864. Sept. 12, 1865, appointed agent for Pima and Maricopa.
Levi Ruggles (special)	Apr. 28, 1866
Capt. F. E. Grossman (special)	July 23, 1869
Edward Palmer (special)	Feb. 8, 1871
J. H. Stout (special)	May 25, 1871
J. H. Stout (agent)	July 23, 1872
Charles Hudson	Mar. 1, 1876
J. H. Stout	Oct. 6, 1876
Abram B. Ludlam	June 30, 1879

Papago Agency

R. A. Wilbur (special)	Feb. 8, 1871
R. A. Wilbur (agent)	July 23, 1872
John M. Cornyn	Jan. 22, 1875

13

AGENTS (cont.)

Colorado River Agency

John C. Dunn (special)	July 1, 1864
John Feudge (special)	Nov. 7, 1865
Lt. J. W. Keller (special)	July 8, 1869
Lt. Helenus Dodt (special)	July 28, 1869
John A. Tonner (special)	Mar. 10, 1871
John A. Tonner (agent)	July 23, 1872
E. S. Hammond	Mar. 26, 1873
John A. Tonner	July 15, 1873
William E. Morford	Sept. 27, 1875
John C. Mallory, Jr.	July 12, 1877
Henry R. Mallory	Aug. 1, 1878
Jonathan Biggs	May 27, 1880

Moqui Pueblo Agency

Capt. A. D. Palmer (special)	Aug. 20, 1869
William D. Crothers (special)	Oct. 22, 1870
William D. Crothers (agent)	July 23, 1872
William S. Defrees	June 18, 1873
William B. Truax	Mar. 19, 1875
Alexander G. Irvine (acting)	Oct. 24, 1876
William R. Mateer	Dec. 3, 1877
Edward S. Merritt (acting)	Began service Nov. 2, 1879
Galen Eastman (acting)	Nov. 21, 1879
Milo A. Boynton	Appointed Feb. 2, 1880, but did not serve
Capt. F. T. Bennett (acting)	Began service July 1, 1880
John H. Sullivan	June 25, 1880

Camp Grant Agency

Lt. Royal E. Whitman (special)	Nov. 13, 1871
Edward C. Jacobs (special)	Mar. 4, 1872
Charles F. Larrabee (special)	Dec. 9, 1872

Rio Verde Agency

Josephus W. Williams (special)	Mar. 4, 1872
Oliver Chapman (special)	Sept. 25, 1874

Chiricahua Agency

Thomas J. Jeffords (special)	Sept. 16, 1872
Thomas J. Jeffords (agent)	July 13, 1874

Camp Apache Agency

Milan Soule (acting)	Aug. 11, 1872
James E. Roberts (special)	Sept. 28, 1872
James E. Roberts (agent)	July 13, 1874
William E. Morford	May 11, 1875

San Carlos Agency

George H. Stevens (acting)	Sept. 1, 1872
Charles F. Larrabee (special)	Transferred from Camp Grant Jan., 1873
Maj. W. W. Brown (acting)	June, 1873
John P. Clum (special)	Feb. 26, 1874
John P. Clum (agent)	July 13, 1874
Henry L. Hart	June 22, 1877
Capt. Adna R. Chaffee (acting)	Began service July 19, 1879
Joseph C. Tiffany	Apr. 22, 1880

ARKANSAS SUPERINTENDENCY
1824-1834

The Arkansas Superintendency was established in 1819, the same year that the Territory of Arkansas was established. The Superintendency was under the immediate supervision of the Secretary of War until the Bureau of Indian Affairs was established in 1824. The Territorial Governor at Little Rock acted as *ex officio* superintendent throughout the existence of the superintendency. The principal Indian tribes in Arkansas were Cherokee, Quapaw and Choctaw. Some Osage, Shawnee, Caddo and Delaware Indians occasionally entered the Territory, but they were regarded as intruders not as residents.

Even before 1819 the War Department had designated Indian agents for the Arkansas area. In 1807 the factor at the Government Indian factory (trading post) at Arkansas Post on the Arkansas River was appointed temporary agent for the Indians "at Arkansas." In 1813 an assistant agent subordinate to the Cherokee agent in Tennessee was appointed for Arkansas. An assistant agent responsible to the Governor of the Territory of Missouri was appointed for the Indians of Arkansas in 1817 and the following year was made a full agent. The agency continued after the Arkansas Superintendency was established, but by 1823 it was restricted to the supervision of the Cherokee Indians in Arkansas. Most of the records concerning this agency are filed under the heading "Cherokee West" rather than with the records concerning the Arkansas Superintendency itself.

An agency for the Choctaw living west of the Mississippi River established in 1825 remained under the Arkansas Superintendency until 1828. Most of the records concerning this agency are filed under "Choctaw." Although most of the Quapaw in Arkansas were removed to the Caddo or Red River Agencies on the Red River west of Arkansas in 1825 and 1826, some of them soon returned to Arkansas. Some of the records concerning these Indians are filed under "Neosho."

By 1834 most of the Indians had been removed from Arkansas to areas farther west. In that year the Arkansas Superintendency and the agencies for the Cherokee and Choctaw were abolished. The Cherokee, Choctaw, Quapaw and other tribes living in the area west of Arkansas were placed under the new Western Superintendency.

See also Western and St. Louis Superintendencies and Cherokee, Choctaw, Caddo, Red River, Osage and Neosho Agencies.

GOVERNORS AND *EX OFFICIO* SUPERINTENDENTS

Name	Date of Appointment
James Miller	Mar. 3, 1819
George Izard	Mar. 24, 1825
John Pope	Mar. 9, 1829

BLACKFEET AGENCY
1855-1869

The Blackfeet Agency was established in 1855 at Fort Benton in the present State of Montana. The agency, under the supervision of the Central Superintendency, had jurisdiction over Blackfeet (Siksika), Piegan, Blood (Kainah) and Grosventre Indians. These Indians previously had been assigned to a special agent appointed by the Governor of the Territory of Washington.

When the Dakota Superintendency was established in 1861 the Blackfeet Agency was claimed by both the Dakota and the Central Superintendencies. In 1862 the agency was definitely assigned to the Dakota Superintendency, but in 1863 it was assigned to the new Idaho Superintendency. The following year, 1864, when the Montana Superintendency was established, the agency was assigned to it.

In 1869, as a result of treaties negotiated the previous year by Special Agent William Cullen, a new Blackfeet Agency was built on the Teton River about 35 miles from Fort Shaw, Montana. The following year the Milk River (later Fort Peck) Agency was established for the Grosventre Indians. In 1876 the Blackfeet Agency was moved from the Teton River to Badger Creek, and in 1879 it was moved to another location on the south bank of Badger Creek.

There is only one letter filed under "Blackfeet" for 1869. Beginning in that year most correspondence relating to the Blackfeet Agency was filed under the heading "Montana." After the Montana Superintendency was abolished in 1873, the Blackfeet agent reported directly to the Bureau of Indian Affairs in Washington.

See also Washington, Central, Dakota, Idaho and Montana Superintendencies.

AGENTS

Name	*Date of Appointment*
Edwin A. C. Hatch	Mar. 3, 1855
Alfred J. Vaughn	May 9, 1857
Luther Pease	Apr. 22, 1861
Henry W. Reed	Apr. 4, 1862
Gad E. Upson	Oct. 13, 1863
George B. Wright	Apr. 10, 1866
Nathaniel Pope (acting)	Aug. 25, 1868
Lt. William B. Pease	June 11, 1869
M. M. McCauley	Sept. 9, 1870

17

Jesse Armitage	Feb. 25, 1871
William F. Ensign	July 23, 1872
Richard F. May	Nov. 6, 1873
John S. Wood	Oct. 24, 1874
John Young	Oct. 20, 1876

CADDO AGENCY
1824-1842

"Caddo Agency" is another designation for the Red River Agency. Most of the correspondence relating to this agency that was received by the Bureau until 1831 is filed under the heading "Red River." A few letters, chiefly relating to the Quapaw Indians, are filed under the heading "Caddo" for the years 1824-30. In 1831 the "Red River" heading was discontinued, and thereafter correspondence concerning the agency was filed under "Caddo." This was a change in filing procedure only and reflects no change in the operations of the agency itself.

In 1820 or 1821 the agency that had been located at Natchitoches since 1804 was moved to Sulphur Fork on the Red River; thereafter it was known as the Red River Agency. In 1825 the agency was moved about 25 miles farther down the river to Caddo Prairie. The "Great Raft" caused the flooding of this site, and in 1831 the agency was moved about 50 miles still farther down the river to Peach Tree (or Orchard) Bluff on the Bayou Pierre Channel, south of the site of Shreveport, Louisiana. The agency was not assigned to any superintendency, and the agent reported directly to the Bureau of Indian Affairs in Washington.

The principal tribes of the agency were Caddo and Quapaw. Most of the Quapaw returned to their old home on the Arkansas River in 1830, but many of them came back to the Red River in 1833, even though they now had a reservation in Indian Territory. There were also Pascagoula, Apalachee, Biloxi, Koasati, Taensa, Alabama, Shawnee and Delaware Indians, and members of other small bands, including roaming Indians from Texas (then part of Mexico).

The Caddo Agency was discontinued in 1834. Provision was made for a military officer to assume the duties of the agent. Agent Jehiel Brooks reported, however, that the officer designated, Lt. Col. Josiah Vose, had refused to take charge of the agency and that he had closed the agency office on September 15, 1834. Thereafter, since there was no regular agent for the Indians in Louisiana, the superintendent of the Western Superintendency was sometimes entrusted with duties relating to them. The correspondence filed under the heading "Caddo" from 1835 through 1842 relates mainly to the payment of annuities to the Caddo Indians. Following a treaty negotiated in 1835 most of the Caddo moved to Texas. In 1859 they were moved to the Wichita Agency in Indian Territory. Eventually most of the Quapaw settled on their reservation in Indian Territory under the Neosho Agency.

See also Arkansas and Western Superintendencies and Red River, Choctaw, Osage, Neosho, Texas and Wichita Agencies.

AGENTS

Name	*Date of Appointment*
George Gray	Dec. 1, 1819
Thomas Griffith	Mar. 18, 1829
Jehiel Brooks	Notified Mar. 29, 1830

CALIFORNIA SUPERINTENDENCY 1849-1880

The California Superintendency was established in 1852. Between 1847 and 1849 subagents appointed by the military governor served in California. The military appointees were John Sutter, Mariano Vallejo and J. D. Hunter. In April, 1849 the Bureau of Indian Affairs established a subagency for the Indians of the San Joaquin and Sacramento Valleys. In November of the same year this subagency was divided into two subagencies, one for the Sacramento Valley and one for the San Joaquin Valley. John Sutter, the appointee for the Sacramento Subagency, declined the appointment and this subagency was never in operation. The San Joaquin Subagency, with headquarters on the Merced River Reservation, was in charge of the Indians scattered on several reservations in the valley and continued to operate until the beginning of 1852. The Salt Lake Agency, also established in 1849, was originally considered to be in California. The boundary between Utah and California was soon established, however, and the

Salt Lake Agency was never directly concerned with Indian affairs in California.

In September, 1850 three agents were appointed for California. They worked together through April, 1851, acting as commissioners rather than agents. On May 1, 1851, they divided California into three districts—Northern, Middle and Southern—and drew lots for assignments. These districts operated for a time after the California Superintendency was established in 1852, but they were discontinued on March 26, 1853 by order of the Commissioner of Indian Affairs.

Since California had been admitted as a State before the California Superintendency was established, there was no Territorial Governor to serve as *ex officio* superintendent, and a separate official was appointed from the beginning. The headquarters of the superintendency was at San Francisco.

There were many small tribes and bands living in California including Tejon, Tule (Tulareños), Mono, Kern River (Tubatulabal), Wikchamni, Nomelaki, Kings River, Fresno, Kawia, Nuimok, Noi-sas, Wailaki, Yupu, Yuki, Klamath, Hupa, Saia, Mattole, Pit River, Redwood (Whilkut), Wappo, Yokaia (Ukiah), Kianamaras, Pomo, Salan Pomo (Potter), Concow (Konkau) and Mission Indians.

The first superintendent, Edward Beale, introduced a program of establishing reservations on which Indians were to be trained in the ways of "civilization." These reservations, located on either Government or on private land, differed from the earlier reservations or reserves that were merely tracts of land recognized as belonging to the Indians. Subagents, and later, agents were gradually appointed to supervise the Indians who were settled on these reservations. The regularly established agencies and subagencies in operation between 1854 and 1860 were the Tejon (Sebastian), Nome Lackee and Klamath Agencies and the Fresno and Mendocino Subagencies. Many other subagencies and special agencies were established by the superintendent, but they were principally for Indians not living on a reservation—most notably the Mission Indians of southern California and the Mojave, Yuma and other Indians living in the vicinity of the Colorado River. There were also special agents assigned to reservations before formal agencies or subagencies were established.

In 1860 the California Superintendency, together with all the agencies and subagencies under it, was abolished. Indian affairs in California were then entrusted to two superintending agents, one for a Northern District and one for a Southern District. The boundary line between the two districts was the southern boundary of Marin, Sonoma, Solano, Sacramento and El Dorado Counties. Supervisors, responsible to one or the other of the superintending agents, were put in charge of the various reservations. The Nome Lackee, Round Valley (Nome Cult), Klamath, Mendocino and Smith River Reservations were in the Northern District. The Tejon, Tule River, Fresno and Kings River Reservations were in the Southern District, which was also responsible for the Mission Indians and—until the establishment of the Arizona Superintendency in 1863—for the Indians of the Colorado River area. Headquarters of the Southern

District was at San Francisco. Headquarters of the Northern District was at Red Bluff in 1860, moved to Yuba City and then to San Francisco in 1861, and to Yreka in 1864.

The California Superintendency was re-established in 1864, with headquarters at San Francisco. The two superintending agencies were discontinued and new agencies were established. In operation between 1864 and 1880 were the Smith River, Round Valley, Tule River, Hoopa Valley and Mission Agencies.

The California Superintendency was abolished permanently on July 1, 1873. Thereafter the agents in California reported directly to the Bureau of Indian Affairs in Washington. Until the change of filing systems in 1881, however, correspondence was still filed under the heading "California" instead of under the names of the individual agencies.

See also Utah, Arizona, Nevada and Oregon Superintendencies.

TEJON (SEBASTIAN) AGENCY

The Tejon or Sebastian Agency (a subagency for a few months) was formally established in 1855. There had been temporary agents on the Tejon Reservation, however, since its establishment by the superintendent in 1853. Tejon Indians lived on the reservation located at the southern end of the San Joaquin Valley at the junction of the Sierra Nevada Mountains and the Coast Range. In 1857 some Tule (Tulareños) Indians were moved to the reservation, and in 1858 a farm for other Tule Indians was established on the Tule River. The Tejon Agency operated until 1860, when the Tejon and Tule River Indians were assigned to the Southern District. By 1864 the Indians at Tejon had been moved to Tule River and the reservation had been abandoned.

NOME LACKEE AGENCY

The Nome Lackee Agency, a subagency until 1856, was established by the superintendent in 1854. In addition to Nomelaki Indians, the agency was responsible for Nuimok, Noi-sas, Wailaki, Yupu, Yuki and other Indians. The agency was located on the Nome Lackee Reservation, on the western side of the Sacramento Valley about 20 miles west of Tehama. After 1856 the agency was also responsible for the Nome Cult farm located about 60 miles southwest of Nome Lackee. The Nome Lackee Agency continued to operate until the California agencies were discontinued in 1860 when the Indians of Nome Lackee and Nome Cult were assigned to the Northern District. Most of the Indians had left Nome Lackee by 1862 and Nome Cult, now known as the Round Valley, became the main reservation for the Indians of the Sacramento Valley.

KLAMATH AGENCY

The Klamath Agency, established in 1856, was responsible principally for the Klamath Indians living on the Klamath Reservation which had been established in 1855 at the mouth of the Klamath River. The agency also had some responsibility for the Indians of Hoopa Valley, Smith River and other places in northern California. When the California agencies were discontinued in 1860, these Indians were assigned to the Northern District. After a flood in 1862 the Klamath Reservation was abandoned. The Smith River Reservation was intended to replace the Klamath Reservation, but few Klamath Indians actually moved there. Most of them were later attached to the Hoopa Valley Agency. The Klamath Agency in California should not be confused with the better known Klamath Agency in Oregon.

FRESNO SUBAGENCY

The Fresno Subagency was not formally established until 1856, although the superintendent had designated a subagent in 1854. The subagency was responsible for 23 small bands of Indians known collectively as Fresno Indians living on the Fresno Reservation or Farm established in 1854 on the Fresno River, and for the Indians living on the Kings River Farm. The Fresno Subagency continued to operate until the closing of the California agencies in 1860, when the two farms were assigned to the Southern District. Fresno and Kings River were abandoned during 1861 and 1862. Later some of the Indians moved to Tule River.

MENDOCINO SUBAGENCY

The Mendocino Subagency was established in 1855. It was responsible for the Yokiah (Ukiah), Wappo, Pomo, Salan Pomo, Kianamaras, Redwood (Whilkut) and other Indians living on the Mendocino Reservation. This reservation, established in 1855, was located on the coast in Mendocino County about 50 miles south of Cape Mendocino. The Mendocino Subagency continued to operate until the California agencies were discontinued in 1860, when the reservation was assigned to the Northern District. In 1864 the Indians moved to Round Valley and the Mendocino Reservation was abandoned.

SMITH RIVER AGENCY

The Smith River Agency was established in 1864. It was responsible for the Indians living on the Smith River Reservation, established in 1862 to replace the Klamath Reservation. Actually few Klamath Indians moved there, and the agency was responsible for Wailaki, Saia, Mattole and other Indians who had formerly lived along the Eel River and at other places in Humboldt County. The Smith River Reservation was located above Crescent City in the northwestern corner of the State. The Smith River Agency was abolished in 1869 and the Indians moved to the Hoopa Valley Agency.

HOOPA VALLEY AGENCY

The Hoopa Valley Agency was established in 1864 for the Indians living on the new Hoopa Valley Reservation on the Trinity River near its junction with the Klamath River. In addition to the Hoopa (Hupa) Indians, the agency was responsible for the Klamath Indians who lived off the reservation in the vicinity of the old Klamath Reservation and, after 1869, for the Indians moved from Smith River. The Hoopa Valley Agency continued to operate beyond 1880.

ROUND VALLEY AGENCY

The Round Valley Agency was established in 1865. Round Valley, known as Nome Cult until 1861, is located in the Coast Range in the northeastern corner of Mendocino County. A farm attached to the Nome Lackee Agency had been established there as early as 1856. After Nome Lackee was abandoned in 1862, Round Valley became the main reservation for the Indians of the Sacramento Valley area. The Round Valley Agency was also responsible for the Indians who until 1864 had lived on the Mendocino Reservation. The individual bands at Round Valley included Yuki, Yupu, Pit River, Konkau (Concow), Yokaia (Ukiah), Wailaki, Redwood (Whilkut), Pomo, Salan Pomo (Potter Valley), Little Lake Valley and other Indians. The Round Valley Agency continued in operation beyond 1880.

TULE RIVER AGENCY

The Tule River Agency was established in 1864. A farm attached to the Tejon Agency had been established on the Tule River as early as 1858. In 1863 the farm was made a reservation and the Indians formerly at Tejon and on the Kings River were moved there. The individual bands at Tule River included Tule (Tulareños), Tejon, Kings River, Mono, Kawia, Wikchamni and Kern River (Tubatulabal). In 1876 the agency was moved from the private farm on which it had been located to a new reservation on the South Fork of the Tule River in southeastern Tulare County. The Tule River Agency continued in operation beyond 1880.

MISSION AGENCY

The Mission Agency was established as a special agency in 1865 for the scattered bands of Indians known collectively as Mission Indians because of their former connection with the Franciscan missions. As early as 1857 special agents had been assigned to the Mission Indians from time to time. Even earlier, one of the three agents appointed in 1850 had assumed general responsibility for the

Indians of southern California. Until 1870 there were no reservations for the Mission Indians, and the agent spent much of his time traveling to the various bands. In 1870 the San Pasqual and Pala Reservations were established in San Diego County with the agency located at Temecula. By 1871 the agent usually stayed on the San Pasqual Reservation. The reservations were abandoned in 1871 and the agency was discontinued. Beginning in 1875 new reservations were established at various locations in southern California. Between 1873 and 1878 several special agents and commissioners were appointed for the Mission Indians, but there were periods when no agent was on duty. These agents usually made their headquarters at Los Angeles. In 1878 a regular agency was established at San Bernardino for the Mission Indians. The Mission Agency continued to operate beyond 1880.

SPECIAL AGENTS AND COMMISSIONERS

John Ross Browne was appointed in 1857 as special agent to investigate Indian affairs in Oregon, Washington and California. His investigation in California in 1858 resulted in the dismissal of Superintendent Henley. In the same year Special Agent George Bailey investigated the conduct of Indian affairs in California. Special Agent Robert J. Stevens made an extensive investigation of affairs in California in 1866.

AGENTS BEFORE THE ESTABLISHMENT OF THE CALIFORNIA SUPERINTENDENCY

Name	Date of Appointment
Adam Johnston (subagent)	Apr. 13, 1849
George Barbour	Sept. 30, 1850
Oliver M. Wozencraft	Sept. 28, 1850
Redick McKee	Sept. 30, 1850
Samuel Sheldon	Sept. 1, 1852
Benjamin Wilson	Sept. 1, 1852

SUPERINTENDENTS, 1852-60

Edward F. Beale	Mar. 5, 1852
Thomas J. Henley	May 31, 1854
James Y. McDuffie	Mar. 9, 1859

SUPERINTENDING AGENTS, NORTHERN DISTRICT

John A. Driebelbis	June 21, 1860
George M. Hanson	Apr. 9, 1861
Elijah Steele	Aug. 10, 1863

SUPERINTENDING AGENTS, SOUTHERN DISTRICT

James Y. McDuffie   June 21, 1860
Augustus D. Rightmire   Dec. 20, 1860
John P. H. Wentworth   Apr. 16, 1861

SUPERINTENDENTS, 1864-73

Austin Wiley	Apr. 14, 1864
Charles Maltby	Mar. 22, 1865
Billington C. Whiting	Oct. 12, 1866
Bvt. Maj. Gen. John B. McIntosh	June 10, 1869
Billington C. Whiting	Reinstated June 20, 1870

AGENTS

Tejon (Sebastian) Agency

Alonzo Riddle (subagent)	Approved Sept. 3, 1855
James R. Vineyard	Mar. 3, 1855. Arrived at agency Jan. 28, 1856

Nome Lackee Agency

Henry L. Ford (subagent)	Approved Sept. 3, 1855
Edward A. Stevenson	Feb. 27, 1856
Vincent Geiger	Apr. 11, 1857

Klamath Agency

James A. Patterson	Apr. 18, 1856
H. P. Heintzleman (subagent)	June 29, 1857
David E. Buel	May 18, 1858

Fresno Subagency

D. A. Enyart	Sept. 12, 1854
M. L. Lewis	Apr. 17, 1856, but actually on duty in 1855

Mendocino Subagency

Henry L. Ford   Transferred from Nome Lackee, Nov. 5, 1855

H. P. Heintzleman   Transferred from Colorado River *ca.* Aug. 3, 1860

Smith River Agency

William Bryson	Oct. 14, 1864
Henry Orman	Sept. 21, 1866

Hoopa Valley Agency

Robert L. Stockton	Oct. 14, 1864
William H. Pratt	July 19, 1867
Lt. J. L. Spalding	June 11, 1869
Capt. S. G. Whipple	Apr. 21, 1870
David H. Lowry	Jan. 23, 1871
Everett K. Dodge	Sept. 30, 1872
James S. Broaddus	Feb. 26, 1875
Capt. R. C. Parker (acting)	May 15, 1877
Lt. Gordon Winslow (acting)	On duty Aug. 31, 1878
Maj. Henry R. Mizner (acting)	On duty Oct. 22, 1878
Capt. E. B. Savage (acting)	On duty Aug. 1, 1880

Round Valley Agency

B. L. Fairfield	Mar. 22, 1865
Lt. J. S. Styles	July 8, 1869
Lt. W. H. Andrews	Mar. 4, 1870
Hugh Gibson	Jan. 23, 1871
John S. Burchard	Aug. 16, 1872
Henry B. Sheldon	Aug. 25, 1877

Tule River Agency

George S. Hoffman (special)	*ca.* June 1, 1864
Charles Maltby	July 19, 1867
Lt. J. H. Purcell	June 12, 1869

Charles Maltby	Jan. 23, 1871
Joel B. Vosburgh	Sept. 22, 1873
C. G. Belknap	Oct. 2, 1875

Mission Agency

Special Agents, 1865-71

John Q. A. Stanley	Approved May 8, 1865
Lt. Augustus P. Greene	Oct. 6, 1869
John R. Tansey	Dec. 12, 1870

Special Agents, 1873-78

John G. Ames	May 6, 1873
Charles A. Wetmore (special commissioner)	Notified Aug. 10, 1874
D. A. Dryden	Mar. 31, 1875
Justin Colburn	July 12, 1877

Agents, 1878-80

Samuel S. Lawson	July 1, 1878

CENTENNIAL
1875-1878

The U.S. International Exhibition, also known as the Centennial Exhibition, was held at Philadelphia in 1876 in celebration of the 100th anniversary of the independence of the United States.

The correspondence received by the Bureau of Indian Affairs concerning the exhibition was filed under the heading "Centennial." Most of this correspondence relates to the obtaining and display of objects for the exhibit presented by the Bureau. Many of the letters are from Spencer F. Baird of the Smithsonian Institution and John Eaton, Commissioner of Education and representative of the Department of the Interior on the Centennial Board.

Correspondence concerning the exhibition was recorded in the regular registers of letters received by the Bureau of Indian Affairs, as well as in a special centennial register before February 1876; but beginning in that month, only the special register was used, and a separate filing system was begun. Letters were registered alphabetically by the initial of the surname of the writer of each letter and thereunder in numerical order. The numbers began in February 1876 with 10,000 and continue through 1878. There is also a volume of press copies of letters sent relating to the exhibition among the records of the Bureau of Indian Affairs in the National Archives.

CENTRAL SUPERINTENDENCY 1851-1880

The Central Superintendency was established in 1851 as the successor to the St. Louis Superintendency, with headquarters originally at St. Louis. In 1859 headquarters was moved to St. Joseph, Missouri, in 1865 to Atchison, Kansas and in 1869 to Lawrence, Kansas. The superintendency was responsible principally for the agencies and Indians (except the Osage) in present Kansas and Nebraska. The upper regions of the Missouri, Platte and Arkansas Rivers extending into the Dakotas, Wyoming and Colorado were also within the jurisdiction of the superintendency. With the organization of Colorado and Dakota Territories in 1861 and the establishment in them of new superintendencies, these outlying areas were removed from the Central Superintendency, except for the Fort Laramie vicinity in present Wyoming. In 1865 the reorganized Northern Superintendency took over the agencies in Nebraska, including the Upper Platte Agency, whose jurisdiction extended into present Wyoming. At that time, therefore, all of the agencies of the Central Superintendency were located in Kansas. Gradually the superintendency became responsible for agencies located in Indian Territory. After the Southern Superintendency was discontinued in 1870, the Central Superintendency had some control over all of the agencies in Indian Territory as well as those in Kansas.

Delaware, Shawnee, Wyandot, Kickapoo, Kansa, Sauk and Fox of the Mississippi, Sauk and Fox of the Missouri, Iowa, Potawatomi, Chippewa, Ottawa,

Munsee, Peoria, Wea, Kaskaskia, Piankeshaw, Miami, Oto, Missouri, Omaha, Pawnee, Ponca, Kiowa, Apache (Kiowa-Apache), Comanche, Cheyenne, Arapaho, and Sioux and other Indians of the Upper Missouri were the most important tribes originally living within the limits of the Central Superintendency. Some of these tribes were later transferred to other superintendencies, and Osage, Quapaw, Seneca, Eastern Shawnee, Modoc, Mexican Kickapoo, Wichita and affiliated tribes and, for some purposes, Cherokee, Creek, Choctaw, Chickasaw and Seminole Indians were added to the Central Superintendency.

Originally the agencies in the Central Superintendency were the Kansas (Delaware, Shawnee, Wyandot and Munsee Indians), Potawatomi (Potawatomi and Kansa), Sac and Fox (Sauk and Fox of the Mississippi, Chippewa and Ottawa), Great Nemaha (Iowa, Sauk and Fox of the Missouri and Kickapoo), Osage River (Miami, Peoria, Wea, Kaskaskia and Piankeshaw), Council Bluffs (Oto, Missouri, Omaha and Pawnee), Upper Platte (Kiowa, Comanche, Apache, Cheyenne, Arapaho and Sioux) and Upper Missouri.

Four changes were made in 1855. The Kansas Agency was divided into the Delaware Agency and the Shawnee Agency. A new Kansas Agency was established for the Kansa Indians. A separate Kickapoo Agency was established. The Upper Arkansas Agency was established for some of the Indians previously assigned to the Upper Platte Agency.

In 1856 the Blackfeet Agency was established and the Council Bluffs Agency was divided into the Omaha Agency and the Otoe Agency (Oto, Missouri and Pawnee). The Pawnee, Ponca and Yankton Agencies were established in 1859.

The Blackfeet, Upper Missouri, Ponca and Yankton Agencies were transferred in 1861 to the newly established Dakota Superintendency. In the same year the Upper Arkansas Agency was transferred to the new Colorado Superintendency, but by 1866 it was back in the Central Superintendency. The Central Superintendency in 1861, then, was composed of the Delaware, Shawnee, Kansas, Potawatomi, Sac and Fox, Kickapoo, Great Nemaha, Otoe, Omaha, Pawnee, Osage River and Upper Platte Agencies. Except for the Upper Platte Agency, then located in present Wyoming, all of these agencies were in Kansas and Nebraska.

In 1863 the Ottawa Agency was established for some of the Indians previously assigned to the Sac and Fox Agency. In 1865 the Otoe, Omaha, Pawnee, Great Nemaha and Upper Platte Agencies were transferred to the Northern Superintendency. These changes left all of the remaining agencies of the Central Superintendency in Kansas.

The status of the Upper Arkansas Agency had been confused for several years, but in 1866 the agency was definitely located in Kansas and assigned to the Central rather than to the Colorado Superintendency. In 1867 the Neosho Agency (renamed Osage in 1874) for the Osage Indians in southern Kansas and for the Quapaw, Seneca and Shawnee Indians, whose permanent home was east of the Neosho River in Indian Territory, was transferred from the Southern to the Central Superintendency. It should be noted that during the Civil War the Southern Superintendency and the agencies assigned to it were temporarily moved from Indian Territory to Kansas. Except for the Neosho Agency, which remained in Kansas, the agencies were returned to Indian Territory within a few years after the end of the war.

In 1869 the Kiowa Agency in Indian Territory, which had not been assigned to any superintendency since its establishment in 1864, was attached to the Central Superintendency, and the Wichita Agency (Wichita and other Indians) was temporarily consolidated with the Kiowa Agency. When a separate Wichita Agency was re-established in 1870, it was assigned to the Central Superintendency.

The Southern Superintendency was discontinued in 1870. The agencies still assigned to it (Creek, Cherokee, Choctaw and Chickasaw and Seminole) were transferred to the Central Superintendency. Later in the same year it was decided that the Central Superintendent should handle only matters in which treaty stipulations required the services of a superintendent (such as the investigation of certain claims) and that for other matters the agents of the four agencies would report directly to the Bureau of Indian Affairs. In 1874 the four agencies were consolidated into the Union Agency.

In 1871 the Neosho (Osage) Agency was divided when the Quapaw Agency for the Indians other than the Osage was established.

In the meantime the number of agencies in Kansas was being reduced as the Indians moved to Indian Territory and were attached to agencies already in operation there. The Ottawa Agency was abolished in 1867, the Delaware Agency in 1869, the Shawnee and Osage River Agencies in 1871 and the Kansas Agency in 1874. The Sac and Fox, Upper Arkansas (renamed Cheyenne and Arapahoe in 1874) and Osage (Neosho) Agencies were moved from Kansas to Indian Territory when the Indians moved there. In 1874 the Kickapoo Agency was consolidated with the Potawatomi Agency leaving the Potawataomi Agency the only agency in Kansas. In 1876 the Pawnee Agency, having been moved from Nebraska to Indian Territory, was transferred from the Northern to the Central Superintendency. Thereafter the Potawatomi Agency in Kansas and the Osage, Quapaw, Sac and Fox, Wichita, Kiowa, Pawnee and Cheyenne and Arapahoe Agencies in Indian Territory were assigned to the Central Superintendency. The superintendent also had some responsibility for the Union Agency.

In October 1877 the agents were instructed to report directly to the Bureau of Indian Affairs in Washington rather than to the superintendent. In 1878 the superintendency was discontinued, but some correspondence was filed under the heading "Central Superintendency" through 1880.

In addition to the persons assigned to regularly established agencies, special agents were occasionally appointed for specific purposes or for Indians not assigned to a regular agency. These agents were too numerous to mention here, but there is at least one special agency that should be noted. In 1876 a special agency was established at Fort Griffin, Texas for the Tonkawa and Lipan Indians living in that area. The commanding officer at the fort acted as agent. Although this special agency was not located within the limits of the Central Superintendency, the correspondence concerning it is filed with the superintendency correspondence.

The Bureau maintained separate file headings for the correspondence relating to the individual agencies in the Central Superintendency. Both the superintendency and the agency headings should be consulted, however, in order to find all of the correspondence relating to any one agency.

See also St. Louis, Dakota, Northern, Southern and Colorado Superintendencies and Kansa, Potawatomi, Sac and Fox, Osage River, Great Nemaha, Upper Missouri, Upper Platte, Council Bluffs, Kickapoo, Upper Arkansas, Otoe, Omaha, Pawnee, Ponca, Blackfeet, Yankton, Ottawa, Delaware, Shawnee, Kiowa, Cheyenne and Arapahoe, Wichita, Neosho, Osage, Quapaw, Nebraska, Creek, Cherokee, Choctaw, Chickasaw, Seminole and Union Agencies. There are also field records of the Central Superintendency among the records of the Bureau of Indian Affairs in the National Archives.

SUPERINTENDENTS

Name	Date of Appointment
David D. Mitchell	Mar. 13, 1851
Alfred Cumming	Apr. 23, 1853
John Haverty	Aug. 19, 1857
Alexander M. Robinson	Mar. 1, 1858
Harrison B. Branch	Apr. 8, 1861
William M. Albin	Mar. 2, 1864
Thomas Murphy	July 1, 1865
Enoch Hoag	Apr. 22, 1869
William Nicholson	Jan. 19, 1876

CHEROKEE AGENCY
1824-1880

Between 1824 and 1839 there were two Cherokee Agencies in operation, one for the Cherokee Indians living east and one for those living west of the Mississippi River. The correspondence until 1836 relating to these two agencies is filed separately under the subheadings "Cherokee East" and "Cherokee West." Beginning in 1836 some correspondence was filed simply under "Cherokee," and in 1837 the "East" and "West" subheadings were discontinued. This was a change in filing procedure only and reflects no change in the operations of the agencies.

An agent, Leonard D. Shaw, was appointed for the Cherokee living east of the Mississippi, principally in Tennessee and Georgia, as early as 1792. Information concerning this agent and his successors is sparse, but by 1801 the Cherokee Agency was permanently established at South West Point (now Kingston), Tennessee. Between 1807 and 1820 the agency headquarters was located at or near Hiwassee Garrison at the mouth of the Hiwassee River. After 1820 the agency was located farther up the Hiwassee River opposite Calhoun, Tennessee. Until the Bureau of Indian Affairs was established in 1824, correspondence relating to the agency was transmitted directly to the Secretary of War. Between 1824 and 1834 the agency was not assigned to any superintendency and the agent reported directly to the Bureau.

On December 31, 1834, the Superintendent of Emigration for the Cherokee was designated to perform the duties of the agent for the Cherokee Agency in the east. By 1839 the Bureau considered the removal of the Cherokee Indians to Indian Territory completed, and the Superintendency of Emigration and the Cherokee Agency in Tennessee were discontinued on January 26, 1839. A considerable number of Cherokee had not moved, however, and the continuing correspondence relating to them was filed under the heading "Cherokee." From time to time the Bureau appointed special agents and commissioners to perform various duties relating to the Cherokee still living in the east.

The Cherokee Agency in the west was established in 1813 for the Cherokee then living between the Arkansas and White Rivers in present Arkansas. The agent was an assistant to the Cherokee agent in the east until 1817, when he was made responsible to the Governor of Missouri Territory. In 1818 he was made a full agent. In 1819 the agency was transferred to the new Arkansas Superintendency. The agency was at times known as the Arkansas Agency and was responsible for the Quapaw Indians in Arkansas as well as the Cherokee. At other times there was a separate subagency for the Quapaw. By the time the Bureau of Indian Affairs was established in 1824, the agency was responsible only for the Cherokee Indians in Arkansas. The agency apparently had no permanent buildings until 1826, when the agent was authorized to buy buildings on the Arkansas River in western Arkansas.

Under the terms of a treaty of May 6, 1828, the Cherokee agreed to give up their land in Arkansas for land in the northeastern part of Indian Territory, and in 1829 they moved to their new homes. The agent, Edward Du Val, seems to have remained in Arkansas. In 1830 his successor, George Vashon, established his headquarters at Fort Gibson in Indian Territory. From then until 1851 the agency office was located at or near Fort Gibson. Although buildings for the agency were erected in 1839 on Bayou Menard about 8 miles southeast of Fort Gibson, these buildings were not always in use. With the removal to Indian Territory the agency was no longer within the limits of the Arkansas Superintendency, and the agent reported directly to the Bureau of Indian Affairs in Washington.

From 1829 until 1831 the Cherokee agent supervised the Choctaw Subagency for the Choctaw Indians living west of the Mississippi River. In addition, in 1834 he was made responsible for the Seneca Indians who had moved west. For the period from 1831 until 1834 there are some letters filed under "Cherokee" relating to the activities of several persons designated to act as subagents for the Seneca. The Cherokee Agency also had responsibility for Cherokee who moved from east of the Mississippi as well as for the Arkansas Cherokee. Most of the Eastern Cherokee, however, did not move west until 1838.

In 1834 the Cherokee Agency was reduced to a subagency in the new Western Superintendency. It was made responsible for the Seneca and the Mixed Band of Seneca and Shawnee as well as the Cherokee. Originally it was intended to assign the Quapaw Indians to the Cherokee Subagency, but they were assigned to the Osage Superintendency instead. During 1836 and 1837, however, Subagent Montford Stokes seemed to consider the Quapaw as being under his jurisdiction.

The Cherokee Subagency was made a full agency in 1837, responsible only for the Cherokee Indians. The Seneca, Seneca and Shawnee, and Quapaw were assigned to the new Neosho Subagency.

In 1851 the Southern Superintendency replaced the Western Superintendency. In the same year the Cherokee Agency was moved from the Fort Gibson area to a location near Tahlequah.

At the beginning of the Civil War Confederate troops occupied Indian Territory and many Cherokee joined the Confederacy. Those remaining loyal to the United States were forced to take refuge in Kansas where the Cherokee agent established temporary headquarters at the Sac and Fox Agency. In 1863 when the agent and the Indians attempted to return to Tahlequah they were unable to remain there, and the agent established himself at Fort Gibson. Since the agency at Tahlequah had been destroyed during the war, the agent remained at Fort Gibson even after military operations had ceased. In 1871 the agency was finally moved to Tahlequah.

In 1867 many Delaware, and in 1869 many Shawnee, both then living in Kansas, were admitted to the Cherokee Nation and began moving to Indian Territory. Some remnants of other bands also lived with the Cherokee.

The Southern Superintendency was abolished in 1870, and the Central Superintendent took over such duties of the superintendency as were required by treaty stipulations (such as the investigation of certain claims). For most purposes, however, the Cherokee Agency was now independent and reported directly to the Bureau of Indian Affairs in Washington.

On June 30, 1874, the Creek, Choctaw and Seminole Agencies were consolidated with the Cherokee Agency. On December 22, 1874, this consolidated agency was named the Union Agency. From the beginning of 1875 most of the correspondence relating to the agency was filed under the new name. Some correspondence, however, was still filed under the heading "Cherokee." Some of this correspondence relates to the Cherokee in Indian Territory, although most of it concerns the Eastern Cherokee. Many of these letters were at one time designated "North Carolina" and filed separately. They are now interfiled with the other Cherokee correspondence. During 1875 and 1876 W. C. McCarthy served as special agent for the Eastern Cherokee with headquarters at Quallatown, North Carolina. Thereafter there were persons who served as school superintendents for Cherokee schools in North Carolina, Tennessee and Georgia, but no regular agent was appointed until 1882.

An unusually large amount of the correspondence filed under the heading "Cherokee" relates to claims and litigation. Most of these claims originated from the cession and disposal of Cherokee lands in the east and the removal of the Cherokee to Indian Territory. A bewildering array of agents and commissioners was appointed to investigate claims, evaluate property, prepare census rolls and perform other duties. Most significant, perhaps, was the series of four Boards of Cherokee Commissioners that served between 1836 and 1847 and investigated claims arising from the terms of the treaty of 1835 with the Eastern Cherokee. In addition to Government officials, lawyers and agents hired by the Indians were in frequent correspondence with the Bureau. The Indians themselves wrote numerous letters.

Many letters relating to the removal of the Cherokee are filed under the subheading "Cherokee Emigration," and some letters relating primarily to land claims are filed under the subheading "Cherokee Reserves." A great number of letters relating to these subjects, however, is filed under the main "Cherokee" heading.

See also Arkansas, Western, Southern, St. Louis and Central Superintendencies and Creek, Choctaw, Osage, Neosho, Caddo and Union Agencies. Among the records of the Bureau of Indian Affairs in the National Archives there are also field records of the Cherokee Agency in Tennessee (many of which have been reproducted by the National Archives and Records Service as Microfilm Publication 208) and a few field records of the Cherokee Agency in the west.

AGENTS

Cherokee Agency, East

(Agents serving before 1799 have not been included in this list.)

Name	*Date of Appointment*
Thomas Lewis	Received instructions Mar. 30, 1799
Return J. Meigs	May 15, 1801
Joseph McMinn	Notified Mar. 17, 1823
Hugh Montgomery	Mar. 18, 1825
Benjamin Currey (acting)	Jan. 1, 1835
Nathaniel Smith (acting)	Jan. 3, 1837

Cherokee Agency, West

William L. Lovely (assistant agent)	Jan. 4, 1813
Reuben Lewis (assistant agent)	July 11, 1817
Reuben Lewis (agent)	Notified Apr. 22, 1818
David Brearly	Notified May 1, 1820
Edward Du Val	Apr. 1, 1823
George Vashon	Mar. 12, 1830; became subagent under regulations adopted July 7, 1834
Montford Stokes (subagent)	Accepted Mar. 25, 1836
Montford Stokes (agent)	Mar. 8, 1837
Pierce M. Butler	Sept. 13, 1841
James McKisick	Aug. 19, 1845
Richard C. S. Brown	Feb. 14, 1848
William Butler	May 29, 1849
George Butler	Notified Oct. 31, 1850
Robert J. Cowart	Mar. 12, 1860
John Crawford	Apr. 5, 1861
Charles W. Chatterton	Mar. 6, 1862
Justin Harlan	Sept. 11, 1862
John J. Humphreys	Sept. 25, 1866
William B. Davis	Nov. 29, 1867
Capt. John N. Craig	June 22, 1869
John B. Jones	Dec. 9, 1870

CHEYENNE AND ARAPAHOE AGENCY 1875-1880

The Cheyenne and Arapahoe Agency, located on the North Fork of the Canadian River at Darlington, Indian Territory, was a continuation of the Upper Arkansas Agency originally established in 1855. The change in name took place on December 22, 1874, the agency having become primarily responsible for the Southern Cheyenne and Arapaho Indians who lived on the Cheyenne and Arapahoe Reservation. There were also some Northern Cheyenne on the reservation, especially between 1877 and 1881, and a small number of Apache.

The Cheyenne and Arapahoe Agency was under the supervision of the Central Superintendency until the superintendency was abolished in 1878. Thereafter the agent reported directly to the Bureau of Indian Affairs in Washington. John D. Miles, originally appointed to the Upper Arkansas Agency on January 23, 1873, was the Cheyenne and Arapahoe agent throughout the period from 1875 through 1880. The agency continued in operation beyond 1880.

See also Upper Arkansas Agency and Central Superintendency.

CHEYENNE RIVER AGENCY 1871-1880

The Cheyenne River Agency (sometimes called the Cheyenne Agency), which was established in 1869, was under the Dakota Superintendency until the superintendency was abolished in 1870. Correspondence received by the Bureau relating to the agency during 1869 and 1870 is filed with the correspondence relating to the Upper Platte Agency. During the temporary re-establishment of the Dakota Superintendency from March, 1877 until June, 1878 the Cheyenne River Agency was again placed under the supervision of the superintendency, but the agent continued to report directly to the Bureau of Indian Affairs in Washington.

The agency was located on the west bank of the Missouri River below the mouth of the Big Cheyenne River about 6 miles from Fort Sully in what is now South Dakota. It had charge of bands of Miniconjou, Sans Arcs, Two Kettle (Oohenonpa) and Blackfeet Sioux. The agency continued to operate beyond 1880.

See also Dakota Superintendency and Upper Platte Agency.

AGENTS

Name	*Date of Appointment*
Bvt. Maj. George M. Randall (special)	June 14, 1869
J. Lee Englebert (special)	Oct. 19, 1870
Percival B. Spear (special)	Dec. 16, 1870
Theodore M. Koues (special)	Jan. 31, 1871
Henry W. Bingham (special)	July 8, 1872
Henry W. Bingham (agent)	July 23, 1872
James F. Cravens	June 27, 1876
Capt. Theodore Schwan (acting)	Mar. 28, 1878
Leonard Love	May 27, 1880

CHICAGO AGENCY
1824-1847

The Chicago Agency was established in 1805. Agent Charles Jouett, who moved from Detroit to Chicago, was put in charge of the Sauk and Fox and other tribes living west and north of Detroit, including the Potawatomi who previously had been attached to the Fort Wayne Agency. From 1811 until 1815 there was no agent at Chicago. The agent appointed in 1815 was made responsible only for the Indians, principally Potawatomi, in the vicinity of Chicago. Although located in Illinois Territory, the agency was assigned to the Michigan Superintendency. Until the Bureau of Indian Affairs was established in 1824, correspondence relating to the Chicago Agency was transmitted directly to the Office of the Secretary of War.

In 1821 the Ottawa, Chippewa and Potawatomi of the headwaters of Rock River and Lake Peoria formerly attached to the now defunct Illinois Agency were assigned to the Chicago Agency. Later in the year a subagency subordinate to the Chicago Agency was established at Peoria, but in 1822 it was transferred to the St. Louis Superintendency. In 1832 the Peoria Subagency was discontinued and the Indians were attached to the Chicago Agency. Before the practice of attaching subagencies to agencies was eliminated in 1834, there were other subagencies responsible to the Chicago Agency. The most important of these was at Carey Mission on the St. Joseph River in Michigan. It had charge of the Potawatomi and Ottawa Indians living in that area.

In the reorganization of 1834 the Chicago Agency, by now sometimes called the Illinois Agency, was made responsible for all the Indians in Illinois and those in Michigan Territory south of the Milwaukee River (in present Wisconsin). The agency was also put in charge of the Ottawa, Chippewa and Potawatomi living along Lake Michigan north of the Milwaukee River who previously had resorted to the Chicago Agency. The agency was detached from the Michigan Superintendency; and the agent reported directly to the Bureau of Indian Affairs in Washington.

The Chicago Agency was discontinued on December 31, 1834. The agent, Thomas J. V. Owen, was appointed superintendent for the removal of the Potawatomi, Ottawa and Chippewa Indians of the Chicago Agency to areas west of the Mississippi River, as provided by a treaty of September 26, 1833. In this capacity he continued to perform the duties of the agent at Chicago, mainly the distribution of annuity goods. On September 24, 1835, Capt. J. B. F. Russell was designated to perform the duties of agent while Owen was on furlough. Owen, however, died during his furlough and on July 26, 1836, his successor as Superintendent of Emigration was instructed to take over the duties as agent from Captain Russell who was still serving in Owen's place. In February, 1838 the Superintendency of Emigration for the Chicago Agency was consolidated with that for the Indians of Indiana. The Bureau decided that this superintendency ceased to operate on October 13, 1838, and that the incumbent, Abel C. Pepper, was thereafter considered to have been serving as subagent. By this time, however, most of the Indians from the Chicago area had emigrated, and Pepper was concerned primarily with the Miami Indians of Indiana. Some letters, however, were filed under the "Chicago" heading until 1839.

In addition to correspondence filed under the main "Chicago" heading, there are also many letters for the period 1835-47 (most of them dated before 1839) filed under the subheading "Chicago Emigration." These letters relate to the removal of the Potawatomi, Ottawa and Chippewa from the Chicago area. Most of these Indians moved to Council Bluffs, Iowa, and after 1837 were assigned to the Council Bluffs Subagency. Some of them, however, moved to the Osage River in present Kansas and were attached to the Osage River Subagency.

See also Michigan and St. Louis Superintendencies and Fort Wayne, Indiana, Council Bluffs, Osage River, Sac and Fox and Green Bay Agencies.

AGENTS

Name	*Date of Appointment*
Charles Jouett	July 27, 1802; but resided at Detroit until 1805. Served until 1811.
John Bowyer	July 14, 1815 (From 1811 until 1815 there was no agent at Chicago.)
Charles Jouett	Mar. 15, 1816
Alexander Wolcott	Assigned Mar. 27, 1819
Thomas J. V. Owen	Feb. 8, 1831; after Dec. 31, 1834 he was Superintendent of Emigration and acting agent.
Capt. J. B. F. Russell (acting)	Sept. 24, 1835
Gholson Kercheval (acting)	July 26, 1836
Col. L. H. Sands (acting)	July 14, 1837
Abel C. Pepper (acting)	Superintendent of Emigration and acting agent in Indiana. Assigned additional duties as Superintendent of Emigration and acting agent at Chicago on Feb. 26, 1838.

CHICKASAW AGENCY
1824-1870

The Chickasaw Agency was established in 1800. Before that time the agent for the Choctaw Indians had been assigned some responsibility for the Chickasaw Indians. The Chickasaw Agent was responsible only for the Chickasaw Indians, who then lived in present Mississippi and in adjacent parts of Alabama and Tennessee.

Until the Bureau of Indian Affairs was established in 1824, correspondence relating to the agency was transmitted directly to the Office of the Secretary of War. By 1824 the agency was not under the supervision of any superintendency and the agency reported directly to the Bureau in Washington. The location of the agency buildings was reported in 1824 as being on the headwaters of the Holky, a branch of the Tombigbee River, near the ridge dividing the waters of the Yazoo River from those of the Tombigbee. This site is in northeastern Mississippi. In 1825 the agent selected a new site for the agency near the Tennessee River and Tuscumbia, Alabama and new buildings were erected in 1826. In 1837 Pontotoc, Mississippi was designated as the headquarters of the agency. The agent, however, reported from both Pontotoc and the agency office in Alabama. In August, 1838 he reported that he had moved the agency records from Pontotoc to the agency buildings in Alabama.

During 1837 and 1838 the Chickasaw moved to Indian Territory, where they settled on the western part of the Choctaw reserve. In 1837 Gaines P. Kingsbury was designated to act as agent for the Chickasaw who had emigrated. The Chickasaw Agency in the east was discontinued in 1839 and a regular agency was established for the Chickasaw in Indian Territory. The agency was under the supervision of the Western Superintendency until 1851 and thereafter its successor, the Southern Superintendency. The agent usually stayed in the vicinity of Fort Towson until in 1842 permanent buildings were erected east of the Washita River near Fort Washita.

When the Chickasaw agent was removed in 1855, the Choctaw agent was put in charge of the agency business. The following year the Chickasaw were permanently assigned to the Choctaw Agency. Some letters, however, were filed under the heading "Chickasaw" until 1870.

Many letters relating to the removal of the Chickasaw Indians and to the disposition of their lands are filed under the subheadings "Chickasaw Emigration" and "Chickasaw Reserves." There are also letters relating to these subjects under the main "Chickasaw" heading.

See also Western and Southern Superintendencies and Choctaw and Union Agencies. There are a few field records of the Chickasaw Agency in the east among the records of the Bureau of Indian Affairs in the National Archives.

AGENTS

Chickasaw Agency (in the East)

Name	*Date of Appointment*
Samuel Mitchell	Assignment author-ized Nov. 28, 1800
Thomas Wright	May 27, 1806
James Neelly	July 7, 1809
James Robertson	Notified June 4, 1812
William Cocke	Sept. 28, 1814
Henry Sherburne	Dec. 11, 1817
Robert C. Nicholas	Aug. 8, 1820
Benjamin F. Smith	July 25, 1823
Benjamin Reynolds	Notified Mar. 12, 1830

Chickasaw Agency (in the West)

Gaines P. Kingsbury	June 11, 1837
A. M. M. Upshaw	Mar. 4, 1839
Gabriel W. Long	Nov. 6, 1849
Kenton Harper	June 30, 1851
Andrew Jackson Smith	Sept. 1, 1852

CHIPPEWA AGENCY
1851-1880

The Chippewa Agency, established in 1851 as successor to the Sandy Lake Subagency, was responsible for both the Chippewa of the Mississippi and the Chippewa of Lake Superior living in Minnesota and Wisconsin. After 1853, however, the Mackinac Agency in Michigan handled the affairs of the Chippewa living along Lake Superior in Minnesota and Wisconsin as well as in Michigan. In 1858 a separate agency was established for the Lake Superior Chippewa. Initially this agency was known as the Chippewa of Lake Superior or Lake Superior Agency, but for correspondence filing purposes the name "La Pointe" was used. The Chippewa Agency was often called the Chippewa of the Mississippi Agency to distinguish it from the agency for the Lake Superior Chippewa. In addition to the Chippewa of the Mississippi proper the Chippewa Agency was also responsible for the Pillager and Lake Winnebigoshish (Winnebegoshshiwininewak) and, after 1863, the Red Lake (Miskwagamiwisagaigan) and Pembina (Anibi-minanisibiwininiwak) Chippewa.

The Chippewa Agency was first located at the site of the Sandy Lake Subagency. The subagency had been at Sandy Lake, Minnesota only since 1850, when it had been moved from La Pointe, Wisconsin. In 1852 the Chippewa Agency was moved from Sandy Lake to the Crow Wing River a few miles above its junction with the Mississippi River. Permanent buildings were erected about five miles from the Mississippi on the Gull Lake Reservation, which was established under the terms of the treaty of February 22, 1855. There were Chippewa Indians living on several reservations in Minnesota. During 1866 and 1867 new agency buildings were erected on the southeast side of Leech Lake on the reservation for the Pillager and Lake Winnebigoshish Chippewa. The buildings on the Crow Wing River, however, were also retained until 1870. In 1872 the agency was moved from Leech Lake to the White Earth Reservation.

The Chippewa Agency was under the Minnesota Superintendency until 1856, when it was transferred to the Northern Superintendency. Beginning in 1865 the agency was no longer assigned to any superintendency, and the agent reported directly to the Bureau of Indian Affairs in Washington.

In 1873 a separate agency was established on the Red Lake Reservation for the Red Lake Chippewa. In 1874 another agency was established at Leech Lake for the Pillager and Lake Winnebigoshish Chippewa living in that area and the Chippewa of the Mississippi living at White Oak Point (near Grand Rapids). After these changes the Chippewa Agency at White Earth had charge of the other Chippewa of the Mississippi (including those living at Mille Lacs), the Otter Tail Pillagers and the Pembina Chippewa. Correspondence relating to all three agencies is filed under the heading "Chippewa." In 1879 the Red Lake and Leech Lake Agencies were consolidated into the White Earth Agency. The White Earth or Chippewa Agency continued to operate beyond 1880.

Some letters relating to the removal of Chippewa Indians are filed under the subheading "Chippewa Emigration," and a few letters relating to Chippewa lands are filed under the subheading "Chippewa Reserves."

See also Minnesota and Northern Superintendencies and Mackinac, La Pointe, Winnebago, Sandy Lake and Green Bay Agencies and Subagencies. For correspondence relating to Chippewa Indians in Michigan, see Mackinac Agency and Sault Ste. Marie Agency. For correspondence relating to Chippewa who had moved to Kansas, see Osage River, Sac and Fox, Ottawa and Potawatomi Agencies. There are field records of the White Earth Agency among the records of the Bureau of Indian Affairs in the National Archives, but most of them are dated later than 1880. There are also field records of the later Leech Lake and Consolidated Chippewa Agencies.

AGENTS

Chippewa Agency

Name	*Date of Appointment*
John S. Watrous	June 30, 1851
David B. Herriman	Apr. 18, 1853
Cyrus K. Drew	Mar. 3, 1858
Joseph W. Lynde	Apr. 30, 1858
Lucius C. Walker	Mar. 23, 1861
A. Lawrence Foster	Sept. 29, 1862
Ashley C. Morrill	Feb. 14, 1863
Edwin Clark	Apr. 12, 1865
Joel B. Bassett	Nov. 9, 1866
Charles T. Brown	Apr. 8, 1869
Bvt. Capt. J. J. S. Hassler	June 17, 1869
Bvt. Capt. George Atcheson	Dec. 8, 1869
John P. Bardwell	Sept. 21, 1870
Edward P. Smith	Feb. 18, 1871
Ebenezer Douglass	May 12, 1873
Lewis Stone	May 13, 1874
Charles A. Ruffee	Feb. 18, 1878

Red Lake Agency

Richard M. Pratt (special)	June 14, 1873
Asa D. Baker	July 1, 1878

Leech Lake Agency

James Whitehead (special)	Apr. 8, 1874
Henry J. King (special)	Oct. 21, 1875
Henry J. King (agent)	July 1, 1878

CHOCTAW AGENCY 1824-1876

Actually there were two separate Choctaw Agencies, one for the Choctaw Indians living east of the Mississippi River and one for those living west of that river.

An agent for the Choctaw Indians living east of the Mississippi River, principally in the present state of Mississippi, was appointed as early as 1792, and the Choctaw Agency was permanently established before 1800. Until the Bureau of Indian Affairs was established in 1824, correspondence relating to the agency was transmitted directly to the Office of the Secretary of War. By 1824 the agency was not under any superintendency, and the agent reported directly to the Bureau in Washington. At the end of 1822, by order of the Secretary of War, the agency headquarters was located in eastern Mississippi near Oaknoxubee Creek on the road from Natchez, Tennessee to Columbus, Mississippi.

In 1832, since most of the Choctaw had been moved to Indian Territory, the Choctaw Agency in the east was discontinued. There were, however, Choctaw Indians still living in Mississippi, and from time to time the Bureau sent persons to perform duties concerning them.

The Choctaw Agency west of the Mississippi River was established in 1825. Much of the correspondence relating to this agency for the period from 1825 until 1835 and some letters dated as late as 1838 are filed under the sub-heading "Choctaw West." Later correspondence was filed under the main "Choctaw" heading.

In 1821 the Choctaw Indians living west of the Mississippi had been assigned to the Red River or Caddo Agency. In 1825 these Indians had a reserve in what is now the southeastern part of Oklahoma. They were considered to be in Arkansas, and the Choctaw Agency established in that year was placed under the supervision of the Arkansas Superintendency. The western boundary of Arkansas was established to the east of Choctaw country in 1828. On August 1, 1828 the Choctaw Agency was made independent of the Arkansas Superintendency, and thereafter the agent reported directly to the Bureau of Indian Affairs in Washington.

At the end of 1828, after the agent reported that he had only eight Indians under his immediate care, the Choctaw Agency was reduced to a subagency under the Cherokee Agency. In 1831, under the provisions of the Treaty of Dancing Rabbit Creek made in 1830, the eastern Choctaw began to move west. In September, 1831 a full agent was again assigned to the Choctaw in the west. The subagent continued to serve under the agent until the practice of using subagents as assistants to agents was discontinued in 1834. The headquarters of the agency was on the Arkansas River above the site of Fort Coffee.

In 1834 the Choctaw agent was designated superintendent of the new Western Superintendency. From 1834 until 1837 the agency for the Choctaw Indians was called the Southern Agency. This name, however, was never used for filing purposes. Since the same person was both agent for the Choctaw and superintendent, letters from the Choctaw agent are filed under the headings "Choctaw" and "Western" as well as the names of the other agencies and subagencies in the superintendency. In 1851 the Southern Superintendency replaced the Western Superintendency. A full-time superintendent was appointed, and the Choctaw agent was now responsible for only the Choctaw Indians.

The Choctaw Agency was moved in 1854 from the Arkansas River to the abandoned garrison at Fort Towson on the Red River. In 1855 the Choctaw agent was also put in charge of the Chickasaw Agency, and in 1856 the Chickasaw Indians were permanently assigned to the Choctaw Agency. The consolidated agency was often called the Choctaw and Chickasaw Agency. Until 1870 some letters were filed under the heading "Chickasaw." Thereafter only the heading "Choctaw" was used. In 1856 the Choctaw agent moved from Fort Towson to the old Chickasaw Agency buildings near Fort Washita.

At the beginning of the Civil War Confederate troops occupied Indian Territory, and most of the Choctaw and Chickasaw joined the Confederacy. Those Indians who remained loyal to the United States took refuge in Kansas. The Choctaw agent established temporary headquarters in Kansas, first at Leroy and then at the Sac and Fox Agency. During 1865 and 1866 the agent stayed at Fort Gibson and Fort Smith. In 1866 the agency headquarters was located at Scullyville, but beginning in 1867 the agent stayed at Boggy Depot.

The Southern Superintendency was discontinued in 1870. The Central superintendent took over such duties of the superintendent as were required by treaties (such as the investigation of certain claims), but for most purposes the agent reported directly to the Bureau of Indian Affairs in Washington. In 1874 the Choctaw, Creek and Seminole Agencies were consolidated with the Cherokee Agency to form the Union Agency. Some letters, however, were filed under the heading "Choctaw" until 1876.

Much of the correspondence relating to the removal of the Choctaw to Indian Territory and to the disposal of their lands is filed under the subheadings "Choctaw Emigration" and "Choctaw Reserves." Other letters relating to these subjects, however, are filed under the main "Choctaw" heading.

See also Arkansas, Western, Southern, St. Louis and Central Superintendencies and Red River, Caddo, Chickasaw, Cherokee, Creek, Seminole, Neosho, Osage and Union Agencies. There are a few field records of the Choctaw Agency in the east among the records of the Bureau of Indian Affairs in the National Archives, and there are many field records of the Western Superintendency.

AGENTS

Choctaw Agency, East

(Agents serving before 1799 have not been included in this list.)

Name	*Date of Appointment*
John McKee	1799
Silas Dinsmoor	Mar. 12, 1802
John McKee	Notified Apr. 30, 1814
William Ward	Notified Mar. 1, 1821

Choctaw Agency, West

William McClellan	Notified Mar. 18, 1825; reduced to subagent Jan. 1, 1829
David McClellan (subagent)	July 31, 1829
Francis W. Armstrong	Assigned Sept. 7, 1831
William Armstrong	Sept. 8, 1835
Samuel M. Rutherford	July 10, 1847
John Drennen	May 29, 1849
William Wilson	June 30, 1851
Douglas H. Cooper	Apr. 18, 1853
Isaac Coleman	July 31, 1861
Martin W. Chollar	Aug. 22, 1866
Capt. George T. Olmsted	June 23, 1869
Theophilus D. Griffith	Oct. 21, 1870
Albert Parsons	Apr. 1, 1873

COLORADO SUPERINTENDENCY 1861-1880

The Colorado Territory and the Colorado Superintendency were both established in 1861. The territory previously had been divided among the New Mexico, Utah, Kansas and Nebraska Territories and Indian administration had been divided among the New Mexico, Utah and Central Superintendencies.

The principal Indians in Colorado were different bands of Ute (Grand River, Uinta, Yampa, Tabaquache or Uncompahgre, Wiminuche, Capote and Moache). In the early years there were also Cheyenne and Arapaho living there. Part of the Navajo Reservation was in Colorado, but the Navajo Agency was assigned to the New Mexico Superintendency.

The Territorial Governor served as *ex officio* superintendent throughout the existence of the Colorado Superintendency. Except for a few months when it was at Golden, the superintendency headquarters was located at Denver.

The Upper Arkansas (Cheyenne and Arapaho Indians) and Conejos (Tabaquache Ute Indians) Agencies—previously assigned, respectively, to the Central and New Mexico Superintendencies—were the original agencies in the Colorado Superintendency. The Upper Arkansas Agency was soon transferred back to the Central Superintendency. During 1861 and 1862 Harvey Vaile was stationed at Breckenridge as subagent for the Ute Indians. Later the Conejos Agency became the Los Pinos Agency and three more agencies were established for the several bands of Ute: White River (originally Middle Park), Denver Special and Southern Ute.

The Colorado Superintendency was discontinued in 1870. Thereafter the agents in Colorado reported directly to the Bureau of Indian Affairs in Washington. Until the change of filing systems in 1881, however, correspondence relating to the several agencies in Colorado was still filed under the heading "Colorado" rather than under the names of the individual agencies.

See also New Mexico, Central, Arizona and Wyoming Superintendencies and Upper Arkansas and Kiowa Agencies.

UPPER ARKANSAS AGENCY

The Upper Arkansas Agency was established under the Central Superintendency in 1855 for the Indians living along the Arkansas River in what is now eastern Colorado and western Kansas. These were primarily the Southern Cheyenne and Southern Arapaho Indians, but, until the Kiowa Agency was established in 1864, the Upper Arkansas Agency also had some responsibility for Kiowa, Comanche and Apache (Kiowa-Apache) Indians and for some Caddo Indians who left Texas during the Civil War. The agency was transferred to the Colorado Superintendency in 1861. During 1861 and 1862 the agent usually stayed at Fort Wise and thereafter at Fort Lyon. The Indians remained nomadic, however, and by 1866 they were no longer in Colorado and the agency had been transferred back to the Central Superintendency. Most of the correspondence relating to the Upper Arkansas Agency is filed under the name of the agency rather than that of either of the superintendencies to which it was assigned.

CONEJOS-LOS PINOS AGENCY

The Conejos Agency was established in 1860 for the Tabaquache Ute Indians who lived north of the Utah Agency area in New Mexico. Until the Colorado Superintendency was established in 1861, the Conejos Agency was assigned to the New Mexico Superintendency. In 1869 the agency was moved from Conejos to a site on Los Pinos Creek (a tributary of the Cochetopa River) on the Ute reservation established under the provisions of a treaty of March 2, 1868. Thereafter the agency was called the Los Pinos Agency, but it was sometimes referred to as the Lower or Southern Ute Agency. It should not be confused with the Southern Ute Agency established in 1877. In 1875 the agency was moved to the Uncompahgre Valley, but the name "Los Pinos" was retained. In 1881 the Tabaquache, now usually called Uncompahgre, moved to a reservation on the Green River in Utah next to the Uintah Reservation. The agency was also moved and renamed the Ouray Agency in honor of the late chief of the Tabaquache. In 1886 the Uintah and Ouray Agencies were combined to form the Uintah and Ouray Agency.

MIDDLE PARK-WHITE RIVER AGENCY

The Middle Park Agency was established in 1862 for the Grand River and Uinta Ute. Later there were also Yampa Ute at the agency. Until 1869 the agency had no permanent headquarters. In that year it was moved from the Middle Park area to the White River on the Ute reservation established under the provisions of the treaty of March 2, 1868. Thereafter the agency was called either the White River Agency or the Upper Agency. In 1879 the agency headquarters was moved about 15 miles down the river from its original site to Powell Valley. Later that year Agent Meeker and the other employees were killed by the Indians and the agency was destroyed. It was never restored. Later the Indians were moved to the Uintah Reservation in Utah. The White River Agency in Colorado should not be confused with the Lower Brulé Agency in Dakota, which was known briefly as the White River Agency.

DENVER SPECIAL AGENCY

The Denver Special Agency was established in 1871 after the Colorado Superintendency was discontinued. It was responsible for the roving groups of Ute Indians that frequented Denver. The agency was discontinued in November, 1874, reestablished in February, 1875 and finally discontinued on December 31, 1875.

SOUTHERN UTE AGENCY

The Southern Ute Agency was established in 1877 on the Rio de los Pinos in southeastern Colorado just north of the New Mexico border. It was responsible for the Capote, Wiminuche and Moache Ute who previously had been attached to the Abiquiu and Cimarron Agencies in New Mexico. There were also a few Navajo at the agency. It should be noted that the Southern Ute Agency was completely distinct from the Los Pinos Agency, which was sometimes called the Southern Ute Agency. The Rio de los Pinos and Los Pinos Creek are two separate streams. The Southern Ute Agency continued in operation beyond 1880 and after 1881 was the only agency in Colorado.

SPECIAL COMMISSIONS

Special commissions were sent to negotiate with the Ute Indians in 1878 and 1880. The 1878 Ute Commission consisted of Edward Hatch, N. C. McFarland and William Stickney (replaced by Lot M. Morrill). The 1880 Ute Commission, which secured the removal of the Indians of the White River and Los Pinos Agencies to Utah, consisted of George W. Manypenny, Alfred B. Meacham, John Bowman, John J. Russell and Otto Mears.

GOVERNORS AND *EX OFFICIO* SUPERINTENDENTS

Name	*Date of Appointment*
William Gilpin	Mar. 25, 1861
John Evans	Mar. 26, 1862
A. Cameron Hunt	May 10, 1867
Edward M. McCook	Apr. 17, 1869

AGENTS

Upper Arkansas Agency

(See Upper Arkansas Agency for earlier and later agents.)

Albert G. Boone	Oct. 17, 1860
Samuel G. Colley	July 26, 1861
Ichabod C. Taylor	Aug. 3, 1865

Conejos-Los Pinos Agency

Conejos

Lafayette Head	June 27, 1860

Los Pinos

Lt. Calvin T. Speer	June 26, 1869
Capt. William H. Merrill	July 23, 1869

Los Pinos (cont.)

Lt. Calvin T. Speer	Assigned Sept. 29, 1869
Jabez Nelson Trask	Feb. 8, 1871
Charles Adams	May 28, 1872
Henry F. Bond	May 20, 1874
Willard D. Wheeler	Sept. 4, 1876
Joseph B. Abbott	Dec. 3, 1877
Leverett M. Kelley	Sept. 26, 1878
Wilson M. Stanley	Apr. 28, 1879
George Sherman (acting)	Jan. 1, 1880
William H. Berry	Apr. 22, 1880

Middle Park-White River Agency

Middle Park

Simeon Whiteley	Dec. 23, 1862
Daniel C. Oakes	May 11, 1865

White River

Lt. W. W. Parry	June 26, 1869
Capt. William H. Merrill	Assigned Oct. 23, 1869
Capt. H. Latimer Beck	Mar. 29, 1870
John S. Littlefield	Feb. 8, 1871
Edward H. Danforth	May 8, 1874
Nathan C. Meeker	Feb. 6, 1878

Denver Special Agency

James B. Thompson	Jan. 17, 1871

Southern Ute Agency

Francis H. Weaver	Apr. 10, 1877
Henry Page	Jan. 29, 1879

COUNCIL BLUFFS AGENCY
1836-1857

Both the Council Bluffs Agency and the Council Bluffs Subagency were established in 1837. The correspondence for 1836 filed under the "Council Bluffs" heading actually relates to the Upper Missouri Agency. The Council Bluffs Agency was responsible for the Oto, Missouri, Omaha and Pawnee Indians who lived west of the Missouri River in present Nebraska. These Indians previously had been assigned to the Upper Missouri Agency. The Upper Missouri Agency was now moved farther up the Missouri River to the site of the former Sioux Subagency. Until 1839 the Council Bluffs agent usually stayed at Fort Leavenworth and visited the Indians only occasionally. Thereafter he stayed at Bellevue on the west side of the Missouri River about 20 miles below Council Bluffs. Between 1849 and 1851 the agency was reduced to a subagency. The Council Bluffs Agency was discontinued in 1856 and was replaced by the Otoe Agency for the Oto, Missouri and Pawnee Indians and the Omaha Agency for the Omaha Indians. Two 1857 letters relating to the affairs of the Council Bluffs Agency are filed under the "Council Bluffs" heading.

The Council Bluffs Subagency was responsible for the United Band of Ottawa, Chippewa and Potawatomi. These Indians had moved from Michigan and Illinois and in 1837 were living on the east side of the Missouri River in the vicinity of Council Bluffs (now in Iowa). The Council Bluffs Subagency, therefore, was on the opposite side of the river and north of the Council Bluffs Agency at Bellevue. In 1847 the Council Bluffs Subagency was discontinued. The Ottawa and Chippewa had moved to the Osage River Agency. The Potawatomi joined the Osage River Potawatomi and for a short time were assigned a subagent of their own. Early in 1848, however, they were attached to the Fort Leavenworth Agency.

The Council Bluffs Agency was under the St. Louis Superintendency until 1851 and thereafter under its successor, the Central Superintendency. The Council Bluffs Subagency was in Wisconsin Territory until 1838 and then in Iowa Territory until 1846. The subagency, however, was always under the St. Louis Superintendency rather than the Wisconsin or Iowa Superintendency.

See also St. Louis, Iowa and Central Superintendencies and Upper Missouri, Fort Leavenworth, Osage River, Great Nemaha, Otoe and Omaha Agencies.

AGENTS AND SUBAGENTS

Council Bluffs Agency

Name	*Date of Appointment*
John Dougherty	Apr. 13, 1837
Joseph V. Hamilton	June 27, 1839
Daniel Miller	Oct. 22, 1841
Jonathan Bean	July 25, 1845
John Miller	July 22, 1846
John E. Barrow (subagent)	Apr. 13, 1849
John E. Barrow (agent)	June 30, 1851
James M. Gatewood	Apr. 18, 1853
George Hepner	May 19, 1854

Council Bluffs Subagency

Edwin James	Notified Apr. 28, 1837
Stephen Cooper	Apr. 4, 1839
James Deaderick	Sept. 2, 1841
John B. Luce	Transferred from Neosho, July 12, 1842
Richard S. Elliot	Mar. 24, 1843
Robert B. Mitchell	Oct. 14, 1845

CREEK AGENCY
1824-1876

Actually there were two separate Creek Agencies—one for the Creek Indians living east of the Mississippi River, principally in Georgia and Alabama, and one for the Creek Indians living in Indian Territory. Most of the correspondence for the years from 1826 to 1836 relating to the western Creek Agency is filed under the subheading "Creek West," and the correspondence under the main "Creek" heading relates principally to the eastern agency. The "Creek West" subheading was not used after 1836.

An agent was appointed for the Creek Indians in the east as early as 1792. The agency was permanently established before 1800, although between 1796 and 1803 the agent was designated as principal agent for the entire area south of the Ohio River and east of the Mississippi River. Until the Bureau of Indian Affairs was established in 1824, correspondence relating to the Creek Agency was transmitted directly to the Office of the Secretary of War. By 1824 the agency was not subordinate to any superintendency and the agent reported directly to the Bureau. At that time the agency was located east of the Flint River near Knoxville, Georgia. At the end of 1832 the agency was reduced to a subagency. The subagent, Leonard Tarrant, was also an agent for the locating of Creek reserves. He usually stayed at Mardisville, Alabama. In 1836, when he resigned as subagent in order to devote full time to his work as location agent, he was not replaced. Thereafter military officers attended to any essential business formerly handled by the subagent.

The western Creek Agency was established in 1826 although few Creek Indians had yet moved west. The first agent, David Brearly, was put in charge of the Indians while they were emigrating as well as after they had arrived in Indian Territory. In 1829 Brearly was dismissed and the agent in the east was notified that he would be in charge of all the Creek—those in the east, those in the west and those in transit. Before this change went into effect, however, another agent was appointed for the western Creek. He was warned that he would probably serve only a few months until the agent in Georgia moved to Indian Territory. Actually, however, both agencies continued to operate until 1836, when the agency in the east was discontinued. There was never a formal removal of the eastern agency to Indian Territory.

The western Creek agent reported directly to the Bureau of Indian Affairs in Washington until 1834, when the agency was attached to the new Western Superintendency and was reduced to a subagency. Again made a full agency in 1837, the Creek Agency was also in charge of the Seminole Indians who had moved west. In 1842 a separate subagency was established for the Seminole.

The headquarters of the Creek Agency was located at various places in the vicinity of Fort Gibson and the confluence of the Arkansas, Grand and Verdigris Rivers. For many years the agency was at a place on the Arkansas River 6 miles from Fort Gibson. In 1851 the agency was moved about 5 miles up the Arkansas River farther away from Fort Gibson.

In 1851 the Southern Superintendency replaced the Western Superintendency. The Creek Agency remained under the Southern Superintendency until it was discontinued in 1870. The central superintendent then took over those duties that were required by terms of treaties, such as the investigation of certain claims and, particularly in the case of the Creek Agency, the selection of a site for the agency buildings. On other matters the agent reported directly to the Bureau of Indian Affairs in Washington.

At the beginning of the Civil War Confederate troops occupied Indian Territory. Many of the Creek remained loyal to the United States and took refuge in

Kansas. The Creek Agent established temporary headquarters in Kansas, first at Leroy and later at the Sac and Fox Agency. By 1865 the agent had returned to Indian Territory, staying first at Fort Gibson and then about 12 miles up the Arkansas River near the old agency site. This was intended to be a temporary location, but permanent buildings had not yet been erected anywhere when the agency was discontinued in 1874. In that year the Creek, Choctaw and Seminole Agencies were consolidated with the Cherokee Agency to form the Union Agency; however some correspondence was still filed under the heading "Creek" until 1876. Under the subheadings "Creek Emigration" and "Creek Reserves," there is correspondence relating to the emigration of the Indians and the disposition of their land holdings, but correspondence relating to these subjects is also filed under the "Creek" and "Creek West" headings.

In addition to the regular agents, there were various special agents and commissioners designated to perform particular duties. Most of these duties related to the settlement of Creek affairs in Georgia and Alabama.

See also Western, Southern and Central Superintendencies and Choctaw, Seminole, Cherokee and Union Agencies. There are some field records of the Creek Agency, East among the records of the Bureau of Indian Affairs in the National Archives.

AGENTS

Creek Agency, East

Name	*Date of Appointment*
James Seagrove	Feb. 20, 1792
Benjamin Hawkins	Dec. 1, 1796
David B. Mitchell	Oct. 3, 1816
John Crowell	Mar. 1, 1821
Leonard Tarrant (subagent)	Jan. 1, 1833

Creek Agency, West

David Brearly	May 13, 1826
John Campbell	Oct. 1, 1829
Luther Blake (acting)	Mar. 26, 1830
John Campbell	Aug. 10, 1830
Robert A. McCabe (subagent)	Notified July 8, 1834
Wharton Rector (subagent)	Aug. 19, 1835
Francis Audrain (subagent)	Aug. 29, 1836
John W. A. Sandford	Mar. 8, 1837
James Logan	Feb. 23, 1838
James L. Dawson	May 16, 1842
James Logan	June 8, 1844
Philip H. Raiford	Apr. 5, 1849

William H. Garrett	Apr. 18, 1853
George A. Cutler	July 16, 1861
James W. Dunn	June 9, 1865
Capt. F. A. Field	July 15, 1869
Francis S. Lyon	Jan. 23, 1871
Edward R. Roberts	Apr. 9, 1873

CROW CREEK AGENCY
1871-1876

The Crow Creek Agency succeeded the Upper Missouri Agency, which had been established in 1819. Although the name was not officially changed to Crow Creek until December 22, 1874, the agency had been commonly known by that name since 1866. Between 1871 and 1874 correspondence was filed under both names, but principally under "Upper Missouri."

By 1871 the Upper Missouri or Crow Creek Agency was located at Sneotka or Soldier Creek on the east side of the Missouri River, about 8 miles from Crow Creek itself in what is now South Dakota. It was responsible for the Lower Yanktonai Sioux Indians living on the Crow Creek Reservation and for the Lower Brulé Sioux Indians living on the opposite side of the river about 8 miles from the agency. In 1875 a separate agency was established for the Lower Brulé.

The Crow Creek agent reported directly to the Bureau of Indian Affairs in Washington, except during the temporary re-establishment of the Dakota Superintendency in 1877 and 1878. Beginning in July, 1876 correspondence concerning the Crow Creek Agency was filed under the heading "Dakota." Much of the correspondence relating to the agency has been segregated into Special File 248, which relates to charges against Agent Henry Livingston of Crow Creek and Agent Henry Gregory of Lower Brulé.

During the period 1882-96 the Crow Creek Agency was consolidated with the Lower Brulé Agency to form the Crow Creek and Lower Brulé Agency. In 1896 they again became separate agencies.

See also Dakota Superintendency and Upper Missouri and Lower Brulé Agencies. For correspondence concerning earlier agencies in the Crow Creek area see St. Peters and Winnebago Agencies.

AGENTS

Name	Date of Appointment
Henry F. Livingston	Oct. 18, 1870
Capt. William E. Dougherty (acting)	Mar. 21, 1878

CROW WING SUBAGENCY 1835-1840

The Crow Wing Subagency was established in 1835 to supervise the Chippewa Indians who were residing on the upper Mississippi. Previously those Indians had been assigned to the Mackinac and Sault Ste. Marie Agency. The headquarters of the subagency was first located at a trading post of the American Fur Company near the mouth of the Crow Wing River in Minnesota. After the trading post was discontinued in 1837, the subagent remained at the St. Peters Agency near Fort Snelling. In 1839 the subagency was discontinued and its duties were absorbed by the La Pointe Subagency.

The Crow Wing Subagency was under the supervision of the St. Louis Superintendency from its establishment until 1836, when it became part of the newly created Wisconsin Superintendency.

See also St. Louis and Wisconsin Superintendencies and La Pointe, Mackinac and Sault Ste. Marie Agencies.

SUBAGENTS

Name	Date of Appointment
James B. Dallam	Notified Sept. 11, 1835
William Sinn	Notified May 28, 1836
Myles M. Vineyard	Feb. 22, 1837

DAKOTA SUPERINTENDENCY
1861-1880

The Dakota Superintendency was established in 1861, the year Dakota Territory was organized. Originally the Territory extended from the 43rd parallel to Canada and from Minnesota and Iowa to the Continental Divide. The Indians and agencies in this area previously had been under the jurisdiction of the Central Superintendency. In 1863 that part of Dakota Territory west of the present states of North and South Dakota was made part of Idaho Territory. With the organization of Montana Territory in 1864 most of present Wyoming was attached to Dakota Territory, where it remained until Wyoming Territory was established in 1868. Thereafter Dakota Territory comprised present North and South Dakota except that the southern boundary had not been finally determined. The Dakota Superintendency at times had under its supervision some agencies located in Nebraska and Wyoming.

Most of the Indians in Dakota belonged to various bands of Sioux including Hunkpapa, Oglala, Yankton, Blackfeet, Brulé, Sisseton, Wahpeton, Yanktonai, Sans Arcs, Miniconjou, Two Kettles (Oohenonpa), Cut Head (Pabaska) and Santee. There were also Cheyenne, Arapaho, Arikara (Arickaree), Mandan, Ponca, Crow and Winnebago.

The Territorial Governor at Yankton served as *ex officio* superintendent from the beginning of the superintendency until it was discontinued in 1870. Thereafter the agents in Dakota reported directly to the Bureau of Indian Affairs in Washington. The superintendency was reactivated in 1877, with headquarters again at Yankton but with a full-time superintendent in charge. It was terminated in 1878.

Until July, 1876 correspondence concerning individual agencies in Dakota was filed under names of agencies, but after that date correspondence relating to the Crow Creek, Lower Brulé and Yankton Agencies was filed under "Dakota." Correspondence concerning other agencies was still filed under the agency names. Much of the correspondence filed under "Dakota" relates to Indians who were not yet located on reservations and were not under the control of any agency.

Operating in Dakota when the superintendency was established in 1861 were the Blackfeet, Ponca, Upper Missouri and Yankton Agencies. In 1863 the Blackfeet Agency was transferred to the Idaho Superintendency and the following year to the Montana Superintendency. The Ponca Agency was moved to Indian Territory in 1877. The Upper Missouri Agency was renamed the Crow Creek Agency in 1874, but some correspondence was filed under the name "Crow Creek" as early as 1871.

In 1863 many of the Sioux of the Mississippi and the Winnebago Indians from the St. Peters and Winnebago Agencies in Minnesota were moved to an area on the Missouri River near the mouth of Crow Creek (later the location of the Upper Missouri-Crow Creek Agency). Until 1865 the Winnebago agent was in charge of both tribes, but he was under the supervision of the Northern rather than the Dakota Superintendency. In 1865 the Winnebago Agency was moved to the new reservation for the Winnebago in Nebraska and the successor to the St. Peters agent was assigned to the Sioux Indians at Crow Creek. In 1866, however, the Indians, now known as the Santee Sioux, moved to Nebraska, and the St. Peters or Santee Sioux Agency was again within the limits of the Northern Superintendency.

The Fort Berthold Agency was established in 1864. Until 1867 correspondence concerning it was filed with that for the Upper Missouri Agency.

The Grand River (renamed Standing Rock in 1874), Whetstone (successor to the Upper Platte Agency and renamed Spotted Tail in 1874) and Cheyenne River Agencies were all established in 1869. Until 1871 correspondence concerning them was filed under the heading "Upper Platte." Beginning in 1878 Spotted Tail was usually known as the Rosebud Agency, but for filing purposes the name Spotted Tail was retained through 1880.

The Red Cloud Agency, established in 1871, was usually known as Pine Ridge after 1878, but for filing purposes the name Red Cloud was retained through 1880. The Lower Brulé Agency (known briefly as White River) was established in 1875.

Assigned to the revived superintendency in 1877 were the Standing Rock, Cheyenne River, Crow Creek, Lower Brulé, Yankton, Red Cloud and Spotted Tail Agencies. The Fort Berthold Agency was not included. The Sisseton Agency, established in 1867; the Devil's Lake Agency, established in 1871; and the Flandreau Agency, established in 1873, were located in Dakota Territory but were never under the supervision of the Dakota Superintendency.

See also St. Louis, Central, Idaho, Montana, Northern and Wyoming Superintendencies and Blackfeet, Cheyenne River, Crow Creek, Devil's Lake, Flandreau, Fort Berthold, Grand River, Lower Brulé, Nebraska, Ponca, Red Cloud, St. Peters, Santee Sioux, Sisseton, Spotted Tail, Standing Rock, Upper Missouri, Upper Platte, Whetstone, Winnebago and Yankton Agencies. There are also field records of the Dakota Superintendency among the records of the Bureau of Indian Affairs in the National Archives.

GOVERNORS AND *EX OFFICIO* SUPERINTENDENTS, 1861-70

Name	Date of Appointment
William Jayne	Mar. 27, 1861
Newton Edmunds	Oct. 6, 1863
Andrew J. Faulk	Aug. 4, 1866
John A. Burbank	Apr. 5, 1869

John H. Hammond   Apr. 5, 1877
William J. Pollock   Feb. 21, 1878

AGENTS, 1876-80

Listed below are the agents of the three agencies for which the correspondence for the period July, 1876–December, 1880 is filed under the heading "Dakota" rather than the agency name. For complete lists of agents see the individual agencies.

CROW CREEK

Henry F. Livingstone   Oct. 18, 1870
Capt. William E. Dougherty (acting)   Mar. 21, 1878

YANKTON

John G. Gasmann   Feb. 23, 1872
John W. Douglas   Mar. 28, 1878
Robert S. Gardner (special)   On duty May 16, 1879
William D. E. Andrus   June 30, 1879

LOWER BRULÉ

Thomas A. Reily   July 2, 1875
Henry E. Gregory   July 18, 1876
Capt. William E. Dougherty (acting)   Mar. 21, 1878
William H. Parkhurst   May 27, 1880

DELAWARE AGENCY
1855-1873

The Delaware Agency was established in 1855 for the Delaware Indians of eastern Kansas. These Indians had been assigned to the Fort Leavenworth Agency and its predecessors until 1851 and from 1851 until 1855 to the Kansas Agency. The Delaware Agency was under the supervision of the Central Superintendency. The agency headquarters occupied, at different times, various places between present-day Leavenworth and Kansas City.

The Delaware were granted a reserve north of the Kansas River under the provisions of an 1829 treaty. This reserve was reduced in area by a treaty of 1854. A few Stockbridge and Munsee Indians (known jointly as "Christian" Indians) also lived on the Delaware Reservation, but by 1859 they had joined the Chippewa then attached to the Sac and Fox Agency. In 1863 the Wyandot Indians were transferred from the Shawnee Agency to the Delaware Agency. A treaty of 1860 provided for the further reduction of the area of the Delaware Reserve and for the allotment of tribal lands to individual Indians. In 1866 and 1867 the Delaware Tribe agreed to buy a tract of land on the Caney River in Indian Territory from the Cherokee Nation, and Delaware Indians who wished to retain their tribal status were expected to move to this new area. Those who remained behind to occupy their allotted land were no longer considered tribal members. By 1869 most of the Delaware had moved and were assigned to the Cherokee Agency, although some settled temporarily on land within the jurisdiction of the Neosho Agency (after 1871 the Quapaw Agency). Most of the Wyandot Indians also had moved to the Neosho Agency. The Delaware Agency was, therefore, discontinued in 1869. Some correspondence, relating largely to the settlement of Delaware affairs in Kansas and the administration of Delaware tribal funds, was filed under "Delaware" until 1873. For the years 1870-72 there is correspondence concerning the Wyandot Indians, filed under the heading "Wyandot."

A band of Delaware left the main tribe early in the 19th century and settled with the Caddo Indians in Texas. In 1859 they moved to the Wichita Agency in Indian Territory. Other small groups of Delaware Indians dispersed to other parts of the country.

See also St. Louis and Central Superintendencies and Kansas, Shawnee, Cherokee, Union, Neosho, Osage River, Fort Leavenworth, Texas, Wichita and Wyandot Agencies and Subagencies. For correspondence concerning the Delaware before their removal west, see Piqua and Ohio Agencies.

AGENTS

Name	Date of Appointment
Benjamin F. Robinson	Mar. 3, 1855
Thomas B. Sykes (special)	May 3, 1859
Thomas B. Sykes (agent)	Mar. 12, 1860
Fielding Johnson	Mar. 27, 1861
John G. Pratt	Apr. 14, 1864

DEVIL'S LAKE AGENCY
1871-1880

The Devil's Lake Agency, sometimes called the Fort Totten Agency, was established in 1871 for the Indians who lived on the Devil's Lake Reservation, which had been established in 1867. The reservation was located on the south side of Devil's Lake in the northern part of Dakota Territory. Before 1871 the Indians in this area—who belonged to the Sisseton, Wahpeton and Cut Head (Pabaska) bands of Sioux—had been assigned to the Sisseton Agency. The agency was never assigned to any superintendency and the agent reported directly to the Bureau of Indian Affairs in Washington. The agency continued in operation beyond 1880.

See also Dakota Superintendency and Sisseton Agency.

AGENTS

Name	*Date of Appointment*
William H. Forbes	Jan. 23, 1871
Paul Beckwith	Aug. 7, 1875
James McLaughlin	June 8, 1876

FLANDREAU AGENCY
1873-1876

The Flandreau Agency was established in 1873 for a group of Santee Sioux who had left the Santee Sioux Agency in Nebraska and moved to the head of the Big Sioux River in Dakota Territory. Although the agency was located at Flandreau, the agent spent much of his time at Greenwood, Dakota. The agency was not attached to any superintendency and the agent reported directly to the Bureau of Indian Affairs in Washington.

Beginning in July, 1876 correspondence concerning the agency was filed under "Nebraska." In 1879 it was consolidated with the Santee Sioux Agency, but the Indians continued to live at Flandreau.

See also Dakota Superintendency and Santee Sioux and Nebraska Agencies.

AGENTS

Name	Date of Appointment
John P. Williamson (special)	Sept. 10, 1873
William H. H. Wasson	July 1, 1878

FLORIDA SUPERINTENDENCY 1824-1853

The Florida Superintendency was formally established in 1822, the year Florida Territory was organized, but officials had been assigned to Florida the previous year. Until the establishment of the Bureau of Indian Affairs in 1824, the superintendency was under the direct supervision of the Secretary of War. The Territorial Governor, who resided permanently in Tallahassee beginning in 1824, acted as *ex officio* superintendent throughout the existence of the superintendency. The principal Indian tribe in Florida was the Seminole.

On March 21, 1821 a subagent for Indians in Florida, responsible to the newly appointed provisional Governor, Andrew Jackson, was appointed. In September of the same year a temporary agent was appointed to handle Indian affairs during the absence of the Governor and the subagent was made responsible to him. When the regular Territorial Government was organized the following year, an agent and a subagent were authorized to serve under the Governor. In practice, the agent usually served on the Seminole Reservation and the subagent was used wherever needed. In 1826 an additional subagent was appointed for the Indians on the Apalachicola River. Correspondence was filed under the headings "Seminole" and "Apalachicola" as well as "Florida," and it is necessary to consult all three classifications for records concerning the Florida Superintendency, the Seminole or Florida Agency and the Apalachicola Subagency.

With the contemplated removal of the Indians from Florida, both the superintendency and the subagencies were abolished on June 30, 1834. In November the agent, Wiley Thompson, became Superintendent of Emigration and he served in this capacity until his death in 1835. Thereafter the control of Indians in Florida was entrusted to the Army, except that there were some Bureau officials on the Apalachicola River until 1839 and in 1849 there was a short-lived subagency for the Seminole still in Florida. Some correspondence concerning the Indians in Florida was filed under "Florida" until 1850. Thereafter any such correspondence was filed with that relating to the Seminole Agency in Indian Territory. Some records concerning the emigration of Indians from Florida were filed under the subheading "Florida Emigration" and there is some correspondence concerning Indian lands in Florida under the subheading "Florida Reserves."

See also Seminole Agency and Apalachicola Subagency .

GOVERNORS AND *EX OFFICIO* SUPERINTENDENTS

Name	*Date of Appointment*
Andrew Jackson (provisional)	Mar. 31, 1821
William DuVal	Apr. 17, 1822

FORT BERTHOLD AGENCY 1867-1880

The agency that came to be known as the Fort Berthold Agency was established when the Upper Missouri Agency was divided in 1864. The incumbent Upper Missouri agent was left in charge of the Sioux Indians of the upper Missouri River area, while a new agent was made responsible for the Mandan, Grosventre, Arikara (Arickaree), Assiniboin and Crow Indians living farther up the Missouri River in the vicinity of Fort Berthold and Fort Union in the present State of North Dakota and in eastern Montana.

Correspondence concerning both agencies was filed under "Upper Missouri" until 1867. In that year the Bureau began filing correspondence relating to the upper agency under the name "Fort Berthold," which had become the agency headquarters. As late as 1870, however, the agency was frequently referred to as the Upper Missouri Agency, and it was not until 1871 that an agent was specifically assigned to the "Fort Berthold Agency."

During 1869 and 1870 the Assiniboin, Crow and some of the Grosventre were transferred to the Crow and Milk River Agencies. Thereafter the Fort Berthold Agency was responsible for only the Mandan, Arikara (Arickaree) and Grosventre Indians living on the Fort Berthold Reservation, which was established in 1870.

The Dakota Superintendency had jurisdiction over the Fort Berthold Agency until 1870, when the superintendency was discontinued. Fort Berthold was not assigned to the revived Dakota Superintendency in 1877, and the agent continued to report directly to the Bureau of Indian Affairs in Washington.

The Fort Berthold Agency continued in operation beyond 1880.

See also Dakota and Montana Superintendencies and Upper Missouri Agency.

AGENTS

Name	*Date of Appointment*
Mahlon Wilkinson	Mar. 2, 1864
Capt. Walter Clifford	June 25, 1869
John E. Tappan	Feb. 17, 1871
Lyman B. Sperry	Sept. 22, 1873
Charles W. Darling	Sept. 23, 1875
Edwin H. Alden	Nov. 20, 1876
Thomas P. Ellis	Sept. 26, 1878
Robert S. Gardner (special)	In charge Aug. 31, 1879
Jacob Kauffman	Apr. 16, 1880

FORT LEAVENWORTH AGENCY
1824-1851

The Fort Leavenworth Agency was established in 1837. The correspondence for the years 1824-37 that is filed under the heading "Fort Leavenworth" relates to predecessor agencies. In 1821 an agency was established for the Osage, Delaware and Kickapoo Indians. In 1824 this agency was divided, one agent being made responsible for the Osage and a second agent for the Delaware, Kickapoo and other scattered bands living near them. The second agency came to be known as the Delaware and Shawnee Agency. The Indians, who had been living in diverse parts of Missouri, Illinois and adjacent areas, were supplemented by others moved from the east, and they were gradually concentrated on reserves on both sides of the Kansas River west of Missouri. The agent made St. Louis his headquarters until 1829 when he moved to the Kansas River. In 1832 permanent buildings were erected about 7 miles south of the mouth of the Kansas River on Shawnee land. The nearest city was Westport, Missouri, now part of Kansas City. Much of the correspondence relating to the Delaware and Shawnee Agency is filed with the correspondence relating to the St. Louis Superintendency to which the agency was assigned rather than under "Fort Leavenworth."

The Kansas Agency for the Kansa (Kaw) Indians was also located in the Kansas River area. It was established as a subagency by the St. Louis superintendent in 1825 and in 1832 it was made a full agency. Correspondence relating to this agency is filed under both "St. Louis" and "Fort Leavenworth."

In 1834 the Delaware and Shawnee Agency and the Kansas Agency were discontinued. The Delaware, Kansa and Kickapoo Indians were assigned to the new Northern Agency of the Western Territory. A subagency was established for the other Indians living west of Missouri by this time—Shawnee, Ottawa, Peoria, Kaskaskia, Piankeshaw and Wea. In 1835 the subagency was discontinued and these Indians were also attached to the Northern Agency. The Northern Agency, which used the Delaware and Shawnee Agency buildings as its headquarters, was assigned to the St. Louis Superintendency. There was also a Southern Agency, but this was in the Western Superintendency.

In 1837 the Fort Leavenworth Agency replaced the Northern Agency and was made responsible for the Delaware, Shawnee, Kansa and Kickapoo Indians. The other Indians that had been assigned to the Northern Agency were attached to the new Osage River Subagency. The Fort Leavenworth agent continued to stay at the headquarters of the Northern Agency near Westport and the agency was never located at Fort Leavenworth. The Fort Leavenworth Agency should not be confused with the Upper Missouri or the Council Bluffs Agency. Although John Dougherty—Upper Missouri agent from 1827 until 1837 and Council Bluffs agent from 1837 until 1839—usually stayed at Fort Leavenworth, he had no responsibility for the Indians assigned to the Fort Leavenworth Agency or its predecessors.

In 1839 some Munsee and Stockbridge Indians moved onto Delaware land. In 1847 the Kansa Indians were transferred to the Osage River Agency. At the same time Alfred Vaughn was designated subagent for the Potawatomi Indians previously assigned to the Council Bluffs Subagency and the Osage River Subagency. A few months later, however, in 1848, this Pottawatomie Subagency was discontinued and the Indians were attached to the Fort Leavenworth Agency. The correspondence relating to this short-lived subagency is filed under the heading "Fort Leavenworth."

As part of the general reorganization of 1851 the Fort Leavenworth Agency was discontinued and the former Fort Leavenworth agent was assigned to the Potawatomi Agency (Potawatomi and Kansa Indians). The Kansas Agency was established for the Delaware, Shawnee, Wyandot, Munsee and Stockbridge Indians. The Kickapoo were attached to the Great Nemaha Agency.

See also St. Louis, Western and Central Superintendencies and Osage River, Upper Missouri, Council Bluffs, Great Nemaha, Pottawatomie and Kansas Agencies. For correspondence concerning the Indians while they were living in the east see Michigan Superintendency and Piqua, Ohio, Fort Wayne, Indiana, Chicago, Green Bay and New York Agencies.

AGENTS

Osage, Delaware and Kickapoo Agency

Name	*Date of Appointment*
Richard Graham	Assigned Apr. 2, 1821

Delaware and Shawnee Agency

Richard Graham	Assigned June 7, 1824
George Vashon	Apr. 15, 1829
Richard W. Cummins	June 1, 1830

Kansas Agency

A. Baronet Vasquez (subagent)	Assignment reported Apr. 13, 1825
Marston G. Clark (subagent)	Feb. 19, 1829
Marston G. Clark (agent)	Notified July 12, 1832

Northern Agency

Richard W. Cummins	Notified July 14, 1834

Subagency for Ottawa, Shawnee, etc.

Marston G. Clark	Notified July 8, 1834

Fort Leavenworth Agency

Richard W. Cummins   Apr. 13, 1837
Luke Lea   Aug. 9, 1849

Pottawatomie Subagency

Alfred J. Vaughn   Transferred from
                                                     Osage River, Dec.
                                                     8, 1847

FORT WAYNE AGENCY
1824-1830

The Fort Wayne Agency was established in 1802. The principal Indians living in the Fort Wayne area were Miami (including the Eel River Indians) and Potawatomi, but, particularly in the earlier years, there were also Wea, Wyandot, Kickapoo, Ottawa, Shawnee and other tribes.

The Fort Wayne Agency was assigned to the Indiana Superintendency until Indiana became a State in 1816 and the superintendency was discontinued. By 1817 the agency was attached to the Michigan Superintendency and in 1818 the Fort Wayne Agency was consolidated with the Piqua Agency. Within a short time, however, the former Fort Wayne agent was appointed as a subagent, and in 1819 a full agent was again assigned to Fort Wayne. At this time Miami, Eel River, Wea and Potawatomi Indians were designated as belonging to the agency. Other Potawatomi Indians were living in Michigan and Illinois.

In 1821 the Vincennes Agency, the only other agency in Indiana, was discontinued, most of the Indians previously assigned to it having emigrated. Any Indians who had remained in the area were to be attached to the Fort Wayne Agency. There were subagents subordinate to the Fort Wayne Agency stationed at various places in Indiana.

Until the Bureau of Indian Affairs was established in 1824, correspondence relating to the Fort Wayne Agency was transmitted directly to the Office of the Secretary of War. Letters received by the Bureau of Indian Affairs relating to the Fort Wayne Agency and its Indians are filed under three different headings: "Fort Wayne," "Indiana" and "Miami." Most of the letters are filed under "Fort

Wayne" until 1828, when the agency was moved from Fort Wayne to the south side of the Wabash River between the mouths of Pipe Creek and Eel River. Later, however, the agent usually reported from Logansport at the mouth of the Eel River.

A larger part of the letters dated after 1828 are filed under "Indiana," but there is no apparent logic to the filing pattern. The "Fort Wayne" heading was not used for letters dated after 1830 and most of this correspondence is filed under "Indiana." There are only a few letters relating to the affairs of the Miami Indians filed under the heading "Miami" before 1838.

See also Michigan Superintendency and Indiana, Miami, Chicago, Piqua and Ohio Agencies and Subagencies.

AGENTS

Name	Date of Appointment
William Wells	Jan. 1, 1802
John Johnston	Jan. 27, 1809
Benjamin Franklin Stickney	Mar. 7, 1812
John Johnston	Piqua agent; put in charge of Fort Wayne on Apr. 22, 1818
Benjamin Franklin Stickney (subagent serving under Johnston)	July 14, 1818
William Turner	Mar. 6, 1819
John Hays	May 24, 1820
John Tipton	Mar. 28, 1823

GRAND RIVER AGENCY 1871-1875

The Grand River Agency was established under the Dakota Superintendency in 1869, but until 1871 correspondence relating to the agency was filed with that relating to the Upper Platte Agency. After the Dakota Superintendency was discontinued in 1870, the agent reported directly to the Bureau of Indian Affairs in Washington. The Grand River Agency was responsible primarily for Upper and Lower Yanktonai, Hunkpapa, Cut Head (Pabaska) and Blackfeet Sioux, but there were also members of the Two Kettle (Oohenonpa), Sans Arcs, Oglala and Brulé bands of Sioux.

In July, 1873 the Grand River Agency was moved from its original location at the junction of the Grand and Missouri Rivers in present-day South Dakota to Standing Rock, about 50 miles upstream on the Missouri River in present-day North Dakota. On December 22, 1874, the name of the agency was changed to Standing Rock. Beginning in 1875 correspondence (except for two letters) was filed under the new name.

See also Dakota Superintendency and Upper Platte and Standing Rock Agencies.

AGENTS

Name	*Date of Appointment*
Bvt. Maj. J. A. Hearn (special)	June 14, 1869
William F. Cady (special)	Sept. 30, 1870
J. C. O'Connor (special)	Feb. 14, 1871
J. C. O'Connor (agent)	July 23, 1872
Edmond Palmer	May 19, 1873

GREAT NEMAHA AGENCY
1837-1876

The Great Nemaha Agency was successor to the Ioway Subagency which was established in 1825. By a treaty of September 17, 1836, the Iowa and the Sauk and Fox of the Missouri agreed to move to new reserves south of the Missouri River along the Great Nemaha River in what is now southeastern Nebraska and northeastern Kansas immediately west of Missouri. The Indians moved in 1837, and beginning in that year the subagency for them was known as the Great Nemaha Subagency. A few letters concerning the removal are filed under the subheading "Great Nemaha Emigration." From January, 1838 until June, 1840, while the position of subagent was vacant, the Council Bluffs agent or a special agent sent out by the superintendent at St. Louis handled the business of the subagency, mainly the distribution of annuity goods to the Indians. By 1842 the agency headquarters was permanently located on Sauk and Fox land about 5 miles south of Iowa Point in present-day Kansas.

The Great Nemaha Subagency was assigned to the St. Louis Superintendency until 1851. As part of the general reorganization of that year, it was made a full agency in the Central Superintendency, successor to the St. Louis Superintendency. The Kickapoo Indians previously assigned to the Fort Leavenworth Agency were transferred to the Great Nemaha Agency until 1855, when a separate Kickapoo Agency was established. There were some Potawatomi Indians living with the Kickapoo, and some Winnebago Indians lived with the Iowa until 1860.

In 1854 and 1861 the Iowa and the Sauk and Fox of the Missouri signed new treaties by which they gave up most of their land except for small reserves on the Kansas-Nebraska border. In 1858 a new agency headquarters was built on the Iowa reserve just east of the Great Nemaha River and just north of the Kansas line in Nebraska. In 1860 a post office named Nohart was established at the agency.

In 1865 the Great Nemaha Agency was transferred from the Central Superintendency to the reorganized Northern Superintendency. After the Northern Superintendency was discontinued on June 30, 1876, the agent reported directly to the Bureau of Indian Affairs in Washington. Beginning July 1, 1876, correspondence received by the Bureau relating to the Great Nemaha Agency was filed under the heading "Nebraska." In 1882 the Great Nemaha Agency was consolidated with the Potawatomi Agency to form the Potawatomi and Great Nemaha Agency.

See also St. Louis, Central and Northern Superintendencies, Ioway Subagency and Council Bluffs, Fort Leavenworth, Kickapoo and Nebraska Agencies. For correspondence concerning other bands of Sauk and Fox see Sac and Fox Agency.

SUBAGENTS

Name	*Date of Appointment*
Andrew S. Hughes	Sept. 5, 1828, for Ioway Subagency; position vacant Jan. 8, 1838, until June 5, 1840
Congrave Jackson	June 5, 1840
William P. Richardson	June 25, 1841
Armstrong McClintock	July 25, 1845
William E. Rucker	June 17, 1846
Alfred J. Vaughn	Mar. 1, 1848
William P. Richardson	Dec. 18, 1849

AGENTS

William P. Richardson	June 30, 1851
Daniel Vanderslice	Apr. 18, 1853
John A. Burbank	Mar. 25, 1861
Chauncey H. Norris	Mar. 21, 1866
Thomas Lightfoot	Apr. 22, 1869
Charles H. Roberts	Sept. 8, 1873
Mahlon B. Kent	Feb. 26, 1875

GREEN BAY AGENCY
1824-1880

The Green Bay Agency was established in 1815. Until the Bureau of Indian Affairs was established in 1824, correspondence concerning the agency was transmitted directly to the Office of the Secretary of War. Originally no specific tribes were assigned to the agency, but Menominee, Winnebago, Chippewa, Ottawa and Potawatomi Indians lived in the Green Bay area. Later the Oneida, Stockbridge, Munsee and Brotherton Indians moved in from New York. The Fort Winnebago and Rock River Subagencies, established in 1829 and 1831, respectively, took charge of the Winnebago Indians previously attached to the Green Bay Agency, and the Prairie du Chien Agency had charge of those Winnebago who lived farther west. By this time the Chippewa, Ottawa and Potawatomi were attached to the Chicago Agency. The Green Bay Agency was then responsible only for the Menominee and the Indians who had emigrated from New York.

Headquarters of the agency was on the Fox River about 3 miles above Fort Howard, but the agent often stayed at other places in the Green Bay area. The agency was under the Michigan Superintendency until 1836, when it was transferred to the new Wisconsin Superintendency.

Under the regulations adopted in 1834, the limits of the agency were defined as north of the Milwaukee River (except for some Chippewa, Ottawa and Potawatomi living north of that river who were assigned to the Chicago Agency), west and south of the line of the Chippewa country (Mackinac and Sault Ste. Marie Agency) and east of a north-south line running through the portage of the Fox and Wisconsin Rivers (except for the Winnebago Indians in the immediate vicinity of the portage who remained in the Fort Winnebago Subagency). This meant that the Green Bay Agency still had charge of the Menominee and New York Indians.

The Green Bay Agency was abolished on December 31, 1836, and the commanding officer at Fort Howard was designated to perform the duties of the agent. The following spring, however, a subagency was established at Green Bay for the Menominee and New York Indians. The agency headquarters remained at Green Bay except for a period in 1842 and 1843 when the agent stayed at Grand Kaukaulin (Kaukalan) farther up the Fox River. In 1839 many of the Stockbridge and Munsee moved to the Delaware reserve in the present State of Kansas, where they were attached to the Fort Leavenworth Agency.

The Wisconsin Superintendency was discontinued in 1848, when Wisconsin became a State. From then until 1851 the Green Bay subagent reported directly to the Bureau of Indian Affairs in Washington. In that year the subagency was assigned to the new Northern Superintendency.

In 1855 the Green Bay Subagency was restored to full agency status. The agency, which was now to be located on the Menominee Reservation on Wolf River rather than at Green Bay, was sometimes called the Menominee Agency. The New York Indians were still attached to the agency, but by this time the Munsee and Brotherton had emigrated, had become citizens (giving up their status as Indians) or had merged with the Stockbridge. The Stockbridge now had a reservation on the southwest corner of the Menominee Reservation and the Oneida lived near Green Bay.

Agent Bonesteel—when he was appointed in 1857—was not instructed to report through the Northern Superintendency, and thereafter the agent reported directly to the Bureau of Indian Affairs in Washington. The agency was located at Keshena on the Menominee Reservation near the falls of Wolf River until 1858, when it was moved to Fond du Lac. The agent appointed in 1861 stayed at Portage until 1863, when he moved to Appleton. From 1866 until 1874 the agent resided at Green Bay. Thereafter the agency headquarters was again located at Keshena, although for a time the agent also kept an office at Green Bay. The Green Bay Agency continued to operate beyond 1880.

See also Michigan, Wisconsin, Northern and St. Louis Superintendencies and Mackinac, Sault Ste. Marie, Chicago, Prairie du Chien, St. Peters, Winnebago, Sac and Fox and Fort Leavenworth Agencies. There are a few field papers of the Green Bay Subagency for the year 1850 among the records of the Bureau of Indian Affairs in the National Archives.

AGENTS AND SUBAGENTS

Agents, 1815-37

Name	*Date of Appointment*
Charles Jouett	June 20, 1815
John Bowyer	Mar. 15, 1816
John Biddle	Mar. 10, 1821
Henry B. Brevoort	July 30, 1822
Samuel C. Stambaugh	Notified June 12, 1830
George Boyd	Transferred from Mackinac Apr. 18, 1832
Bvt. Brig. Gen. George M. Brooks (acting)	Jan. 1, 1837

Subagents, 1837-55

George Boyd	Mar. 31, 1837
George W. Lawe	May 24, 1842
David Jones	Notified Nov. 17, 1843
Albert G. Ellis	Aug. 21, 1845
William H. Bruce	Apr. 2, 1849
George Lawe	Mar. 28, 1851
John V. Suydam	May 11, 1853
Ephraim Shaler	Feb. 21, 1855

Agents, 1855-80

Benjamins Hunkins	May 8, 1855
Frederick Moscowitt	Feb. 16, 1857
Augustus D. Bonesteel	Sept. 23, 1857
Moses M. Davis	Apr. 1, 1861
Morgan L. Martin	May 8, 1866
A. H. Read	Appointed Apr. 9, 1869, but did not serve
Lt. J. A. Manley	June 24, 1869
Lt. W. R. Bourne	Feb. 10, 1870
William T. Richardson	Sept. 8, 1870
Isaac W. Hutchins	Appointed Mar. 3, 1873, but did not serve
Thomas N. Chase	May 31, 1873
Joseph C. Bridgeman	Aug. 22, 1874
Ebenezer Stephens	Mar. 3, 1879

IDAHO SUPERINTENDENCY
1863-1880

The Idaho Superintendency was established in 1863 with the organization of Idaho Territory from parts of Washington Territory and Dakota Territory. The area which comprises the present state of Idaho was, from 1848 to 1853, part of Oregon Territory. In 1853 part of the area was transferred to Washington Territory and the remaining part, in 1859. From 1863 until Montana Territory was organized in 1864, Idaho included Montana and part of Wyoming. Thereafter Idaho had its present boundaries. Indian tribes under the supervision of the Idaho Superintendency after 1864 were Nez Percé, Shoshone and Bannock. Coeur d'Alène, Kutenai, Pend d'Oreille and Spokan Indians also lived or roamed in Idaho, and the Coeur d'Alène Reservation was located in Idaho but the Coeur d'Alène and Spokan Indians were more closely associated with the Washington Superintendency, and the Kutenai and Pend d'Oreille with the Flathead Agency of the Montana Superintendency.

Until 1869 the territorial governor served as *ex officio* superintendent. After that time an army officer was detailed to the position. The superintendency headquarters was at the territorial capital, which was located briefly at Lewiston but was moved to Boise in 1864.

The Nez Percé, Flathead and Blackfeet Agencies were assigned to the Idaho Superintendency in 1863, but the following year the Flathead and Blackfeet Agencies were transferred to the new Montana Superintendency. Later the Flathead Agency was returned temporarily to the Idaho Superintendency and the Fort Hall and Lemhi Agencies were established in Idaho.

The Idaho Superintendency was discontinued in 1870. Thereafter the agents in Idaho reported directly to the Bureau of Indian Affairs in Washington. Until the change of filing systems in 1881, however, incoming correspondence relating to the individual agencies in Idaho was filed under the heading "Idaho" rather than under the names of the agencies.

See also Oregon, Washington, Wyoming, Montana, Dakota and Nevada Superintendencies and Blackfeet Agency. There are also some field records of the Idaho Superintendency among the records of the Bureau of Indian Affairs in the National Archives.

NEZ PERCÉ AGENCY

The Nez Percé Agency was a continuation of an agency for "Washington East of the Cascades" established in 1857 for the Nez Percé and other Indians. After 1861 the agency was called the Nez Percé Agency and was responsible only for the Nez Percé Indians. The agent usually stayed at Lapwai on the Nez Percé Reservation in the western part of present Idaho east of Lewiston. The agency was transferred to the Idaho Superintendency in 1863 and continued in operation beyond 1880.

BLACKFEET AGENCY

The Blackfeet Agency was established in 1855 and continued to operate beyond 1880. It was in the Idaho Superintendency, however, only from the time the superintendency was established in 1863 until the Montana Superintendency was established the following year. During this brief period the agency, with headquarters at Fort Benton, was responsible for Blackfeet (Siksika, Piegan, Blood (Kainah) and Grosventre Indians. Most of the correspondence relating to the agency until 1869 is filed under the name of the agency rather than under the name of the superintendency to which it was responsible.

FLATHEAD AGENCY

The Flathead Agency was estblished under the Washington Superintendency in 1854 and continued to operate beyond 1880. Like the Blackfeet Agency, it was assigned to the Idaho Superintendency for only one year, until the Montana Superintendency was established in 1864. From September, 1865 until February, 1866 it was again assigned to the Idaho Superintendency. During the periods in which the Flathead Agency was in the Idaho Superintendency it was responsible for Flathead, Kutenai and Pond d'Oreille Indians with agency headquarters at the junction of the Flathead and Jocko Rivers on the Jocko Reservation. As late as 1870 some letters relating to the Flathead Agency were filed under "Idaho."

FORT HALL AGENCY

Special Agent Charles F. Powell, appointed in 1867, was assigned to the Boise and Bruneau bands of Shoshoni. In 1869 these Indians as well as some Western Shoshoni and some Bannock were moved to the Fort Hall Reservation in southeastern Idaho. In 1872 the Bannock previously assigned to the Shoshone and Bannock Agency in Wyoming also moved to Fort Hall. From January, 1879 until February, 1880 the Lemhi Agency was consolidated with the Fort Hall Agency, which continued to operate beyond 1880.

LEMHI AGENCY

The Lemhi Agency was established in 1873 for the mixed Bannock, Shoshoni and Tukuarika (Sheepeater) Indians living along the Lemhi River in eastern Idaho. From January, 1879 until February, 1880 the Lemhi Agency was consolidated with the Fort Hall Agency. The restored agency continued to operate beyond 1880. Some letters relating to the Lemhi Agency are filed under "Montana."

SPECIAL AGENTS

George C. Hough served as special agent, without specific assignment, for the Indians in Idaho between 1866 and 1869.

GOVERNORS AND *EX OFFICIO* SUPERINTENDENTS

Name	Date of Appointment
William H. Wallace	Mar. 10, 1863
Caleb Lyon	Feb. 26, 1864
David W. Ballard	Apr. 10, 1876

ARMY OFFICER DETAILED AS SUPERINTENDENT

Col. De L. Floyd-Jones	June 17, 1869

AGENTS

Nez Percé Agency

(See Washington Superintendency for earlier agents.)

John W. Anderson (subagent)	Aug. 23, 1862
James O'Neil	July 2, 1864
Robert Newell	July 23, 1868
Lt. Joseph W. Wham	June 10, 1869
Capt. David M. Sells	Feb. 10, 1870
John A. Simms	Appointed Nov. 5, 1870, but did not serve
John B. Monteith	Feb. 1, 1871
Charles D. Warner	Mar. 3, 1879

Blackfeet Agency

(For complete list see Blackfeet Agency.)

Henry W. Reed	Apr. 4, 1862
Gad E. Upson	Oct. 13, 1863

Flathead Agency

(See Washington Superintendency for earlier agents and Montana Superintendency for later agents.)

Charles Hutchins	Transferred from Nez Percé Agency, Sept. 30, 1862
Augustus H. Chapman	Sept. 22, 1865

Fort Hall Agency

Charles F. Powell (special)	Notified Apr. 18, 1867
Lt. William H. Danilson (special)	June 11, 1869
Johnson N. High (special)	Nov. 8, 1870
Montgomery P. Berry (special)	Mar. 25, 1871
Johnson N. High (special)	Dec. 21, 1871
Henry W. Reed	Nov. 15, 1872
James Wright	Oct. 24, 1874
William H. Danilson	May 21, 1875
John A. Wright (acting)	Sept. 3, 1879
James M. Haworth (special agent at large)	In charge Oct. 9, 1879
John A. Wright	Jan. 19, 1880

Lemhi Agency

Harrison Fuller (special)	Nov. 13, 1873
Charles N. Stowers (special)	July 12, 1877
John A. Wright	June 14, 1878. Starting Jan. 1, 1879, was farmer-in-charge
Elijah A. Stone	Feb. 5, 1880

INDIANA AGENCY
1824-1850

The Indiana Agency was successor to the Fort Wayne Agency established in 1802. Although some letters are filed under the heading "Indiana" for the years 1824-28, most of the correspondence for these years is filed under "Fort Wayne." For the period after the agency was moved in 1828, from Fort Wayne to the south side of the Wabash River between the mouths of Pipe Creek and Eel River, a larger part of the correspondence is filed under "Indiana." The heading "Fort Wayne" was used for letters dated through 1830. Some letters are also filed under "Miami," the name of one of the principal tribes of the agency. The other main tribe was the Potawatomi, and some Wea Indians were also under the jurisdiction of the agency.

Until 1834 the Indiana Agency was responsible to the Michigan Superintendency. Under the reorganization plan of that year the agency was not assigned to any superintendency, and the agent was to report directly to the Bureau of Indian Affairs in Washington. The agency was responsible for all Indians in the State of Indiana. The headquarters of the agency was fixed at Logansport at the mouth of Eel River, from which place the agent usually had been reporting rather than from the site reported in 1828.

When the Indiana Agency was discontinued on July 1, 1835, the Superintendent of Emigration for the Indians in Indiana was designated to perform the duties of the agent. In February, 1838 the superintendent was also assigned the duties of Superintendent of Emigration for the Indians of the Chicago Agency. During the same month a subagent was appointed for the Miami (including the Eel River) Indians who since the emigration of the Potawatomi were now the principal tribe remaining in Indiana. When Subagent John T. Douglas left office in February, 1839, the Superintendent of Emigration was notified to take charge of the affairs of the subagency. It was decided, however, that his services as superintendent had ceased on October 13, 1838, and he was considered as serving in the capacity of subagent thereafter. On May 13, 1839, a subagent, Samuel Milroy, was formally commissioned for the Miami Indians. The subagency was more frequently called the Miami or Miami and Eel River Subagency than Indiana Subagency, but correspondence was filed under both "Indiana" and "Miami."

Subagent Milroy usually stayed at Delphi rather than Logansport, the designated site of the agency. After 1841 the subagent usually resided at Fort Wayne. In 1846 the subagent was appointed Superintendent of Emigration for the Miami Indians, whose removal to the Osage River was completed in 1847 (although many soon returned). The services of the superintendent were discontinued. No agent was appointed for the Indians still in Indiana, and a General Land Office receiver was designated to make the annuity payments. Some letters were filed under the headings "Indiana" and "Miami" until 1850 and under "Miami Emigration" until 1853. Later correspondence relating to the Miami Indians is with that relating to the Osage River Agency and the Central Superintendency.

Some of the correspondence relating to the removal of the Indians from Indiana is filed under the subheading "Indiana Emigration." There is also an "Indiana Reserves" subheading, which contains almost entirely cross-references to correspondence filed with the records of the Land Division of the Bureau. These letters relate mainly to the reserves of Potawatomi Indians.

See also Michigan, St. Louis and Central Superintendencies and Fort Wayne, Miami, Chicago, Piqua, Council Bluffs and Osage River Agencies and Subagencies.

AGENTS

Indiana Agency

Name	*Date of Appointment*
John Tipton	Mar. 28, 1823
William Marshall	Confirmed by Senate, Jan. 13, 1832
Abel C. Pepper (acting)	July 1, 1835

Miami Subagency

John T. Douglas	Feb. 28, 1838
Abel C. Pepper (acting)	Feb. 6, 1839
John Tipton (acting)	Apr. 3, 1839
Samuel Milroy	May 13, 1839
Allen Hamilton	June 21, 1841
Samuel Milroy	Mar. 1, 1845
Joseph Sinclair	June 5, 1845

IOWA SUPERINTENDENCY
1838-1849

The Iowa Superintendency was established in 1838, the year Iowa Territory was created from the western part of Wisconsin Territory. In addition to the present state of Iowa, the territory included most of Minnesota and large parts of the Dakotas. The territorial governor, who served as *ex officio* superintendent throughout the existence of the superintendency, usually stayed at Burlington but spent some time at Iowa City.

The St. Peters (Sioux of the Mississippi Indians) and Sac and Fox (Sauk and Fox of the Mississippi Indians) Agencies were assigned to the Iowa Superintendency in 1838. These agencies had been under the Wisconsin Superintendency since 1836 and before that under the St. Louis Superintendency. The Upper Missouri Agency (Sioux and other Indians) and the Council Bluffs Subagency (United Band of Ottawa, Chippewa and Potawatomi) were located in Iowa Territory, but they were assigned to the St. Louis Superintendency. In 1840 the subagency for the Winnebago Indians at Prairie du Chien was moved to the Turkey River in Iowa, and in 1841 it was transferred from the Wisconsin to the Iowa Superintendency.

Most of the letters filed under the heading "Iowa" are copies. The originals were sent to the Curator of the Historical Department of the State of Iowa in 1901 by authority of Congress. Correspondence relating to the individual agencies for the most part was filed under the names of the agencies rather than with the correspondence relating to the superintendency. There was considerable confusion, however, concerning the names of the agencies. Correspondence concerning the agency for the Sioux of the Mississippi was filed consistently under the name "St. Peters." Most of the correspondence relating to the subagency for the Winnebago was filed under "Prairie du Chien" until 1842. Some letters were filed under "Winnebago" in 1842, but from 1842 until 1846 most of the letters were filed under "Turkey River." Thereafter only "Winnebago" was used.

Some correspondence relating to the agency for the Sauk and Fox of the Mississippi was filed under "Sac and Fox" throughout the period when it was under the Iowa Superintendency. One letter for 1843 and most of the letters for 1844 and 1845 were filed under the name "Raccoon River," the location of the agency during those years. In 1845 the Sauk and Fox moved to the Osage River west of Missouri (now Kansas). Thereafter the agency was within the limits of the St. Louis Superintendency.

In 1846, when Iowa was admitted as a state, the Iowa Superintendency was abolished. The St. Peters Agency and the Winnebago (Turkey River) Subagency were transferred to the St. Louis Superintendency. One letter was filed under "Iowa" in 1849.

See also St. Louis and Wisconsin Superintendencies and St. Peters, Sac and Fox, Raccoon River, Prairie du Chien, Turkey River, Winnebago, Upper Missouri, Council Bluffs and Osage River Agencies and Subagencies.

GOVERNORS AND *EX OFFICIO* SUPERINTENDENTS

Name	*Date of Appointment*
Robert Lucas	July 7, 1838
John Chambers	Mar. 25, 1841
James Clarke	Nov. 8, 1845

IOWAY SUBAGENCY
1825-1837

The Ioway Subagency for the Iowa Indians was established under the St. Louis Superintendency in 1825. As early as 1822 Capt. A. Baronet Vasquez had been authorized to serve as interpreter and acting subagent for the Iowa Indians when needed. He was still serving in this capacity in 1825, when a regular subagent was appointed. For this early period correspondence is filed with that relating to the St. Louis Superintendency. The Iowa Indians were then living in northwestern Missouri and in the area east of the Missouri River known as the Platte Country, which was later (1837) annexed to Missouri. In 1827 Superintendent William Clark reported that the Iowa villages were 40 miles inside the State of Missouri. The next year he reported that the Indians were living at a new village on the Missouri River west of the State line. In 1834 the subagent wrote that the agency headquarters had been for some time on the Platte River (in Missouri, not the more widely known Platte River in Nebraska). The next year he established the location more definitely as 40 miles northeast of Fort Leavenworth.

In 1829 the Sauk and Fox of the Missouri, at that time without an agent, were attached to the Ioway Subagency. When subagent Andrew S. Hughes was reappointed in 1830, the subagency was designated as being within the Upper Missouri Agency. This designation seems to have had little effect and the subagent continued to report to Superintendent Clark in St. Louis. In 1834 the Sauk and Fox of the Missouri were transferred to the jurisdiction of the Prairie du Chien-Sac and Fox Agency at Rock Island. Again the assignment seems to have been ineffective, and the next year they were attached to the Upper Missouri Agency.

In 1836 the Ioway Subagency was transferred from the St. Louis Superintendency to the newly formed Wisconsin Superintendency. By a treaty of September 17, 1836, the Iowa and the Sauk and Fox of the Missouri ceded their land on the Missouri side of the Missouri River and agreed to settle on reserves south of that river in the vicinity of the Great Nemaha River (now southeastern Nebraska and northeastern Kansas). The Indians moved in 1837, and the Ioway Subagency was replaced by the Great Nemaha Subagency, which was placed under the St. Louis Superintendency.

See also St. Louis and Wisconsin Superintendenceis and Upper Missouri, Sac and Fox, Prairie du Chien and Great Nemaha Agencies.

SUBAGENTS

Name	Date of Appointment
Martin Palmer	Mar. 2, 1825
Patrick Henry Ford	Sept. 15, 1825
Charles Bent	Appointed Mar. 9, 1827, but did not serve
Jonathan Bean	Acting Aug. 15, 1827; appointed July 5, 1828
Andrew S. Hughes	Transferred from Sioux Subagency, Sept. 5, 1828

KANSAS AGENCY
1851-1876

The Kansas Agency for the Delaware, Shawnee, Wyandot, Munsee and Stock-bridge Indians who lived along the Kansas River in eastern Kansas was estab-lished in 1851. The Delaware Indians lived on the north side of the Kansas River on a reserve that had been granted to them by treaty in 1829. To the east of the Delaware Indians, at the junction of the Kansas and Missouri Rivers, the Wyandot had a small reserve that they had purchased from the Delaware in 1843. The Shawnee lived south of the Kansas River on a reserve that had been granted to them by treaty in 1825. The Stockbridge and Munsee (known jointly as "Christian" Indians) lived on the Delaware Reserve.

Except for the Wyandot, who had a subagency of their own, these Indians had been assigned previously to the Fort Leavenworth Agency (now discontinued). The Kansas Agency was under the Central Superintendency. The agency head-quarters was briefly situated at the old Wyandot Subagency, but it was located permanently on the Shawnee Reserve.

In 1855 the Kansas Agency was divided into two agencies. The Delaware Agency became responsible for the Delaware and the Stockbridge and Munsee Indians and the Shawnee Agency for the Shawnee and Wyandot. In 1863 the Wyandot were transferred to the Delaware Agency.

A new agency, named the Kansas Agency, was established in 1855 for the Kansa or Kaw Indians. This agency was located at Council Grove, Kansas on the Neosho River. By 1874 the Kansa Indians who had sold or ceded their land in Kansas had moved to a tract in the northwestern corner of the Osage Reser-vation in Indian Territory, which they had purchased from the Osage Indians. The Neosho Agency (renamed the Osage Agency on December 22, 1874) took charge of the Kansa Indians, and the Kansas Agency was discontinued. Some correspondence was filed under "Kansas" until 1876. After 1874 the Pota-watomi Agency—now the only agency in Kansas—was sometimes called the Kansas Agency, but correspondence concerning it was never filed under "Kan-sas."

There was a Kansas Agency (Subagency until 1832) for the Kansa Indians in operation between 1825 and 1834. Correspondence concerning this agency is filed with that relating to the Fort Leavenworth Agency and the St. Louis Superintendency. In 1834 the Kansa Indians were assigned to the Northern Agency (see Fort Leavenworth for correspondence), in 1837 to the Fort Leaven-worth Agency, in 1847 to the Osage River Agency, and in 1851 to the Potawatomi Agency, where they remained until they were given an agency of their own in 1855.

See also St. Louis and Central Superintendencies, Fort Leavenworth, Delaware, Shawnee, Osage River, Potawatomi, Neosho and Osage Agencies and Wyandot Subagency.

AGENTS

Kansas Agency for the Delaware, Shawnee, Wyandot, Munsee and Stockbridge Indians

Name	Date of Appointment
Thomas Mosely, Jr.	June 30, 1851
Benjamin F. Robinson	Apr. 18, 1853

Kansas (Kaw) Agency

John Montgomery	Mar. 3, 1855
Milton C. Dickey	Mar. 3, 1859
H. W. Farnsworth	Apr. 18, 1861
Forrest R. Page	Sept. 1, 1866
E. S. Stover	Mar. 18, 1867
Mahlon Stubbs	June 22, 1869

KICKAPOO AGENCY 1855-1876

The Kickapoo Agency was established under the Central Superintendency in 1855 for the Kickapoo Indians of Kansas. These Indians had been assigned to the Great Nemaha Agency since 1851 and before that to the Fort Leavenworth Agency and its predecessors. There were also a few Potawatomi Indians under the Kickapoo Agency.

Until 1873 the location of the agency headquarters alternated between Kennekuk and Muscotah, both on the eastern edge of the Kickapoo Reservation in northeastern Kansas. In 1873 the agency was moved farther west to Netawaka.

In 1874 the Kickapoo Agency was consolidated with the Potawatomi Agency, but correspondence was filed under the heading "Kickapoo" until 1876. Also filed with the correspondence concerning the Kickapoo Agency are records concerning the removal, to Indian Territory, between 1873 and 1875, of the Kickapoo Indians from Mexico, where they had gone in 1850-51. These Indians were placed in the area between the Deep Fork and North Fork of the Canadian River and were assigned to the Sac and Fox Agency. Special Commissioners Henry M. Atkinson, Thomas G. Williams, William N. Edgar and Andrew C. Williams were in charge of the removal.

See also Central Superintendency and Fort Leavenworth, Great Nemaha, Potawatomi and Sac and Fox Agencies.

AGENTS

Name	Date of Appointment
Royal Baldwin	Apr. 21, 1855
William P. Badger	June 3, 1858
Charles B. Keith	July 16, 1861
Abram Bennett	May 7, 1864
Franklin G. Adams	Mar. 16, 1865
John D. Miles	June 22, 1869
B. H. Miles	Jan. 3, 1873

KIOWA AGENCY
1864-1880

The Kiowa Agency, also known as the Kiowa and Comanche and as the Kiowa, Apache and Comanche Agency, was established in 1864. It was primarily responsible for the Kiowa, Apache (Kiowa-Apache) and Comanche Indians living in the upper Arkansas River area. These Indians had been assigned since 1855 to the Upper Arkansas Agency and before that to the Upper Platte Agency. Between 1865 and 1867 the Apache Indians of the upper Arkansas, affiliated with the Southern Cheyenne during this period, were attached to the Upper Arkansas rather than the Kiowa Agency. Until the removal of the Indians of the upper Arkansas area to Indian Territory, the affairs of the Kiowa Agency and the Upper Arkansas Agency (which was responsible for the Southern Cheyenne and Arapaho) were closely connected. The Kiowa agent briefly had charge of some Caddo Indians who had left Texas during the Civil War and at times was given some responsibility for bands of Comanche living in Texas.

The Kiowa Agency was not assigned to any superintendency for several years, and the agent reported directly to the Bureau of Indian Affairs in Washington. This procedure was followed because the Kiowa, Apache and Comanche were nomadic and did not remain within the boundaries of any one superintendency. They frequently left the upper Arkansas area and made raids into Indian Territory, Colorado, Texas and New Mexico. The agency headquarters was originally intended to be at Fort Larned, Kansas, but in practice the agency had no fixed location.

By a treaty negotiated at Medicine Lodge Creek in 1867 the Kiowa, Apache and Comanche agreed to settle on a reservation south of the Washita River in the "Leased District" in Indian Territory on land previously part of the reservation of the Indians of the Wichita Agency. The Indians did not actually start to move until 1868, and it was not until 1869 that the Kiowa Agency was permanently located on Cache Creek near the site of Fort Sill. From May, 1869 until July 1870 the Wichita Agency was consolidated with the Kiowa Agency and the combined agency was made responsible to the Central Superintendency. After the Wichita Agency again became a separate agency, the Kiowa Agency remained under the Central Superintendency until the superintendency was discontinued in 1878. Thereafter the agent again reported directly to the Bureau of Indian Affairs in Washington.

On September 1, 1878, the Wichita Agency was permanently consolidated with the Kiowa Agency and the Kiowa Agency headquarters was moved from Fort Sill to Anadarko, the headquarters of the Wichita Agency. In addition to the Kiowa, Apache and Comanche Indians previously assigned to the Kiowa Agency, the consolidated agency had charge of the Wichita, Caddo, Kichai, Waco, Tawakoni, Delaware and Penateka Comanche who had been assigned to the Wichita Agency. The combined agency, usually called the Kiowa, Comanche and Wichita Agency, remained in operation beyond 1880.

See also Central, Colorado, Southern and New Mexico Superintendencies and Upper Arkansas, Upper Platte and Wichita Agencies.

AGENTS

Name	*Date of Appointment*
Jesse H. Leavenworth	July 2, 1864
Albert G. Boone	July 23, 1868
Laurie Tatum	Apr. 22, 1869
James M. Haworth	Apr. 1, 1873
Philemon B. Hunt	Feb. 18, 1878

LA POINTE AGENCY 1831-1850, 1855-1880

The correspondence filed under the heading "La Pointe" relates to both a La Pointe Subagency and a La Pointe Agency and to Indian affairs in the La Pointe area during some periods when neither was in operation.

The La Pointe Subagency located on Madeline (Madaline) Island at the head of Lake Superior was established in 1836 by the Governor of Wisconsin Territory in his capacity as *ex officio* superintendent of Indian affairs. The subagent was formally commissioned the following year. Between 1826 and 1829 the Sault Ste. Marie agent had stationed one of his subagents, George Johnston, at La Pointe. The correspondence for the period 1831-36, filed under "La Pointe," relates to the settlement of Johnston's accounts and to Indian affairs in the La Pointe area.

The Indians originally assigned to the La Pointe Subagency were the Chippewa of Lake Superior living west of Michigan in Wisconsin Territory. In 1839 the Crow Wing Subagency for the Chippewa of the Mississippi was abolished and its duties absorbed by the La Pointe Subagency. The Chippewa of the Mississippi were assigned in 1848 to the Winnebago Agency. In the same year Wisconsin became a state, and the Wisconsin Superintendency was discontinued. From then until 1850 the La Pointe subagent reported directly to the Bureau of Indian Affairs in Washington.

In 1850 the La Pointe Subagency was moved to Sandy Lake, Minnesota and was then under the Minnesota Superintendency. The subagency was now responsible for the Chippewa of the Mississippi who had been assigned to the Winnebago Agency as well as the Chippewa of Lake Superior. Correspondence relating to the subagency was now filed under the heading "Sandy Lake" instead of "La Pointe." In 1851 the subagency was made a full agency known as the Chippewa Agency.

In 1853 the Mackinac agent in Michigan took charge of the Chippewa of Lake Superior. The "La Pointe" heading, discontinued in 1851, was revived in 1855, although the Mackinac agent continued to be responsible for these Indians.

An agency was established for the Chippewa of Lake Superior of Wisconsin and Minnesota in 1858. Correspondence concerning this agency was filed under the heading "La Pointe," although the agency was not located at La Pointe and for several years was more commonly known either as the Chippewa of Lake Superior Agency or the Lake Superior Agency.

The La Pointe Agency was under the jurisdiction of the Northern Superintendency until 1865 after which time it was not attached to any superintendency and the agent reported directly to the Bureau of Indian Affairs in Washington. The agency was located at Superior, Wisconsin, until 1860 and again from 1869 until 1871. During other periods it was located either on the Red Cliff Reservation or at Baysfield, Wisconsin, a few miles from the reservation on the mainland opposite La Pointe. The Indians were now living on several reservations in Wisconsin and Minnesota. The La Pointe Agency continued to operate beyond 1880.

See also Wisconsin, Michigan, St. Louis, Minnesota and Northern Superintendencies and Mackinac, Sault Ste. Marie, Sandy Lake, Chippewa, Winnebago and Green Bay Agencies.

AGENTS AND SUBAGENTS

La Pointe Subagency

Name	*Date of Appointment*
Daniel P. Bushnell	Nov. 1, 1836 by superintendent; regular commission on Apr. 25, 1837
Alfred Brunson	Oct. 13, 1842
James P. Hays	Jan. 12, 1844
John Livermore	May 24, 1848
John Watrous	Apr. 20, 1850

La Pointe Agency

Cyrus K. Drew	Transferred from Chippewa Agency, July 19, 1858
Luther E. Webb	Mar. 23, 1861
Asaph Whittlesey	July 16, 1868
Bvt. Lt. Col. John H. Knight	June 17, 1869
Selden N. Clark	Sept. 21, 1870
Ebenezer E. Henderson (acting)	May 12, 1873
Isaac L. Mahan	June 7, 1873
Samuel E. Mahan	July 8, 1880

LOWER BRULE AGENCY
1875-1876

The Lower Brulé Agency, until January, 1876 called the White River Agency (not to be confused with the White River Agency in Colorado), was established in 1875 for the Lower Brulé Sioux. Previously these Indians had been assigned to the Crow Creek Agency and its predecessor, the Upper Missouri Agency. The Lower Brulé Agency was first located on the western side of the Missouri River 10 miles below Crow Creek in the present State of South Dakota. In the summer of 1876 it was relocated at the mouth of American Crow Creek, 12 miles below the old site.

At first the agent reported directly to the Bureau of Indian Affairs in Washington, but in 1877 the agency became part of the revived Dakota Superintendency. The following year, when the superintendency was abolished, the agency again became independent. After July, 1876 correspondence concerning the agency was filed under the heading "Dakota."

In 1882 the Crow Creek and Lower Brulé Agencies were consolidated to form the Crow Creek and Lower Brulé Agency. In 1896 the agencies were again divided.

See also Dakota Superintendency and Crow Creek and Upper Missouri Agencies.

AGENTS

Name	Date of Appointment
Thomas A. Reily	July 2, 1875
Henry E. Gregory	July 18, 1876
Capt. William E. Dougherty (acting)	Mar. 21, 1878
William H. Parkhurst	May 27, 1880

MACKINAC AGENCY
1828-1880

The Mackinac or Michilimackinac Agency, which was established in 1815, was located on Mackinac Island north of the Lower Peninsula of Michigan. No specific tribes or area were assigned to the agency, but the principal Indians living around Mackinac were Chippewa, Ottawa, and Potawatomi. In 1822 another agency was established at Sault Ste. Marie on the Upper Peninsula. Both agencies were under the Michigan Superintendency. Until the establishment of the Bureau of Indian Affairs in 1824 correspondence concerning the Mackinac Agency was transmitted directly to the Office of the Secretary of War. For the years 1824-27 letters relating to the agency are filed under the heading "Michigan."

In 1832 the Mackinac and Sault Ste. Marie Agencies were consolidated. At first the agent remained at Sault Ste. Marie, but in 1833 he moved to Mackinac. There were usually subagents subordinate to the agent until 1834.

Under the regulations adopted in 1834 the Mackinac and Sault Ste. Marie Agency was assigned the northern part of the Lower Peninsula, the islands of Lake Huron, the Upper Peninsula, the country on Lake Superior and the country of the Chippewa of the Mississippi. The commanding officer of Fort Brady at Sault Ste. Marie was put in charge of the Indians in that immediate vicinity.

In 1835 the Crow Wing Subagency was established for the Chippewa of the Mississippi, and in 1836 the La Pointe Subagency was established for the Chippewa of Lake Superior living in the newly established Wisconsin Territory.

In 1836 the Mackinac and Sault Ste. Marie agent was made acting superintendent of the Michigan Superintendency. He was expected to spend the summers at Mackinac and the winters at Detroit. Gradually he spent less and less time at Mackinac, until Detroit became the headquarters of the agency and only occasional trips were made to Mackinac. Since the same person was both agent and superintendent, it was difficult to separate the letters relating to the agency from those relating to the superintendency; there are many letters filed under the heading "Michigan" that relate in large part to the affairs of the Mackinac Agency.

With the reorganization of 1837, a separate Sault Ste. Marie Subagency was established. The Mackinac Agency was assigned the northern part of the Lower Peninsula and islands of Lake Huron, Lake Michigan and Grand Traverse Bay. The Sault Ste. Marie Subagency had charge of the Indians living on the Upper Peninsula and the Saginaw Subagency was made responsible for those living in the southern part of Michigan. The Saginaw Subagency was abolished in 1846 and the Sault Ste. Marie Subagency in 1852; their duties were transferred to the Mackinac Agency. The Mackinac Agency was then in charge of all the Indians in Michigan, and it was now sometimes called the Michigan Agency. The principal bands assigned to the agency were Ottawa and Chippewa of the Upper Lakes; Chippewa of Lake Superior; Saginaw Chippewa; remnants of the United Ottawa, Chippewa and Potawatomi; Black River and Swan Creek Chippewa; and Potawatomi of Huron. These Indians were living on reserves scattered over Michigan.

When the Michigan Superintendency was discontinued in 1851, it was intended that the new Northern Superintendency have charge of Indian affairs in Wisconsin and Michigan. In practice, however, the Mackinac agent had little contact with the new superintendency and he continued to report directly to the Bureau of Indian Affairs in Washington, as he had while serving as both agent and acting superintendent. In 1853 the Northern superintendent was informed that only the Wisconsin Indians were in his superintendency. Thereafter the Mackinac Agency was not attached to any superintendency.

Between 1853 and 1858 the Mackinac Agency had some responsibility for the Chippewa Indians living along Lake Superior in Wisconsin and Minnesota. These Indians had formerly been attached to the La Pointe Subagency, which was moved to Sandy Lake, Minnesota in 1850 and became the Chippewa Agency in 1851. In 1858 the La Pointe or Chippewa of Lake Superior Agency was established for these Indians, and the Mackinac Agency was again responsible for only the Indians in Michigan. Most of the correspondence concerning the activities of the Mackinac agent relating to the La Pointe Indians for the years 1855-58 is filed under the heading "La Pointe." In 1873 the Mackinac Agency was moved from Detroit to Lansing and in 1876 to Ypsilanti. The agency continued in operation beyond 1880.

There are a few letters for 1838 and 1839, mostly relating to an exploring party of Ottawa and Chippewa, filed under the subheading "Mackinac Emigration." Correspondence relating to Indians who actually left Michigan and moved west of the Mississippi River will be found with the correspondence relating to several of the agencies of the St. Louis Superintendency and its successor, the Central Superintendency—particularly the Osage River, Council Bluffs, Sac and Fox, Ottawa and Potawatomi Agencies.

See also Michigan, Wisconsin, Minnesota and Northern Superintendencies and Saginaw, Sault Ste. Marie, La Pointe, Sandy Lake, Chippewa, St. Peters, Chicago and Indiana Agencies and Subagencies. There are also field records of the Michigan Superintendency and the Mackinac Agency among the records of the Bureau of Indian Affairs in the National Archives. (Many of these records have been reproduced by the National Archives and Records Service as Microfilm Publication 1.)

AGENTS

Name	Date of Appointment
William H. Puthuff	Dec. 29, 1815
George Boyd	Notified Aug. 13, 1818
Henry R. Schoolcraft	Assigned to consoli-dated Mackinac and Sault Ste. Marie Agency, Apr. 18, 1832
Robert Stuart	Apr. 17, 1841
William A. Richmond	Apr. 14, 1845
Charles B. Babcock	Apr. 11, 1849
William Sprague	June 30, 1851
Henry Gilbert	Apr. 23, 1853
Andrew M. Fitch	July 1, 1857
DeWitt C. Leach	Mar. 25, 1861
Richard M. Smith	Apr. 29, 1865
William H. Brockway	Apr. 8, 1869
Bvt. Maj. James W. Long	June 14, 1869
Richard M. Smith	Apr. 18, 1871
George J. Betts	Oct. 31, 1871
George Lee	Apr. 25, 1876

MIAMI SUBAGENCY
1824-1853

The Miami, or Miami and Eel River, Subagency was established in 1838. Previously the Miami Indians, including the Eel River Indians, had been assigned to the Indiana Agency and its predecessor, the Fort Wayne Agency. There are only a few letters for the years before 1838 filed under the heading "Miami," and even after the Miami Subagency was established in 1838 most of the correspondence relevant to it was filed under "Indiana." Only for the years 1846-50 is a substantial amount of correspondence filed under "Miami," and there are letters filed under "Indiana" even for these years. Much of the correspondence filed under "Miami" relates to the Miami Indians who had moved to the Osage River Agency in present Kansas rather than to those in Indiana.

The headquarters of the Miami Subagency was originally at Logansport, the site of the former Indiana Agency. From 1839 until 1841 the subagent usually stayed at Delphi, and thereafter at Fort Wayne. The subagency was not attached to any superintendency, and the subagent reported directly to the Bureau of Indian Affairs in Washington.

For several months in 1839 the Superintendent of Emigration for the Indians of Indiana acted as subagent, but, when it became apparent that the Miami would not move in the near future, a regular subagent was again appointed. In 1846 the subagent was appointed Superintendent of Emigration for the Miami Indians. The removal of the Indians to the Osage River was completed in 1847, although many soon returned to Indiana. The services of the superintendent were discontinued and no new subagent was appointed for the Indians in Indiana. For a few years a General Land Office official was designated to make annuity payments.

Some of the letters relating to the emigration of the Miami are filed under the subheading "Miami Emigration." The "Miami Reserves" subheading consists almost entirely of cross-references to correspondence filed with the records of the Land Division of the Bureau.

See also Michigan, St. Louis and Central Superintendencies and Fort Wayne, Indiana, Chicago and Osage River Agencies.

SUBAGENTS

Name	Date of Appointment
John T. Douglas	Feb. 28, 1838
Abel C. Pepper (acting)	Feb. 6, 1839
John Tipton (acting)	Apr. 3, 1839
Samuel Milroy	May 13, 1839
Allen Hamilton	June 21, 1841
Samuel Milroy	Mar. 1, 1845
Joseph Sinclair	June 5, 1845

MICHIGAN SUPERINTENDENCY
1824-1851

The Michigan Superintendency was established in 1805, the year Michigan Territory was organized. The Territorial Governor at Detroit served as *ex officio* superintendent. Michigan Territory originally consisted of only the Lower Peninsula and the eastern tip of the Upper Peninsula, but in 1818 its boundaries were extended to include present Wisconsin and Minnesota east of the Mississippi River, previously part of Illinois Territory. The jurisdiction of the Michigan Superintendency, however, did not coincide with the Territorial boundaries. Some agencies in the west, either located in or having charge of Indians living in Michigan Territory, were assigned to the St. Louis Superintendency (the Missouri Superintendency until 1821). The Michigan Superintendency, on the other hand, at times had charge of agencies and Indians in Illinois, Indiana, Ohio and New York.

The principal tribes under the supervision of the Michigan Superintendency were Chippewa, Ottawa, Potawatomi, Menominee, Winnebago, Wyandot, Seneca, Shawnee, Delaware, Miami, Oneida, Stockbridge and Munsee. The organization of the superintendency for the period before the Bureau of Indian Affairs was established in 1824 is too complicated to describe in this sketch. Correspondence relating to the superintendency for this period was transmitted directly to the Office of the Secretary of War. In 1824 the Mackinac, Sault Ste. Marie, Green Bay, Chicago, Fort Wayne (Indiana) and Piqua (Ohio) Agencies were in the Michigan Superintendency. The Prairie du Chien Agency was located in Michigan Territory but was assigned to the St. Louis Superintendency. The St. Peters Agency, also in the St. Louis Superintendency, was located just west of Michigan Territory, but some of the Sioux Indians belonging to it lived east of the Mississippi in Michigan. No significant changes were made in this arrangement until 1832, when the Mackinac and Sault Ste. Marie Agencies were consolidated.

In addition to the regular agencies, there were also several subagencies in the Michigan Superintendency. Most of the subagents were assistants to agents, but some, not subordinate to any agency, deserve special mention. From about 1827 until 1836 there was a subagent assigned to the Ottawa of Maumee in Ohio. The Fort Winnebago Subagency was established in 1829 for the Winnebago Indians living in the vicinity of the portage of the Fox and Wisconsin Rivers. The Rock River Subagency (Winnebago Indians) was transferred from the St. Louis Superintendency in 1832 and remained in the Michigan Superintendency until it was discontinued in 1834. From 1832 until 1834 the New York (Six Nations) Subagency at Buffalo was attached to the Michigan Superintendency. In 1834 the jurisdiction of the Michigan Superintendency was considerably reduced although in the same year Michigan Territory was extended to the Missouri River. The Chicago, Indiana (formerly Fort Wayne) and Ohio (formerly Piqua) Agencies and the New York Subagency were all made independent. The Chicago Agency, in addition to the Indians living in Illinois, was given charge of the Indians living in Michigan Territory as far north as the Milwaukee River and also of some Chippewa, Ottawa and Potawatomi living north of that river. The Prairie du Chien and St. Peters Agencies remained in the St. Louis Superintendency. Most of the subagencies in the Michigan Superintendency were abolished. The consolidated Mackinac and Sault Ste. Marie Agency was continued, but the commanding officer at Fort Brady was designated to act as agent for the Indians in the immediate vicinity of Sault Ste. Marie. Also in the Michigan Superintendency were the Green Bay Agency, the Fort Winnebago Subagency, a subagency at Detroit for the southern part of Michigan and the Maumee Subagency in Ohio. It was intended that tha Maumee Subagency should be abolished on December 31, 1834, but it continued to operate until the death of the subagent, James Jackson, early in 1836.

Wisconsin Territory was organized in 1836 and Michigan was reduced to the boundaries of the present State. With the transfer of the Green Bay Agency and the Fort Winnebago Subagency to the new Wisconsin Superintendency, the Michigan Superintendency was left responsible primarily only for Chippewa, Ottawa and some Potawatomi Indians.

Also in 1836, since Michigan was shortly to become a state, the Mackinac agent was designated to act as superintendent instead of the Territorial Governor. He was to spend the summers at Mackinac and the winters at Detroit. Over the years, however, the superintendents gradually spent more time at Detroit and less at Mackinac.

Under the regulations adopted in 1837, the Michigan Superintendency was responsible for the Indians in Michigan and the Ottawa of Maumee. There were now two subagencies and one agency in Michigan. The Sault Ste. Marie Subagency was established for the Upper Peninsula and the Mackinac Agency had charge of the northern part of the Lower Peninsula. The Saginaw Subagency replaced the Detroit Subagency for the southern part of Michigan. The Saginaw Subagency was discontinued in 1846 and the Sault Ste. Marie Subagency in 1852, and the duties of both were transferred to the Mackinac Agency.

The Michigan Superintendency was abolished in 1851, and the new Northern Superintendency was put in charge of Indian affairs in Michigan and Wisconsin. In practice, however, the Northern superintendent exercised little control in Michigan, and in 1853 he was informed that he was in charge of the Indians in Wisconsin only. The Mackinac Agency therefore was not in any superintendency, and the agent reported directly to the Bureau of Indian Affairs in Washington.

In addition to the agencies immediately responsible to the superintendency, after 1839—when the use of army officers as disbursing agents was discontinued —the Michigan superintendent also handled disbursements for the Green Bay and La Pointe Subagencies in Wisconsin.

The Bureau maintained separate file headings for correspondence relating to the agencies and the more important subagencies in the Michigan Superintendency. Many letters relating to agencies are filed under "Michigan," however, particularly for the period before 1830. Since from 1836 until 1851 the same person was both superintendent and agent for the Mackinac Agency, it was difficult to separate the correspondence relating to the agency from that relating to the superintendency, and the letters in the "Mackinac" and "Michigan" headings relate to both the agency and the superintendency.

There is correspondence filed under the subheading "Michigan Emigration" relating largely to the removal to present Kansas of the Ottawa of Maumee from Ohio and the Black River and Swan Creek Chippewa from Michigan. There are also some letters filed under the subheading "Michigan Reserves" which relate to land reserves of Michigan Indians.

See also St. Louis, Wisconsin, Minnesota and Northern Superintendencies and Mackinac, Sault Ste. Marie, Saginaw, Green Bay, Piqua, Ohio, Fort Wayne, Indiana, Chicago, Six Nations, New York, La Pointe, St. Peters, Prairie du Chien, Winnebago, Miami and Sac and Fox Agencies and Subagencies. There are also field records of the Michigan Superintendency among the records of the Bureau of Indian Affairs in the National Archives. Many of these records have been reproduced by the National Archives and Records Service as Microfilm Publication 1.

GOVERNORS AND *EX OFFICIO* SUPERINTENDENTS

Name	*Date of Appointment*
William Hull	Mar. 1, 1805
Lewis Cass	Oct. 29, 1813
George B. Porter	Aug. 6, 1831
Stevens T. Mason (acting)	Took charge upon death of Porter, July 6, 1834
John S. Horner (acting)	Sept. 8, 1835

MACKINAC AGENTS AND ACTING SUPERINTENDENTS

Henry R. Schoolcraft	July 2, 1836
Robert Stuart	Apr. 17, 1841
William A. Richmond	Apr. 14, 1845
Charles P. Babcock	Apr. 11, 1849

MINNESOTA SUPERINTENDENCY 1849-1856

The Minnesota Superintendency was established in 1849, the year of the organization of Minnesota Territory. The Territory included the eastern part of the area that later became the Dakotas. The Territorial Governor at St. Paul served as *ex officio* superintendent throughout the existence of the superintendency. The Indians living in Minnesota Territory were principally Sioux, Chippewa and Winnebago. There were also some Assiniboin and Mandan, but these Indians had few contacts with the superintendency.

When the superintendency was established, the Winnebago Agency (known earlier as Prairie du Chien and Turkey River) and the St. Peters Agency (a subagency until 1851) were assigned to it. These agencies had been under the St. Louis Superintendency since 1846 and at different times had been under the Iowa, Wisconsin, St. Louis and Michigan Superintendencies. The Winnebago Agency was responsible for the Winnebago and, until 1850, for the Chippewa Indians in Minnesota. The St. Peters Agency was responsible for the Sioux in Minnesota, who, except for some Yankton Sioux, were known as Sioux of the Mississippi. The individual bands were the Mdewakanton, Wahpetkute, Sisseton and Wahpeton.

In 1850 the La Pointe Subagency, which had been moved from Wisconsin to Minnesota and renamed the Sandy Lake Subagency, was placed under the Minnesota Superintendency. The following year it became the Chippewa Agency. The agency was responsible for the Chippewa of the Mississippi already in Minnesota and previously assigned to the Winnebago Agency, and for the Chippewa of Lake Superior who were being moved into Minnesota from Wisconsin and Michigan. In 1853 the Mackinac Agency took charge of the Chippewa of Lake Superior, and in 1858 a separate agency, which came to be known as the La Pointe Agency, was established for them. Correspondence filed under "Minnesota" relates primarily to matters concerning the superintendency in general; correspondence concerning each agency is filed under its own name.

The Minnesota Superintendency was discontinued in 1856, and its three agencies were transferred to the Northern Superintendency, whose headquarters was moved from Milwaukee, Wisconsin to St. Paul, Minnesota.

See also St. Louis, Iowa, Wisconsin, Michigan, Northern, Central and Dakota Superintendencies and St. Peters, Winnebago, Turkey River, Prairie du Chien, La Pointe, Sandy Lake, Chippewa and Mackinac Agencies and Subagencies. There are also field records of the Minnesota Superintendency among the records of the Bureau of Indian Affairs in the National Archives.

GOVERNORS AND *EX OFFICIO* SUPERINTENDENTS

Name	Date of Appointment
Alexander Ramsey	Apr. 2, 1849
Willis E. Gorman	Apr. 1, 1853

MISCELLANEOUS 1824-1880

The heading "Miscellaneous," as the name implies, was used for correspondence that did not seem to belong with any of the jurisdictional or subject headings in use, and under it is included correspondence relating to Indian affairs in general rather than to the activities of any one agency or superintendency. There are letters relating to more than one jurisdiction and letters that pertain to Indians who were not under the supervision of any field unit of the Bureau. There is also included correspondence pertaining to the operations of the central office of the Bureau and to the rules and regulations of the Bureau; much correspondence relating to applications for employment, appointments, and other personnel matters and to other administrative activities of the Bureau; and correspondence from inspectors and special commissioners and from the Board of Indian Commissioners. There is correspondence concerning a multitude of subjects not directly connected with any one jurisdiction: legislation, trade with the Indians, missionary activities, Indian delegations to Washington, explorations, the procurement of goods for distribtuion to the Indians (particularly guns, flags and medals for chiefs), medical care for Indians (particularly vaccinations for smallpox) and many other matters. Many letters relating to annuity goods, schools and Indian trust funds were filed under the heading "Miscellaneous" during periods when the headings "Annuity Goods," "Schools" and "Stocks" were not in use. The filing practices of the clerks in the Bureau were not always consistent. Letters that might seem to belong in one of the jurisdictional or subject headings are sometimes filed under "Miscellaneous."

In addition to the main heading, there is a subheading "Miscellaneous Emigration." In large part this was used for correspondence relating to supplies and equipment (particularly rifles) needed in the removal of Indians.

MONTANA SUPERINTENDENCY 1864-1880

The Montana Superintendency was established in 1864, the year Montana Territory was organized. Since 1863 Montana had been part of Idaho Territory and before that it was divided between Washington and Dakota Territories. The principal tribes living in Montana were Blackfeet, Piegan, Blood (Kainah), Grosventre, Flathead, Kutenai, Pend d'Oreille, Crow, Assiniboin and several bands of Sioux.

The Territorial Governor served as *ex officio* superintendent until a separate official was appointed in 1869. The superintendency headquarters was located at the Territorial capital, Bannock, until 1865 and after that Virginia City. After 1869 the superintendent stayed at Helena.

The Blackfeet and Flathead Agencies, transferred from the Idaho Superintendency, were the original agencies in the Montana Superintendency. Between 1867 and 1869 several special agents were appointed for Montana; the most important of these was William Cullen. Later the Crow, Fort Peck (Milk River) and Fort Belknap Agencies were established in Montana. The Lemhi Agency for the mixed Shoshoni, Bannock and Tukuarika (Sheepeater) Indians was located in Idaho, but these Indians had lived in Montana before settling on the Lemhi River and some of the correspondence relating to the agency itself is filed under the "Montana" heading.

After the Montana Superintendency was discontinued on June 30, 1873, the agents in Montana reported directly to the Bureau of Indian Affairs in Washington. Until the change of filing systems in 1881, however, incoming correspondence relating to the separate agencies was filed under the heading "Montana" rather than under the names of the individual agencies.

See also Central, Oregon, Washington, Dakota, Idaho and Wyoming Superintendencies and Blackfeet, Upper Missouri and Fort Berthold Agencies. There are also some field office records of the Montana Superintendency among the records of the Bureau of Indian Affairs in the National Archives.

BLACKFEET AGENCY

The Blackfeet Agency was established in 1855 for the Blackfeet, Piegan, Blood (Kainah) and Grosventre Indians. It was successively assigned to the Central, Dakota and Idaho Superintendencies before the establishment of the Montana Superintendency in 1864. The agency was located at Fort Benton until 1869, when it was moved to a site on the Teton River about 35 miles from Fort Shaw. The next year the Grosventre were transferred to the new Milk River (later Fort

99

Peck) Agency. In 1876 the Blackfeet Agency was moved from the Teton River to Badger Creek, and in 1879 it was moved to another location on the south bank of Badger Creek. The Blackfeet Agency continued in operation beyond 1880. From 1855 until 1869 correspondence relating to the agency was filed under its own name, but beginning in 1869 most of the agency correspondence was filed under "Montana."

FLATHEAD AGENCY

The Flathead Agency was established in 1854 under the Washington Super-intendency—principally for the Flathead, Upper Pend d'Oreille and Kutenai Indians. The agency headquarters was located near the junction of the Flathead and Jocko Rivers. The Kutenai and Pend d'Oreille settled on the Jocko Reservation, but most of the Flatheads continued to live in the Bitter Root Valley to the west. In 1857 the Flathead Agency was consolidated into the agency for "Washington East of the Cascades" in the temporarily consolidated Oregon and Washington Superintendency. Special and subagents were assigned to the Flat-heads until the Flathead Agency was re-established as a full agency in 1861. It was transferred from the Washington to the Idaho Superintendency in 1863, to the Montana Superintendency in 1864 and from September, 1865 until February, 1866 was again assigned to the Idaho Superintendency. As late as 1870 some correspondence relating to the Flathead Agency was filed under "Idaho" rather than "Montana." The Flathead Agency continued to operate beyond 1880.

CROW AGENCY

The Crow Agency was permanently established in 1869. Special agents, how-ever, were assigned to the Crow Indians between 1867 and 1869. There were two groups of Crow Indians in Montana—Mountain and River. Originally the Crow Agency was responsible only for the Mountain Crows; the River Crows lived near the Milk River-Fort Peck Agency, but gradually came under the control of the Crow Agency. The headquarters of the agency was located near the Yellowstone River about 25 miles from Fort Ellis, but in 1875 it was moved about 75 miles to Rosebud River about 15 miles from the Yellowstone. The Crow Agency continued to operate beyond 1880.

FORT PECK (MILK RIVER) AGENCY

The Milk River Agency was established in 1870. The agency was intended for the Grosventre and Assiniboin Indians living along the Milk River in northern Montana, but there were also River Crows, Sioux and other Indians living in the area. In 1873 the agency was moved to Fort Peck on the Missouri River where it was responsible for the Assiniboin Indians living at Wolf Point and the Sioux, principally Yanktonai, at Fort Peck itself. The new Fort Belknap Agency took charge of the Grosventre and the Upper Assiniboin on Milk River. On December 22, 1874 the name of the Milk River Agency was changed to Fort Peck. From 1876 until 1878 the Fort Belknap Agency was consolidated with the Fort Peck Agency, and in 1877 the Fort Peck Agency was moved to the mouth of the Poplar River. The Fort Peck Agency continued to operate beyond 1880.

FORT BELKNAP AGENCY

The Fort Belknap Agency was established at Fort Belknap on the Milk River in 1873 for the Grosventre and Upper Assiniboin Indians, who previously had been assigned to the Milk River (Fort Peck) Agency. In 1876 the Fort Belknap Agency was consolidated with the Fort Peck Agency, and some of the Assiniboin moved to Wolf Point. The Grosventre refused to move, however, and in 1878 the Fort Belknap Agency was re-established, first as a subagency and then as a full agency. In addition to the Grosventre there were still Assiniboin and some other Indians under the jurisidiction of the agency. The Fort Belknap Agency continued to operate beyond 1880.

GOVERNORS AND *EX OFFICIO* SUPERINTENDENTS

Name	*Date of Appointment*
Sidney S. Edgerton	June 22, 1864
Green Clay Smith	July 13, 1866

SUPERINTENDENTS

Maj. Gen. Alfred Sully	June 1, 1869
Jasper A. Viall	Sept. 9, 1870
James Wright	Dec. 11, 1872

AGENTS

Blackfeet Agency

(For complete list see Blackfeet Agency.)

Gad E. Upson	Oct. 13, 1863
George B. Wright	Apr. 10, 1866
Nathaniel Pope (acting)	Aug. 25, 1868
Lt. William B. Pease	June 11, 1869
M. M. McCauley	Sept. 9, 1870
Jesse Armitage	Feb. 25, 1871
William F. Ensign	July 23, 1872
Richard F. May	Nov. 6, 1873

Blackfeet Agency (cont.)

John S. Wood	Oct. 24, 1874
John Young	Oct. 20, 1876

Flathead Agency

(For earlier agents see Washington Superintendency.)

Charles Hutchins	Transferred from Nez Percé Agency Sept. 30, 1862
Augustus H. Chapman	Sept. 22, 1865
John W. Wells	Nov. 9, 1866
M. M. McCauley	July 25, 1868
Maj. Alvin S. Galbreath	June 11, 1869
Lt. George E. Ford	July 22, 1870
Charles S. Jones	Sept. 9, 1870
Daniel Shanahan	Nov. 15, 1872
Peter Whaley	Apr. 29, 1874
Charles S. Medary	Apr. 30, 1875
Peter Ronan	Apr. 12, 1877

Crow Agency

Capt. Erskine M. Camp	June 2, 1869
Fellows D. Pease	Sept. 9, 1870
James Wright	July 17, 1873
Dexter E. Clapp	Oct. 7, 1874
Lewis H. Carpenter	Aug. 15, 1876
George W. Frost	Apr. 26, 1877
David Kern	Appointed August 2, 1878, but did not serve
Augustus R. Keller	Nov. 4, 1878

Milk River-Fort Peck Agency

Lt. George E. Ford	Apr. 14, 1870
A. S. Reed (special)	Sept. 14, 1870
Andrew J. Simmons (special)	Jan. 17, 1871
Andrew J. Simmons (agent)	July 23, 1872
William W. Alderson	Sept. 1, 1873
Thomas J. Mitchell	Nov. 10, 1875

Milk River-Fort Peck Agency (cont.)

Wellington Bird	Mar. 27, 1877
Nathan S. Porter	May 23, 1879

Fort Belknap Agency

William H. Fanton (special)	Aug. 12, 1873
Wyman L. Lincoln (subagent)	Apr. 11, 1878
Wyman L. Lincoln (agent)	July 1, 1878

NEBRASKA AGENCIES
1876-1880

The "Nebraska" classification was used by the Bureau of Indian Affairs for filing purposes only; it did not denote any administrative unit. Correspondence concerning the Great Nemaha, Otoe, Omaha, Winnebago, Santee Sioux and Flandreau Agencies was filed under "Nebraska" beginning July 1, 1876. Previously correspondence concerning these agencies had been filed under their own names. With the exception of the Flandreau Agency, these agencies had been under the Northern Superintendency at the time it was discontinued on June 30, 1876. Correspondence concerning the Pawnee Agency, which was in the process of moving to Indian Territory, and the Spotted Tail and Red Cloud Agencies, which were considered to be Dakota Agencies even though they were not moved from Nebraska to Dakota until 1877, was still filed under the name of the agency. The Ponca Agency, located within the present boundaries of Nebraska until 1877, was considered to be in Dakota at that time.

See also Northern, Central and Dakota Superintendencies and Great Nemaha, Omaha, Winnebago, Otoe, Santee Sioux, Flandreau, Ponca, Red Cloud and Spotted Tail Agencies.

GREAT NEMAHA AGENCY

The Great Nemaha Agency was responsible for the Iowa and for the Sauk and Fox of the Missouri Indians living on reservations in southeastern Nebraska and northeastern Kansas. In 1882 it was consolidated with the Potawatomi Agency in Kansas.

103

OMAHA AGENCY

The Omaha Agency for the Omaha Indians was located on the west bank of the Missouri River, north of Decatur in eastern Nebraska. In 1879 the Omaha and Winnebago Agencies were consolidated. The Omaha and Winnebago Agency continued in operation beyond 1880.

WINNEBAGO AGENCY

The Winnebago Agency was responsible for the Winnebago Indians who lived north of the Omaha Indians in eastern Nebraska. The Omaha and Winnebago Agencies were consolidated in 1879. The Omaha and Winnebago Agency continued to operate beyond 1880.

OTOE AGENCY

The Otoe Agency was responsible for the Oto and Missouri Indians who lived on a reservation on the Big Blue River in southern Nebraska and northern Kansas. In 1881 the agency and Indians were moved to Indian Territory and in 1882 the Otoe Agency was consolidated into the Ponca, Pawnee and Otoe Agency.

SANTEE SIOUX AGENCY

The Santee Sioux Agency was responsible for the Santee Sioux Indians living on the west side of the Missouri River below the mouth of the Niobrara River in northern Nebraska and, beginning in 1878, for a few Ponca. In 1879 the Flandreau Agency was consolidated with the Santee Sioux Agency. In April, 1877, when the Senate failed to confirm the appointment of an agent, the Santee Sioux Agency was temporarily put under the jurisdiction of the agent of the Yankton Agency. An agent was appointed the following year and the Santee Sioux Agency continued in operation beyond 1880.

FLANDREAU AGENCY

The Flandreau Agency was responsible for a group of Santee Sioux who had left the reservation in Nebraska and moved to Flandreau, Moody County, Dakota Territory. In 1879 the Flandreau Agency was consolidated with the Santee Agency, but the Indians continued to live at Flandreau.

AGENTS, 1876-80

(For complete lists see individual agencies.)

Great Nemaha Agency

Name	*Date of Appointment*
Mahlon B. Kent	Feb. 26, 1875

Omaha Agency

Theodore T. Gillingham	Sept. 30, 1873
Jacob Vore	July 10, 1876

Winnebago Agency

Howard White	Sept. 4, 1875

Omaha and Winnebago Agency

Howard White	Apr. 30, 1879
Arthur Edwards	Apr. 1, 1880

Otoe Agency

Jesse W. Griest	Apr. 1, 1873
Robert S. Gardner (special)	In charge June 16, 1880
Lewellyn E. Woodin	July 21, 1880

Santee Sioux Agency

Charles H. Searing	Aug. 27, 1875
John G. Gasmann	In charge April 25, 1877
John W. Douglas, Yankton agent also in charge of the Santee Sioux Agency	Mar. 28, 1878
Isaiah Lightner	Farmer in charge from Apr. 25, 1877, until appointment as agent Apr. 24, 1878

Flandreau Agency

John P. Williamson (special)	Sept. 10, 1873
William H. H. Wasson	July 1, 1878

NEOSHO AGENCY
1831-1875

The Neosho Subagency was established under the Western Superintendency in 1837 for the Quapaw, Seneca and Mixed Band of Seneca and Shawnee who lived on reserves east of the Neosho River in what is now the northeastern corner of Oklahoma. These Indians had moved into the area in accordance with treaties negotiated between 1831 and 1833. Before the Neosho Subagency was established, the Quapaw were assigned to the Osage Subagency and the Seneca and Seneca and Shawnee to the Cherokee Subagency. The correspondence filed under "Neosho" before 1837 relates primarily to the Quapaw who were then living along the Arkansas River in Arkansas.

The Neosho Subagency headquarters, originally located on the Seneca reserve, was moved in 1841 to Seneca and Shawnee land. In 1845 it was returned to Seneca country.

In 1851 the Southern Superintendency replaced the Western Superintendency, and in the same year the Osage Subagency in Kansas was combined with the Neosho Subagency to form the Neosho Agency. The agency was under the Southern Superintendency until 1867, when it was transferred to the Central Superintendency. At first the agent stayed at the former Neosho Subagency, but he soon moved to Crawford Seminary on Quapaw land.

During the Civil War, when Confederate troops occupied Indian Territory, the Neosho agent moved to Kansas with many of the Quapaw, Seneca and Shawnee Indians. For a while after the move the agent stayed at Fort Scott, but until 1869 he usually made his headquarters at Baldwin City. From 1869 to 1871 the agent reported from various places, mostly in Montgomery County, Kansas.

In 1864 the Southern superintendent appointed a special agent, George Mitchell, for the Southern refugee Indians in Kansas. After the war most of these Indians returned to Indian Territory, and in 1865 the special agent established a branch of the Neosho Agency on the Spring River in what became Eastern Shawnee country. After the treaty of February 23, 1867, in addition to the Osage Indians in Kansas and the Quapaw, Seneca and Eastern Shawnee (who now separated from the Seneca), the Neosho Agency gradually took charge of Wyandot, Ottawa, Peoria, Kaskaskia, Wea, Piankeshaw and other small groups of Indians formerly living in Kansas who, as a result of the treaty, had secured sections of the old Quapaw and Seneca reserves.

Often the special agency in Indian Territory, subordinate to the Neosho Agency, was called the Neosho Agency, while the Neosho Agency itself, still in Kansas, was referred to as the Osage Agency. In 1871 the Indians of the Neosho

Agency living in Indian Territory and the Indians formerly under the now discontinued Osage River Agency were assigned to the new Quapaw Agency.

During 1871 and 1872 the Neosho Agency was moved from Kansas to a new reservation for the Osage Indians in the north central part of Indian Territory. In 1872 the agent selected a permanent agency site at Deep Ford on Bird Creek, the site of Pawhuska. In 1874, in addition to the Osage Indians, the Neosho Agency was put in charge of the Kansa (Kaw) Indians, who had purchased a plot in the northwestern corner of the reservation.

On December 22, 1874 the Neosho Agency was renamed the Osage Agency. Beginning in 1875 correspondence, with the exception of one letter, was filed under the new name.

See also Arkansas, Western, Southern, St. Louis and Central Superintendencies and Osage, Osage River, Quapaw, Cherokee, Caddo, Red River, Piqua, Ohio, Delaware, Ottawa and Kansas Agencies.

SUBAGENTS

Name	*Date of Appointment*
Alexander S. Walker	Apr. 29, 1837
Robert A. Callaway	Dec. 1, 1837
Congrave Jackson	Jan. 24, 1840
Smallwood V. Noland	June 5, 1840
John B. Luce	Apr. 15, 1841
Montford Stokes	Sept. 8, 1842
Benjamin B. R. Barker	Mar. 24, 1843
James S. Rains	Apr. 25, 1845
Burton A. James	June 1, 1848
Andrew J. Dorn	Mar. 31, 1849

AGENTS

William J. J. Morrow	June 30, 1851
Andrew J. Dorn	Apr. 18, 1853
Peter P. Elder	Apr. 29, 1861
George Mitchell (special; served until 1871 in addition to the regular agent)	Apr. 8, 1864
George C. Snow	Mar. 16, 1865
Isaac T. Gibson	July 14, 1869

NEVADA SUPERINTENDENCY 1861-1880

The Nevada Superintendency was established in 1861, the year Nevada Territory was organized from the western part of Utah. Large parts of present Nevada were still in Utah and New Mexico (later Arizona) territories; Nevada did not get its present boundaries until 1866. The principal tribes living in Nevada were Paiute, Washo and Shoshoni.

The Territorial Governor served as *ex officio* superintendent until Nevada became a state in 1864. The superintendency headquarters was located at Carson City.

The Carson Valley Agency of the Utah Superintendency was transferred to the Nevada Superintendency in 1861. Usually called the Nevada Agency, it continued to operate beyond 1880 and was for much of the time the only regularly established agency in Nevada. There were two other agencies in existence during part of the period 1861-80, the South East Nevada Agency and the Western Shoshone Agency.

The Nevada Superintendency was discontinued in 1870, and thereafter the agents reported directly to the Bureau of Indian Affairs in Washington. Until the change of filing systems in 1881, however, incoming correspondence relating to the separate agencies was filed under the heading "Nevada" rather than under the names of the individual agencies.

See also Utah, California, Wyoming, Idaho and Arizona Superintendencies. There are also some field records of the Nevada Superintendency among the records of the Bureau of Indian Affairs in the National Archives.

NEVADA AGENCY

The Nevada Agency was a continuation of the Carson Valley Agency of the Utah Superintendency, which was established in 1858 for the Paiute and Washo Indians. In western Nevada the Walker River Reservation south of Carson City and the Pyramid Lake or Truckee Reservation north of Carson City were set aside for these Indians in 1859. Most of the Indians, however, refused to move onto the reservations. At different times the agent also had some duties relating to the Paiute Indians in southeastern Nevada and the Shoshoni Indians in eastern Nevada. The agent usually made his headquarters at Carson City but spent much of his time traveling, and for several months in 1871 there were separate agents assigned to the Walker River and Pyramid Lake Reservations. When the Pyramid Lake Agency was discontinued, the agent at Walker River moved to Wadsworth, headquarters for the Pyramid Lake agent, and the consolidated agency was again called the Nevada Agency. In 1873 the headquarters of the Nevada Agency was moved from Wadsworth to the Pyramid Lake Reservation. In 1875 the South East Nevada Agency was consolidated into the Nevada Agency. There was only one agency in Nevada from then until 1878, when an agency was established for the Western Shoshoni.

SOUTH EAST NEVADA AGENCY

The South East Nevada, or Pi-Ute, Agency was established in 1869 for the Paiute Indians living in southeastern Nevada and adjacent parts of Utah and Arizona. The agency was located briefly at St. Thomas and then at Pioche. A reservation known as Muddy Valley or Moapa River was established in 1873 and its boundaries modified in 1874 and 1875. During this period the agents were away from the agency much of the time, but by 1875 the agency was apparently settled at West Point. In that year, however, the South East Nevada Agency was consolidated with the Nevada Agency.

WESTERN SHOSHONE AGENCY

During 1871 and 1872 George Dodge acted as special agent for the Western, Northwestern and Goship Shoshoni Indians. Most of the correspondence relating to this agency is filed under the heading "Utah." After this agency was discontinued, a farmer was assigned to the Western Shoshoni living in Nevada. By 1875 the Nevada Agency had assumed some responsibility for these Indians. The Western Shoshone Agency was established in 1878 at Elko. Some of the Western Shoshoni were living on the "Carlin Farms," and, although an attempt was made to get them and other groups to move to the Duck Valley Reservation on the Nevada-Idaho border, many of the Indians preferred to live off the reservation. The Western Shoshoni Agency continued to operate beyond 1880.

SUPERINTENDENTS

Name	Date of Appointment
James W. Nye (Governor and *Ex Officio* Superintendent)	Mar. 22, 1861
Hubbard G. Parker	July 18, 1865
Theodore T. Dwight	Sept. 21, 1866
Hubbard G. Parker	Mar. 2, 1867
Bvt. Col. A. D. Nelson	Appointed June 17, 1869, but did not serve
Maj. Henry Douglas	Sept. 22, 1869

AGENTS

Nevada Agency

Frederick Dodge	June 12, 1858 for Carson Valley Agency of the Utah Superintendency
Jacob T. Lockhart	Aug. 31, 1861
Franklin Campbell	Nov. 1, 1865
Lt. Jesse M. Lee (special)	June 28, 1869
George Balcom (Special for Pyramid Lake)	Dec. 12, 1870
Calvin A. Bateman	Mar. 3, 1871
A. J. Barnes	Transferred from South East Nevada Agency, Dec. 7, 1875
William M. Garvey	Mar. 3, 1879
James E. Spencer	Aug. 18, 1879

South East Nevada Agency

Capt. Reuben N. Fenton (special)	Aug. 5, 1869
Henry G. Stewart (special)	Dec. 12, 1870
Charles F. Powell (special)	Aug. 3, 1871
George W. Ingalls	Mar. 26, 1873
A. J. Barnes	Sept. 30, 1874

Western Shoshone Agency

John How	July 1, 1878

NEW MEXICO SUPERINTENDENCY 1849-1880

The New Mexico Superintendency was established with the organization of the Territory of New Mexico on September 9, 1850. It replaced the Santa Fe Agency which had been established on March 28, 1849, with James S. Calhoun as agent. At that time New Mexico included most of Arizona and parts of Colorado and Nevada, and its area was increased in 1853 by the Gadsden Purchase. With the establishment of Colorado Territory in 1861 and Arizona Territory in 1863, however, New Mexico was reduced to its present boundaries. Until 1857 the Territorial Governor served as *ex officio* superintendent after which time a separate official was appointed. The superintendency headquarters was at Santa Fe throughout the existence of the superintendency.

On February 27, 1851 Congress authorized the appointment of four agents to serve under the superintendent. At first these men did not have specific assignments but were used wherever the superintendent believed they were needed. Gradually regular agencies were established for the different tribes. These agencies were the Navajo, Southern Apache, Utah (Ute Indians), Abiquiu (Ute and Jicarilla Apache), Conejos (Tabaquache Ute), Pueblo, Tucson (Pima, Papago, Maricopa and Apache), Cimarron (Jicarilla Apache and Moache Ute) and Mescalero.

The New Mexico Superintendency was abolished in 1874, and thereafter the agents in New Mexico reported directly to the Bureau of Indian Affairs in Washington. Until the change of filing systems in 1881, however, correspondence relating to the separate agencies in New Mexico was filed under the heading "New Mexico" rather than under the names of the individual agencies.

See also Arizona, Utah and Colorado Superintendencies and Santa Fe and Pima Agencies. There are also field records of the New Mexico Superintendency among the records of the Bureau of Indian Affairs in the National Archives.

NAVAJO AGENCY

The Navajo Agency was established in 1852 at Fort Defiance, in what is now Arizona. It had charge of the Navajo Indians who lived in the northwestern part of New Mexico and adjoining areas in Arizona, Utah and Colorado. After the Navajo War (1858-63) the Army gradually moved part of the Navajo to the Bosque Redondo Reservation on the Pecos River. The Navajo Agency was moved to Fort Sumner on the Bosque Redondo Reservation in 1866. The reservation was abandoned in 1868, and the agency was returned to Fort Defiance where it continued beyond 1880. From October, 1876 until December, 1877 the Navajo agent handled the business of the Moqui Pueblo Agency. Although its headquarters was in Arizona, the Navajo Agency was considered a New Mexico agency.

SOUTHERN APACHE (APACHE, GILA APACHE) AGENCY

The Southern Apache Agency was established in 1852 with jurisdiction over the Mimbreño, Mogollon, Coyotero and, temporarily, the Mescalero Apache. Over the years it was located at various places in the vicinity of Ojo Caliente (Hot Springs), but in 1873 the agency was moved to a new Apache reservation in

111

the Tulerosa Valley. The following year the reservation and agency were moved to Ojo Caliente. Both were abolished in 1877 when the Indians were moved to the San Carlos Reservation in Arizona.

UTAH AGENCY

The Utah Agency was established in 1853 with jurisdiction over various bands of Ute in New Mexico and, at times, the Jicarilla Apache. Located briefly at Abiquiu, it was permanently established at Taos. In 1854 the Abiquiu Agency was established and took nominal charge of the Capote Ute and the Jicarilla Apache; the Utah Agency retained jurisdiction over the Tabaquache and Moache Ute. The division of tribes between the two agencies, however, was indistinct. In general, the Utah Agency was in charge of the Indians of northeastern New Mexico. In 1860 the Conejos Agency was established for the Tabaquache Ute. The Utah Agency was replaced in 1862 by the Cimarron Agency.

ABIQUIU AGENCY

The Abiquiu Agency was established at Abiquiu in 1854 to take charge of the Capote Ute and the Jicarilla Apache in the northwestern part of present New Mexico. After the Cimarron Agency was established in 1862, the Abiquiu Agency had charge of the Capote and Wiminuche Ute. In 1878, when the Ute were moved to Colorado, the agency was consolidated with the Pueblo Agency.

CONEJOS AGENCY

The Conejos Agency was established in 1860 for the Indians (Tabaquache Ute) living north of the Utah Agency area. The Conejos Agency was located at Conejos in present Colorado, and when the Territory of Colorado was organized in 1861, the Conejos Agency was transferred to the Colorado Superintendency.

CIMARRON AGENCY

In 1862 the Cimarron Agency replaced the Utah Agency and assumed jurisdiction over the Jicarilla Apache and Moache Ute. After the resignation of Agent Roedel in April, 1872, no agent was appointed until after the New Mexico Superintendency was discontinued in 1874. Because of the contemplated removal of the Indians from the area, the Cimarron Agency was consolidated with the Pueblo Agency in 1876. The Moache Ute were later assigned to the Southern Ute Agency in Colorado.

PUEBLO AGENCY

The Pueblo Agency was established at Santa Fe in 1854. It had charge of 19 Pueblo villages in the vicinity of Sante Fe and Albuquerque and in 1876 it also

112

took charge of the Jicarilla Apache. The agency continued to operate beyond 1880.

TUCSON AGENCY

The Tucson Agency was established at Tucson in 1857 to supervise those Indians (Pima, Papago, Maricopa and Apache) who lived chiefly on the land acquired by the Gadsden Purchase. In 1861 Confederate troops occupied the area and the agency was abandoned. Control was not re-established until after Arizona had been made a separate superintendency.

See also the separate correspondence relating to the Pima Agency that was in operation during 1859 and 1860.

MESCALERO AGENCY

When Tucson fell to Confederate troops in 1861, the agent there was transferred to Fort Stanton to assume control of the Mescalero Apache. Fort Stanton soon fell also and the Mescalero Agency, although nominally in existence, was inoperative until 1871. In 1875 the agency was moved from Fort Stanton to South Fork, Lincoln County, on the reservation newly established for the Mescalero. The agency remained in that location beyond 1880.

SPECIAL AGENTS AND COMMISSIONERS

The principal special agent during the period 1849-80 was J. K. Graves, who visited New Mexico in 1865 and 1866 and made an important report on Indian affairs there. In 1871 Vincent Colyer, secretary of the Board of Indian Commissioners, visited New Mexico and Arizona in a futile effort to make peace with the warring Apache.

GOVERNORS AND *EX OFFICIO* SUPERINTENDENTS

Name	*Date of Appointment*
James S. Calhoun	Jan. 7, 1851
William Carr Lane	July 15, 1852
David Meriwether	May 6, 1853

SUPERINTENDENTS

James L. Collins	Mar. 12, 1857
Michael Steck	Mar. 16, 1863
Felipe Delgado	Mar. 3, 1865
A. Baldwin Norton	Feb. 15, 1866
Luther E. Webb	Feb. 10, 1868

SUPERINTENDENTS (cont.)

Jose Manuel Gallegos	Oct. 17, 1868
Maj. William Clinton	July 7, 1869
Nathaniel Pope	Oct. 29, 1870
Levi Edwin Dudley	Nov. 18, 1872

AGENTS

Agents Without Specific Assignments

Edward H. Wingfield	Mar. 12, 1851
Richard H. Weightman	Mar. 12, 1851
Abraham R. Woolley	Mar. 12, 1851
John Greiner (Acted as superintendent on occasion)	Mar. 12, 1851
Michael Steck	Sept. 1, 1852

Navajo Agency

Spencer M. Baird	Jan. 22, 1852
Henry Dodge	Apr. 11, 1853
William R. Harley	June 25, 1857
Robert J. Cowart	Sept. 11, 1858
Silas F. Kendrick	July 1, 1859
John Ward	Apr. 30, 1861
Theodore H. Dodd	Mar. 21, 1865
James C. French	Transferred from Abiquiu Jan. 23, 1869
Capt. F. T. Bennett	July 1, 1869
James H. Miller	Nov. 22, 1870
W. F. Hall	July 23, 1872
William F. M. Arny	June 18, 1873
Alexander G. Irvine	Sept. 23, 1875
John E. Pyle	Dec. 3, 1877
Capt. F. T. Bennett (acting)	July 1, 1880

Southern Apache Agency

Charles Overman (special)	Feb. 29, 1852
Edward H. Wingfield	Assigned Oct. 27, 1852
James M. Smith	May 3, 1853
Edmund A. Graves	Transferred from Utah Agency, Jan. 9, 1854

Southern Apache Agency (cont.)

Michael Steck	May 4, 1854
Amos J. Chipman	July 26, 1861
Ferdinand Maxwell	July 28, 1862
Louis Baca	Mar. 18, 1867
John Ayres	July 23, 1868
Lt. Charles E. Drew	July 6, 1869
Orlando F. Piper	Oct. 25, 1870
Benjamin M. Thomas	Oct. 29, 1872
John M. Shaw	Sept. 17, 1874
James Davis	Aug. 15, 1876

Utah Agency

Edmund A. Graves	May 1, 1853
Christopher Carson	Mar. 22, 1853; on duty Jan. 9, 1854
William F. M. Arny	May 20, 1861

Abiquiu Agency

Lorenzo Labadi	July 24, 1854
Diego Archuleta	May 13, 1857
Jose A. Manzanares	Apr. 30, 1861
Diego Archuleta	Mar. 21, 1865
William F. M. Arny	Mar. 12, 1867
James C. French	July 16, 1868
John Ayres	Transferred from Southern Apache Agency, Jan. 23, 1869
Lt. J. B. Hanson	July 1, 1869
John S. Armstrong	July 17, 1871
William D. Crothers	May 12, 1873
Samuel A. Russell	Aug. 3, 1874

Conejos Agency

Lafayette Head	June 27, 1860

Cimarron Agency

Levi J. Keithly	Aug. 4, 1862
Manuel S. Salazar	Mar. 21, 1865
Erasmus B. Dennison	July 16, 1866
Lt. A. S. B. Keyes	July 1, 1869

Cimarron Agency (cont.)

Maj. W. P. Wilson	Apr. 5, 1870
Charles E. Roedel	Nov. 2, 1870; Position vacant after Apr., 1872
Alexander G. Irvine (special)	July 31, 1874
John E. Pyle (special)	Nov. 16, 1875

Pueblo Agency

Abraham G. Mayers	Oct. 27, 1854
Samuel M. Yost	Apr. 9, 1857
John T. Russell	Nov. 5, 1859
Ramon Luna	Apr. 30, 1861
Toribio Romero	Mar. 21, 1865
John D. Henderson	June 18, 1866
Nicholas Quintana	July 25, 1868
Lt. Charles Cooper	July 1, 1869
Lt. George E. Ford	July 6, 1869
Lt. J. A. Manley	Apr. 5, 1870
William F. N. Arny	Jan. 27, 1871
John O. Cole	June 7, 1872
Edwin C. Lewis	May 30, 1873
Benjamin M. Thomas	Sept. 17, 1874

Tucson Agency

John Walker	Mar. 12, 1857
Lorenzo Labadi	Mar. 28, 1861

Mescalero Agency

Lorenzo Labadi	Transferred from Tucson, Aug. 11, 1861
Lt. A. G. Hennisee	July 1, 1869
Robert S. Clark	Nov. 22, 1870
Andrew J. Curtis	Feb. 8, 1871
Samuel B. Bushnell	Jan. 11, 1873
William D. Crothers	Jan. 23, 1874
Frederick C. Godfroy	Apr. 25, 1876
John A. Broadhead	Aug. 2, 1878
Samuel A. Russell	Dec. 19, 1878

NEW YORK AGENCY
1829-1880

The New York Agency, a subagency until 1855, was a continuation of the Six Nations Agency. Under the regulations adopted by the Bureau of Indian Affairs in 1834, the subagency responsible for the Indians living in New York was designated as the New York Subagency, and correspondence beginning in 1835 is filed under the new name. Some earlier letters are filed under the subheading "New York Emigration."

Most of the Indians living in New York were Seneca. There were also members of four of the other "Six Nations" of Iroquois—Cayuga, Tuscarora, Onondaga and Oneida—and there were members of the St. Regis Band of Iroquois. Most of the Oneida had moved to Green Bay in what became Wisconsin, as had most of the Stockbridge, Munsee and Brotherton Indians who had formerly lived in New York. Almost all the members of the sixth of the principal Iroquois tribes, the Mohawk, had long since moved to Canada. Most of the New York Indians lived on reservations in the western part of the state. During the 1870's the New York agent considered that the small group of Seneca living on the Cornplanter reservation along the Allegheny River in Warren County, Pennsylvania were under his supervision.

The New York Agency was not responsible to any superintendency after 1834, and the agent reported directly to the Bureau of Indian Affairs in Washington. Until 1846 the agency headquarters was at Buffalo, except for a period during 1840 and 1841 when the acting subagent lived at Williamson. After 1846 each agent selected his own headquarters and the agency site changed many times. The locations were: Ellicottville, 1846-49; Versailles, 1849-51; Ellicottville, 1851; Buffalo, 1851-53; Randolph, 1853-57; Buffalo, 1857-61; Ellicottville, 1861-64; Akron, 1864-66; Buffalo, 1866-69; Forestville, 1869; Dunkirk, 1869-70; and Forestville, 1870-80.

The New York Agency continued in operation beyond 1880. There are some letters filed under the subheading "New York Emigration" for the years 1829-51. Most of these letters relate to plans for and the actual removal of some Indians to present Kansas rather than to the earlier removals to Green Bay. Most of the Indians remained in New York.

See also Six Nations and Seneca Agencies. For correspondence concerning Indians who had left New York and concerning other groups of Seneca see Green Bay, Cherokee, Osage River, Fort Leavenworth, Neosho, Quapaw, Kansas, Delaware, Sac and Fox, Ottawa, Potawatomi, Piqua and Ohio Agencies. There are also field records of the New York Agency among the records of the Bureau of Indian Affairs in the National Archives, but for a much later period.

SUBAGENTS

Name	Date of Appointment
James Stryker	Assigned to Six Nations Agency, Apr. 1, 1832
Griffith M. Cooper (acting)	Dec. 30, 1840
Stephen Osborne	Dec. 23, 1841
William P. Angel	July 1, 1846
Robert H. Shankland	Aug. 11, 1848
Stephen P. Mead	June 27, 1849
Charles P. Washburn	Apr. 3, 1851
Stephen Osborne	Sept. 30, 1851
Marcus H. Johnson	Apr. 26, 1853

AGENTS

Marcus H. Johnson	June 8, 1855
Bela H. Colgrove	Nov. 30, 1857
Delos E. Sill	Mar. 8, 1861
Charles B. Rich	Nov. 18, 1864
Henry S. Cunningham	Oct. 25, 1866
Daniel Sherman	Apr. 21, 1869
Capt. E. R. Ames	June 12, 1869
Daniel Sherman	May 30, 1870

NORTHERN SUPERINTENDENCY 1851-1876

The Northern Superintendency was established in 1851 as part of the general reorganization of that year. The superintendent was informed that he would have charge of the Indians living in Wisconsin and Michigan—the Indians of the Mackinac Agency and Sault Ste. Marie Subagency in Michigan (Chippewa, Ottawa and Potawatomi Indians) and the Indians of the Green Bay Subagency in Wisconsin (Menominee, Oneida and Stockbridge Indians). There were also some stray Potawatomi and other Indians in Wisconsin. Mackinac and Sault Ste. Marie previously had been in the Michigan Superintendency, and the Green Bay Subagency had not been assigned to any superintendency since the Wisconsin Superintendency was discontinued in 1848. In practice the Northern superintendent had little contact with Indian affairs in Michigan. The Sault Ste. Marie Subagency was consolidated with the Mackinac Agency in 1852, and the Mackinac agent usually reported directly to the Bureau of Indian Affairs in Washington. When the superintendent inquired concerning his authority in 1853, he was informed that his superintendency included only the Menominee, Stockbridge and Oneida Indians (the Green Bay Subagency). In 1855 Green Bay was made a full agency.

The superintendent made his headquarters briefly at Green Bay and then at Sheboygan. The superintendent appointed in 1853 established his office at Milwaukee. In 1856 the Minnesota Superintendency was discontinued, its agencies were transferred to the Northern Superintendency, and the superintendent was ordered to move his headquarters to St. Paul, Minnesota. Actually, until 1857, he alternated between St. Paul and Milwaukee. The agencies in Minnesota were the St. Peters (Sioux of the Mississippi Indians), Winnebago and Chippewa (Chippewa of the Mississippi Indians). Beginning in 1857 the Green Bay Agency was no longer responsible to the Northern Superintendency, and the agent reported directly to the Bureau of Indian Affairs in Washington. In 1858 the La Pointe Agency for the Chippewa of Lake Superior living in Minnesota and Wisconsin was established under the Northern Superintendency. In 1863 many of the Winnebago and Sioux Indians and the Winnebago Agency were moved to Dakota Territory, but they remained under the jurisdiction of the Northern Superintendency.

The Northern Superintendency was completely reorganized in 1865, and its office was moved from St. Paul, Minnesota to Omaha, Nebraska. It was put in charge of the Omaha, Pawnee, Otoe (Oto and Missouri Indians), Great Nemaha (Sauk and Fox of the Missouri and Iowa Indians) and Winnebago Agencies in Nebraska and the Upper Platte Agency (Cheyenne, Arapaho and Sioux), then located near Fort Laramie but later moved east into Nebraska. Only the Winnebago Agency, which had been moved again from Dakota to Nebraska, previously had been assigned to the Northern Superintendency. The other agencies were transferred from the Central Superintendency. The Chippewa and La Pointe Agencies were no longer attached to a superintendency, and thereafter the agents reported directly to the Bureau of Indian Affairs in Washington. The St. Peters Agency, now located in Dakota, was transferred to the Dakota Superintendency; in 1866 it was moved to Nebraska and was again within the limits of the Northern Superintendency. This agency was now often called the Santee Sioux Agency, and in 1871 the Bureau adopted this name for filing purposes, abandoning the old name "St. Peters."

The Upper Platte Agency was moved to Dakota in 1868. It was transferred to the Dakota Superintendency in 1869 and renamed the Whetstone Agency, although the name "Upper Platte" continued to be used for filing purposes through 1870. By 1876 the Pawnee had moved to Indian Territory and the Pawnee Agency was transferred from the Northern to the Central Superintendency.

The Northern Superintendency was discontinued on June 30, 1876. Thereafter the Otoe, Omaha, Great Nemaha, Winnebago and Santee Sioux agents reported directly to the Bureau of Indian Affairs in Washington. Until this time correspondence relating to the individual agencies in the Northern Superintendency had been filed under the respective names of the agencies rather than under the name of the superintendency. From July 1, 1876, however, correspondence relating to the Otoe, Omaha, Great Nemaha, Winnebago and Santee Sioux Agencies in Nebraska and the Flandreau Agency in Dakota was filed under the heading "Nebraska."

See also Michigan, Wisconsin, Minnesota, Central and Dakota Superintendencies and Green Bay, Mackinac, Sault Ste. Marie, St. Peters, Santee Sioux, Winnebago, Chippewa, La Pointe, Omaha, Otoe, Pawnee, Great Nemaha, Upper Platte, Whetstone, Flandreau and Nebraska Agencies. There are also field records of the Northern Superintendency among the records of the Bureau of Indian Affairs in the National Archives.

SUPERINTENDENTS

Name	Date of Appointment
Elias Murray	Mar. 12, 1851
Francis Huebschmann	Apr. 18, 1853
William J. Cullen	May 13, 1857
Clark W. Thompson	Mar. 27, 1861
Edward B. Taylor	July 1, 1865
Hampton B. Denman	Oct. 29, 1866
Samuel M. Janney	Apr. 22, 1869
Barclay White	Oct. 1, 1871

OHIO AGENCY
1831-1843

The Ohio Agency was a continuation of the Piqua Agency that had been established in 1812. The agency office was moved from Piqua to Columbus in 1829, but correspondence through 1830 is filed under "Piqua."

The Ohio Agency was responsible for the Indians, principally Wyandot, Shawnee and Seneca, living in Ohio. The Delaware, who had been one of the major tribes assigned to the Piqua Agency, were in the process of moving west in 1831. Also living in Ohio were some Ottawa Indians and remnants of other bands. Since the Indians assigned to the Ohio Agency were widely dispersed, the agent was assisted by a number of subagents, notably for the Wyandot at Upper Sandusky, the Seneca at Fort Ball and the Mixed Band of Seneca and Shawnee at Lewiston. Until 1836 there was a separate subagency for the Ottawa of Maumee who were more closely identified with the Michigan Superintendency than the Ohio Agency.

By the end of the 1832 most of the Seneca and Shawnee had moved west of the Mississippi River, leaving the Wyandot as the major responsibility of the Ohio Agency. In February, 1832 the agent had been ordered to move from Columbus to Upper Sandusky on the Wyandot reserve. On December 31, 1832, the Ohio Agency was reduced to a subagency which was often called the Wyandot Subagency.

The Ohio Agency and the successor subagency were assigned to the Michigan Superintendency, but the agent usually reported directly to the Bureau of Indian Affairs in Washington. Following the reorganization of 1834, the Michigan Superintendency no longer had any supervision over the Ohio Subagency.

In 1842 the Wyandot agreed to move west of Missouri (present Kansas) and the Ohio Subagency was discontinued in April of that year. It was revived from October, 1842 until September, 1843, by which time the Indians had actually moved. The Wyandot Subagency was established for them in the west.

Some of the correspondence relating to the emigration of the Indians from Ohio for the years 1831-39 is filed under the subheading "Ohio Emigration." For 1834-43 there are separate records under the subheading "Ohio Reserves" that relate primarily to the sale of Wyandot lands in Ohio.

James B. Gardiner was the principal special agent in charge of negotiating with the Indians to move west and of superintending the removal during the years 1831-33. John Johnston was the commissioner in charge of negotiating the 1842 treaty by which the Wyandot agreed to leave Ohio.

See also Michigan Superintendency and Piqua Agency. For correspondence concerning the Indians after they had moved west see St. Louis and Western Superintendencies and Fort Leavenworth, Neosho and Wyandot Agencies and Subagencies.

AGENTS

Name	Date of Appointment
John McElvain	Apr. 20, 1829

John McElvain	Jan. 1, 1833
Purdy McElvain	Mar. 13, 1835
John W. Bear	June 1, 1841
Purdy McElvain	Oct. 1, 1842

OMAHA AGENCY
1856-1876

The Omaha Agency was established in 1856 to supervise the Omaha Indians previously under the Council Bluffs Agency. The agency was located on the west bank of the Missouri River, north of Decatur, Nebraska.

Originally under the Central Superintendency, the agency was transferred to the Northern Superintendency in 1865. On June 30, 1876 the Northern Superintendency was discontinued, and thereafter the Omaha agent reported directly to the Bureau of Indian Affairs in Washington. Beginning July 1, 1876, correspondence relating to the agency was filed under the heading "Nebraska." In 1879 the Omaha and Winnebago Agencies were united to form the Omaha and Winnebago Agency.

See also Central and Northern Superintendencies and Council Bluffs and Nebraska Agencies.

AGENTS

Name	*Date of Appointment*
John B. Robertson	July 15, 1856
William F. Wilson	June 3, 1858
William E. Moore	Sept. 13, 1859
George B. Graff	June 21, 1860
Orsamus H. Irish	Apr. 30, 1861
Robert W. Furnas	Mar. 2, 1864
Lewis Lowry	Oct. 26, 1866
William P. Callon	Apr. 11, 1867
Edward Painter	Apr. 30, 1869

Theodore T. Gillingham   Sept. 30, 1873
Jacob Vore   July 10, 1876

OREGON SUPERINTENDENCY
1842-1880

The Oregon Superintendency was established in 1848, the year Oregon Territory was organized. The superintendency was preceded by a subagency for the "country West of the Rocky mountains," which was established in 1842 and located in the Willamette Valley. Originally Oregon Territory included all of the area west of the Rocky Mountains and north of the 42d parallel. In 1853 the region north of the Columbia River and the 36th parallel was organized as Washington Territory. When Oregon became a state in 1859, it was reduced to its present boundaries and the remainder of Oregon Territory became part of Washington. Between 1857 and 1861, however, the Oregon and Washington Superintendencies were combined. Correspondence for this period is filed with that relating to the Oregon Superintendency.

The territorial governor acted as *ex officio* superintendent of Indian affairs until 1850, when a separate official was appointed. In 1851 the superintendency headquarters was moved from its original location at Oregon City to Milwaukee; in 1853 to Dayton; in 1856 back to Oregon City; in 1857 to Salem; in 1859 to Portland; and in 1861 to Salem again.

There were many bands of Indians in Oregon, including Umpqua, Umatilla, Cayuse, Wallawalla, Wasco, Shoshoni (Snake), Kalapuya, Clackamas, Rogue River, Warm Springs, Shasta, Klamath, Modoc, Paiute, Tenino, Nez Percé, Molala, Yamel, Joshua, Sixes (Kwatami), Chastacosta, Chetco and Bannock.

When the Oregon Superintendency was organized in 1848, three subagents were appointed for assignment by the superintendent wherever they might be needed. The first full agents were appointed in 1850 and were also assigned at the discretion of the superintendent. Gradually permanent agencies were established, usually on a geographic basis rather than for particular Indians. The agencies in Oregon were Rogue River, Warm Springs (also known by other names), Puget Sound District, Southeastern District, Port Orford, Siletz, Grand Ronde, Umatilla, Klamath and Malheur. During the period from 1857 to 1861 the Puget Sound, Columbia River District-Yakima and Washington East of the Cascades—Nez Percé Agencies were included in the combined Oregon and

Washington Superintendency. There were also many subagencies, special agencies and local agencies, especially following the wars of 1855, when an attempt was being made to move the Indians to reservations.

The Oregon Superintendency was abolished in 1873. Thereafter the agents in Oregon reported directly to the Bureau of Indian Affairs in Washington. Until the change of filing systems in 1881, however, correspondence relating to the separate agencies was filed under the heading "Oregon" rather than under the names of the individual agencies.

See also Washington, Idaho, Montana, California and Nevada Superintendencies. There are also field records of the Oregon Superintendency and of the Malheur Agency among the records of the Bureau of Indian Affairs in the National Archives. Many of the records of the Oregon Superintendency have been reproduced by the National Archives and Records Service as Microfilm Publication 2.

ROGUE RIVER AGENCY

In 1850 an agent was assigned to the Southwestern or Southern District of Oregon, which included the Umpqua and Rogue River Valleys. The following year the agent was specifically assigned to the Rogue River Valley, and the agency was usually called the Rogue River or Rogue River Valley Agency. By 1856 most of the Rogue River and Umpqua Indians had been removed to the Coast Reservation, and the agent was transferred to Grand Ronde.

WARM SPRINGS AGENCY

In 1851 an agency was established for the Indians east of the Cascade Mountains. This agency was known by many names, including Utilla, Eastern Oregon, Northeastern Oregon, Middle Oregon, Dalles and, finally, the Warm Springs Agency. The agency was originally located at the Lower Crossing of the Utilla (Umatilla) River and was primarily responsible for the Cayuse, Shoshoni and Nez Percé Indians. In 1854 the agency was moved to The Dalles. The principal tribes in eastern Oregon at that time were Wasco, Wallawalla, Cayuse, Shoshoni and Umatilla. With the reductions in the boundaries of Oregon in 1853 and 1859, the jurisdiction of the agency also diminished. Between 1854 and 1856 that part of Oregon south of the 44th parallel was assigned to a separate agency for the Southeastern District. Beginning in 1860 the agent spent much of his time at the Warm Springs Reservation, which had been established in 1856, and in 1861 the superintendent specifically assigned the agent to the Warm Springs Agency. By this time principal Indian bands under its charge were Wasco, Tenino and Warm Springs. The Warm Springs Agency continued in operation beyond 1880.

PUGET SOUND DISTRICT AGENCY

An agent was assigned to the Puget Sound area and located at Steilacoom in 1851. The agency became part of the new Washington Superintendency in 1853. From 1857 to 1861 the agency, then located at Olympia, was under the combined Oregon and Washington Superintendency.

PORT ORFORD AGENCY

The Indians in the Port Orford area were usually assigned to a subagent. In 1854 and again in 1856, when the Indians were to be moved to the Coast Reservation, a full agent was stationed at Port Orford.

SOUTHEASTERN DISTRICT AGENCY

This agency, established in 1854 with headquarters at The Dalles, was in charge of the Indians east of the Cascade Mountains and south of the 44th parallel. In 1856 the agent was transferred to Port Orford and was not replaced.

GRAND RONDE AGENCY

An agent was assigned to the eastern part of the Coast Reservation in 1856. The agency there had charge of remnants of various bands, mainly from the Willamette and Rogue River Valleys, including Molala, Clackamas, Yamel, Kalapuya, Umpqua, Shasta and Rogue River Indians. The agency continued to operate beyond 1880.

SILETZ AGENCY

In 1856 the Siletz Agency was established on the Siletz River on the Coast Reservation near Toledo. The agency had charge of the Indians who had been removed from along the coast, from the Rogue River area and from other parts of Oregon. The principal tribes were Joshua, Sixes (Kwatami), Chetco, Rogue River, Chastacosta and Klamath. The agency continued in operation beyond 1880.

UMATILLA AGENCY

The Umatilla Agency on the Umatilla Reservation in northeastern Oregon was transferred from the Washington Superintendency in 1862. There had been a subagency under the Oregon and Washington Superintendency on the reservation in 1860, but in 1861 it was made an agency of the Washington Superintendency. The agency was responsible for Umatilla, Cayuse and Wallawalla Indians. It continued in operation beyond 1880.

KLAMATH AGENCY

The Klamath Agency was established for the Klamath, Modoc and Shoshoni Indians who had moved into southern Oregon after the Rogue River, Umpqua and other groups had been removed to the Coast Reservation. A special agent was appointed for the Klamath Lake area in 1861 and a subagent, who resided in Jacksonville, was appointed in 1862. In 1867 the subagency was moved to the Klamath Reservation and in 1872 it was made a full agency. The Klamath Agency remained in operation beyond 1880. (The Klamath Agency in Oregon should not be confused with the earlier Klamath Agency in California.)

MALHEUR AGENCY

The Malheur Agency for the Shoshoni (Snake), Bannock and Paiute Indians in eastern Oregon was established in 1873. It was abolished in 1882 after most of the Indians had been removed to the Yakima Agency in Washington.

WASHINGTON AGENCIES, 1857-1861

In addition to the Puget Sound District Agency discussed above, there were two regular agencies in Washington during the period of the combined Oregon and Washington Superintendency. At Vancouver there was an agency for the Indians of the Columbia River District, which extended from the mouth of the Columbia River to The Dalles. In 1858 the agency was moved to White Salmon. It was moved to Fort Simcoe in 1859, after which it was known as the Yakima Agency.

The other of the two regular agencies, originally established in 1854, was known as the Flathead Agency. The superintendent discontinued this agency and stationed the agent at The Dalles, where he was to act as agent for that part of Washington east of the Cascade Mountains. This move put the agent in charge of Nez Percé and Coeur d'Alène as well as Flathead Indians. In 1859 the agent was assigned to the Walla Walla Valley, where he was in charge of Nez Percé, Cayuse, Paloos and, at times, Spokan and Coeur d'Alène Indians. After 1861 the agent usually stayed at Lapwai on the Nez Percé Reservation in present Idaho.

SUBAGENT FOR COUNTRY WEST OF THE ROCKY MOUNTAINS

Name	Date of Appointment
Elijah White	Jan. 27, 1842

GOVERNORS AND *EX OFFICIO* SUPERINTENDENTS

Joseph Lane	Aug. 18, 1848
John P. Gaines	Oct. 2, 1849

SUPERINTENDENTS

Anson Dart	June 21, 1850
Joel Palmer	Mar. 17, 1853
Absalom F. Hedges	Notified June 21, 1856
James W. Nesmith	Mar. 12, 1857
Edward R. Geary	Mar. 22, 1859
William H. Rector	June 13, 1861
J. W. Perit Huntington	Jan. 19, 1863
Alfred B. Meacham	Mar. 29, 1869
T. B. Odeneal	Jan. 8, 1872

AGENTS

Rogue River Agency

Henry H. Spaulding	June 28, 1850
Alonzo A. Skinner	July 10, 1851
Samuel H. Culver	Apr. 28, 1853
George H. Ambrose	Nov. 2, 1854
John F. Miller	Aug. 13, 1856

Warm Springs Agency

At Utilla

Elias Wampole	Sept. 24, 1850

At The Dalles

Robert R. Thompson	Apr. 28, 1853
Ami P. Dennison	Feb. 3, 1857

At Warm Springs

William Logan	June 13, 1861
John Smith	Nov. 4, 1865
Bvt. Capt. W. W. Mitchell	June 21, 1869
John Smith	Reinstated, Oct. 4, 1870

Puget Sound District Agency

(Before transfer to Washington.)

Edmund A. Starling	July 10, 1851
Joseph M. Garrison	Mar. 22, 1853

(1857-1861)

Michael T. Simmons   Feb. 27, 1856
Wesley B. Gosnell   Nov. 21, 1860

Port Orford Agency

Josiah M. Parrish   Jan. 11, 1854
Nathan Olney   Transferred from
                                        Southeastern Dis-
                                        trict, Mar. 14, 1856

Southeastern District

Nathan Olney   Nov. 2, 1854

Grand Ronde

John F. Miller   Transferred from
                                        Rogue River, Nov.
                                        22, 1856
James B. Condon   July 16, 1861
Amos Harvey   May 18, 1864
Charles Lafollett   Mar. 31, 1869
Patrick B. Sinnott   Jan. 8, 1872

Siletz Agency

Robert B. Metcalf   Aug. 13, 1856
Daniel Newcomb   Sept. 30, 1859
Benjamin R. Biddle   July 16, 1861
Benjamin Simpson   Jan. 19, 1863
Joel Palmer   Mar. 2, 1871
James H. Fairchild   Dec. 20, 1872
William Bagley   Oct. 16, 1875
Edmund A. Swan   Apr. 28, 1879

Umatilla Agency

William H. Barnhart   July 16, 1861
Lt. W. H. Boyle   July 14, 1869
Narcisse A. Cornoyer   Mar. 2, 1871
Theophilus W. Taliaferro   July 14, 1875
Narcisse A. Cornoyer   Jan. 19, 1876
Richard H. Fay   June 16, 1880

Klamath Agency

Subagents

Amos E. Rogers	Jan. 21, 1862
Lindsay Applegate	June 28, 1865
Bvt. Col. Edmund Rice	June 23, 1869
Capt. O. C. Knapp	July 26, 1869
Johnson High	Mar. 27, 1871
Leroy S. Dyar	Dec. 29, 1871

Agents

Leroy S. Dyar	July 23, 1872
John H. Roork	Mar. 1, 1877
Linus M. Nickerson	Sept. 13, 1878

Malheur Agency

Harrison Linville (special)	Sept. 20, 1873
Samuel B. Parrish (special)	Apr. 18, 1874
Samuel B. Parrish (agent)	July 13, 1874
William V. Rinehart	Apr. 26, 1876

Columbia River District-Yakima Agency

John Cain	Jan. 4, 1855
Richard H. Lansdale	Transferred from Washington East of Cascades, Apr. 1, 1858

Washington East of the Cascades—Nez Percé Agency

Richard H. Landsdale	Appointed for Flathead Agency, Aug. 4, 1854. Transferred, June 2, 1857
Andrew J. Cain	Aug. 19, 1858

OSAGE AGENCY 1824-1853, 1874-1880

As early as 1807 Peter Chouteau, originally appointed in 1804 as agent for the Indians of Upper Louisiana, was specifically appointed agent for the Great and Little Osage. From 1812 until 1821 subagents responsible to the Governor of the Territory of Missouri had charge of the Osage. In 1821 an agent, who usually made his headquarters at St. Louis, was designated for the Osage, Delaware and Kickapoo Indians. Until the Bureau of Indian Affairs was established in 1824, correspondence concerning the Osage and their agents was transmitted directly to the Office of the Secretary of War.

In 1824 an agent was assigned solely to the Osage Indians. He was responsible to the St. Louis Superintendency, but in 1834 the Osage Agency was reduced to a subagency and assigned to the new Western Superintendency. By this time the agent usually stayed at a place on the Neosho River on the Osage Reservation in what is now southeastern Kansas. From 1834 until the Neosho Subagency was established in 1837, the Osage Subagency also had charge of the Quapaw Indians.

In 1843 the Osage Superintendency was transferred to the St. Louis Superintendency, in 1847 back to the Western Superintendency, and in 1849 to the St. Louis Superintendency again. In 1851 the Osage and Neosho Subagencies were combined to form the Neosho Agency under the Southern Superintendency, the successor to the Western Superintendency. From then until 1874, except for one item dated 1853, correspondence concerning the agency and the Osage Indians was filed under "Neosho."

On December 22, 1874 the Neosho Agency was renamed the Osage Agency. By this time the agency was responsible for the Osage Indians who had moved to a new reservation in the northern part of Indian Territory, for the Kansa (Kaw) Indians who lived in the northwestern corner of the Osage Reservation and, after 1879, for some Quapaw Indians who lived on the Osage Reservation. The agency headquarters was in the center of the reservation at Deep Ford on Bird Creek, the site of Pawhuska.

The Osage Agency was under the Central Superintendency until the superintendency was abolished in 1878; thereafter the agent reported directly to the Bureau of Indian Affairs in Washington. The Osage Agency, sometimes called the Osage and Kaw Agency, remained in operation beyond 1880.

See also St. Louis, Western, Southern, Central and Arkansas Superintendencies and Neosho and Kansas Agencies.

AGENTS AND SUBAGENTS

Agents, 1824-1834

Name	*Date of Appointment*
Alexander McNair	Notified June 1, 1824
John Francis Hamtramck	Notified May 4, 1826
Paul L. Chouteau	Notified May 3, 1830

Subagents, 1834-1851

Paul L. Chouteau	July 2, 1834
Edwin James	Transferred from Council Bluffs, Jan. 8, 1838
Congrave Jackson	Mar. 27, 1839
Robert Callaway	Jan. 24, 1840
John Hill Edwards	Feb. 14, 1844
Joel Cruttenden	Sept. 6, 1844
Samuel H. Bunch	Notified Feb. 13, 1846
John M. Richardson	Nov. 15, 1847
William H. Bell	Appointed July 23, 1849, but did not serve
Henry Harvey	Dec. 18, 1849

Agents, 1874-1880

Isaac T. Gibson	July 14, 1869, for Neosho Agency
Cyrus Beede	Jan. 19, 1876
Laban J. Miles	June 24, 1878

OSAGE RIVER AGENCY
1824-1871

The Osage River Agency, a subagency until 1847, was established under the St. Louis Superintendency in 1837. The few letters filed under "Osage River" for earlier years were those from Superintendent William Clark at St. Louis and from agents and subagents with responsibility for tribes later in the Osage River Agency. In general, until 1837, the Indians of the Osage River area were under the jurisdiction of the predecessors of the Fort Leavenworth Agency, particularly the Delaware and Shawnee Agency, 1824-34; a subagency for the Ottawa, Shawnee and other Indians, 1834-35; and the Northern Agency, 1835-37. Most of the correspondence relating to these agencies and subagencies is filed under "Fort Leavenworth." There is correspondence filed under "Osage River" relating to subagencies farther east, particularly the Kaskaskia Subagency of Pierre Menard and the Peoria Subagency of Peter Menard, Jr.

The Osage River Subagency, with headquarters near the site of Paolo, Kansas, was responsible for Potawatomi, Ottawa, Piankeshaw, Wea, Kaskasia and Peoria Indians; others moved in later, particularly Chippewa and Miami. The name of the Sac and Fox Agency was changed to the Osage River Agency in December, 1847. Placed under its jurisdiction were the Sauk and Fox of the Mississippi who had moved to the Osage River area from Iowa, the Kansa Indians who were transferred from the Fort Leavenworth Agency and the Chippewa, Ottawa, Peoria, Kaskasia, Piankeshaw, Wea, Miami and New York Indians who were at that time under the Osage River Subagency. A separate subagency was established for the Potawatomi Indians, but the next year this subagency was discontinued and the Indians were assigned to the Fort Leavenworth Agency.

In the reorganization of 1851 the Sauk and Fox, Ottawa and Chippewa were assigned to a new Sac and Fox Agency. The Kansa Indians were assigned to the new Potawatomi Agency. The Wea, Piankeshaw, Kaskasia, Peoria and Miami Indians remained in the Osage River Agency, which was now responsible to the Central Superintendency, successor to the St. Louis Superintendency.

The Osage River Agency was discontinued in 1871. The Miami Indians still in Kansas were placed briefly in the immediate charge of the Central Superintendency and then were placed under the Shawnee Agency. Most of the other Indians had moved or were moving to Indian Territory, where they were under the jurisdiction of the Neosho Agency until 1871 and thereafter under the Quapaw Agency.

See also St. Louis and Central Superintendencies and Fort Leavenworth, Sac and Fox, Council Bluffs, Potawatomi, Shawnee, Neosho and Quapaw Agencies. For correspondence concerning the Indians while they were still living in the east, see particularly *Michigan Superintendency* and *Chicago, Fort Wayne, Indiana, Miami, Piqua, Ohio* and *Mackinac Agencies and Subagencies*.

SUBAGENTS

Name	Date of Appointment
Anthony L. Davis	Apr. 24, 1837
Joshua Carpenter	Nov. 23, 1843
Alfred J. Vaughn	July 5, 1844

AGENTS

Solomon P. Sublette	Oct. 21, 1847, as Sac and Fox Agent; assigned to Osage River Agency on Dec. 8, 1847
James S. Rains	May 18, 1848
Charles N. Handy	Mar. 30, 1849
John R. Chenault	Notified Oct. 12, 1850
Asbury M. Coffey	June 30, 1851
Ely Moore	May 12, 1853
Maxwell McCaslin	Mar. 3, 1855
Seth Clover	Apr. 1, 1858
Gustavus A. Colton	Apr. 15, 1861
James Stanley	Apr. 22, 1869

OTOE AGENCY
1856-1876

The Otoe Agency (usually called the Otoe and Missouria Agency until 1869) was established under the Central Superintendency in 1856. It was located in the Big Blue River Valley in southern Nebraska and was responsible for the Oto and Missouri Indians. The Pawnee Indians were also under the Otoe Agency until a separate agency was established for them in 1859. Until 1865 the Council Bluffs Agency had had charge of these tribes.

In 1865 the Otoe Agency was transferred from the Central to the Northern Superintendency. The Northern Superintendency was abolished on June 30, 1876, and thereafter the agent reported directly to the Bureau of Indian Affairs in Washington. From July 1, 1876 correspondence relating to the Otoe Agency was filed under the heading "Nebraska." In 1881 the Otoe Agency was moved to Red Rock, Indian Territory, and the following year was consolidated into the Ponca, Pawnee and Otoe Agency.

See also Central and Northern Superintendencies and Council Bluffs, Pawnee and Nebraska Agencies.

AGENTS

Name	*Date of Appointment*
John A. Alston	July 15, 1856
William W. Dennison	Feb. 3, 1857
John Baker	Mar. 13, 1861
William Daily	Mar. 2, 1864
John L. Smith	May 31, 1866
Albert L. Green	Apr. 22, 1869
Jesse W. Griest	Apr. 1, 1873
Robert S. Gardner (special)	In charge, June 16, 1880
Lewellyn E. Woodin	July 21, 1880

OTTAWA AGENCY
1863-1873

The Ottawa Agency was established in 1863 for the Ottawa Indians of Kansas (the Blanchards Fork and Roche de Boeuf bands), the Chippewa of Swan Creek and Black River and the Munsee or "Christian" Indians who had affiliated with the Chippewa in 1859. The Ottawa lived on a reserve along the Marais des Cygnes River in Franklin County, Kansas, which they had received under the terms of a treaty made in 1831, and the Chippewa and Munsee lived to the west of the Ottawa. The Ottawa and Chippewa had been assigned to the Sac and Fox Agency since 1851 and before that to the Osage River Agency. The Munsee had lived with the Delaware Indians before they joined the Chippewa. The office of the Ottawa Agency was at Ottawa, Kansas and the agency was under the Central Superintendency.

In 1864 the Chippewa and Munsee were transferred back to the Sac and Fox Agency. In 1867 the Ottawa agent, Clinton C. Hutchinson, was suspended and not replaced. Thereafter either the Sac and Fox agent or the Central superintendent handled the affairs of the Ottawa in Kansas.

By a treaty of June 24, 1862 the Ottawa agreed to make allotments of land to individual members of the tribe and to sell the surplus land to white settlers. The Ottawa were to become citizens of Kansas and to dissolve their tribal government within five years. Those Indians who did not wish to become citizens arranged with the Shawnee Indians of the Neosho Agency to purchase a tract of land in Indian Territory. This agreement was confirmed by the Omnibus Treaty of 1867. As the Indians moved to Indian Territory, they came under the jurisdiction of the Neosho Agency until 1871 and thereafter the Quapaw Agency. Some correspondence, relating principally to the Ottawa still in Kansas, was filed under "Ottawa" until 1873.

See also Central Superintendency and Sac and Fox, Osage River, Delaware, Neosho and Quapaw Agencies. For correspondence concerning the Ottawa and Chippewa before they left the east and concerning Indians who remained in the east see particularly Michigan Superintendency and Mackinac and Chicago Agencies.

AGENT

Name	Date of Appointment
Clinton C. Hutchinson	Mar. 7, 1863; changed to special agent on Mar. 8, 1864

PAWNEE AGENCY
1859-1880

The Pawnee Agency was established under the Central Superintendency in 1859. The Pawnee Indians had been assigned to the Otoe Agency since 1856 and before that to the Council Bluffs Agency. The Pawnee Agency headquarters was at Genoa, Nebraska until 1875. During 1875 and 1876 the agency was moved to the new Pawnee Reservation in Indian Territory, and buildings were erected on Black Bear Creek about eight miles from the Arkansas River.

The Pawnee Agency was transferred to the Northern Superintendency in 1865 but was returned to the Central Superintendency in 1876 following the agency's removal to Indian Territory. The Central Superintendency was abolished in 1878, and thereafter the agent reported directly to the Bureau of Indian Affairs in Washington. In 1882 the Pawnee Agency was consolidated into the Ponca, Pawnee and Otoe Agency.

See also Central and Northern Superintendencies and Otoe, Council Bluffs and Wichita Agencies.

AGENTS

Name	*Date of Appointment*
James L. Gillis (special)	June 16, 1859
James L. Gillis (agent)	June 26, 1860
Henry DePuy	Apr. 29, 1861
Benjamin F. Lushbaugh	May 16, 1862
Daniel H. Wheeler	July 1, 1865
John P. Becker	Aug. 24, 1866
Charles H. Whaley	Apr. 20, 1867
Jacob M. Troth	Apr. 22, 1869
William Burgess	Jan. 1, 1873
Charles H. Searing	Mar. 16, 1877
Samuel Ely	Feb. 18, 1878
A. C. Williams (acting)	Sept. 16, 1878
John C. Smith	May 23, 1879
Edward H. Bowman	Mar. 29, 1880

PIMA AGENCY
1859-1861

The Pima Agency was a special agency established on February 18, 1859 for the Pima and Maricopa Indians, who lived along the Gila River in what is now Arizona but was then part of New Mexico Territory. The agent, Silas St. John, was an employee of the Overland Mail Company and was appointed at the request of the company, which ran stage coaches through Pima and Maricopa land and was anxious to maintain friendly relations with the Indians. St. John was not allowed any compensation by the Bureau for his services as Indian agent.

The Pima and Maricopa Indians were included in the jurisdiction of the Tucson Agency of the New Mexico Superintendency, but St. John reported directly to the Bureau of Indian Affairs in Washington and had little communication with either the Tucson agent or the New Mexico superintendent. St. John resigned in May, 1860 and was not replaced. Some correspondence relating to the affairs of the Pima and Maricopa Indians, however, was filed under "Pima" until 1861. Included with the correspondence relating to the Pima Agency are communications from Sylvester Mowry, who supervised the survey of a reservation for the Pima and Maricopa and for a time was in charge of purchasing and distributing goods for them.

With the closing of the Pima Agency, the Pima and Maricopa Indians were solely the responsibility of the Tucson Agency. In 1861 Confederate troops occupied Arizona and the Tucson Agency was abandoned. Federal control was re-established in 1863, and in the same year Arizona was made a separate territory and the Arizona Superintendency was established. In 1865 the Pima and Maricopa were assigned to the Pima, Papago and Maricopa Agency—known later as the Gila River Agency—and, after 1875, as the Pima agency. Correspondence concerning this agency is filed with the correspondence relating to the Arizona Superintendency.

See also New Mexico Superintendency.

AGENT

Name	*Date of Appointment*
Silas St. John	Feb. 18, 1859

PIQUA AGENCY
1824-1830

The Piqua Agency was established in 1812, primarily for the Shawnee Indians living near Piqua in east central Ohio, but by 1816 the agency was also responsible for the Shawnee, Wyandot, Delaware and Shawnee Indians living in Ohio. During 1818 and 1819 the Fort Wayne Agency in Indiana was consolidated with the Piqua Agency, and at times the Piqua Agency was given responsibility for other Indians. The number of Indians living in Ohio was gradually reduced as the Indians moved west of the Mississippi River, but in 1830 some members of all the tribes assigned to the Piqua Agency were still in Ohio. At different times subagents responsible to the Piqua Agency were assigned to groups of Indians living in Ohio, mainly to the Wyandot and Delaware Indians at Upper Sandusky, to the Mixed Band of Seneca and Shawnee at Lewiston and to the Seneca at Fort Seneca.

The Piqua Agency was under the Michigan Superintendency after 1817, but the agent normally reported directly to the Secretary of War until 1824 and thereafter to the Bureau of Indian Affairs. In 1829 the agency office was moved from Piqua to Columbus. Correspondence beginning in 1831 is filed under the heading "Ohio" instead of "Piqua."

See also Michigan Superintendency and Ohio and Fort Wayne Agencies. For correspondence concerning the Indians after they moved west of the Mississippi see St. Louis and Western Superintendencies and Fort Leavenworth, Neosho and Wyandot Agencies and Subagencies.

AGENTS

Name	*Date of Appointment*
John Johnston	Mar. 5, 1812
John McElvain	Apr. 20, 1829

PONCA AGENCY
1859-1880

In April, 1859 J. Shaw Gregory was appointed special agent for the Ponca Indians, who had been neglected by the Bureau for some years but had formerly been assigned to the Upper Missouri Agency. The following year the Ponca Agency was established as a regular agency, located between the Niobrara and Missouri Rivers near their junction. It was within the present boundaries of Nebraska, but from 1861 until its removal in 1877 the agency was considered to be in Dakota Territory. Originally the agency was under the Central Superintendency, but it was transferred to the new Dakota Superintendency in 1861. After the Dakota Superintendency was discontinued in 1870, the agent reported directly to the Bureau of Indian Affairs in Washington.

The Indians and agency were moved in 1877 to the Quapaw Reservation in the northeastern corner of Indian Territory, and in 1878 to the Salt Fork River west of the Arkansas River and the Osage Reservation. Also in 1878 a small number of Ponca left Indian Territory to live at the Santee Sioux Agency in northern Nebraska, near the old Ponca Agency. Beginning in June, 1879 members of Chief Joseph's band of Nez Percé Indians were attached to the agency. In 1882 the Ponca Agency was consolidated into the Ponca, Pawnee and Otoe Agency.

See also Central, Dakota and Idaho Superintendencies and Santee Sioux, Upper Missouri and Quapaw Agencies.

AGENTS

Name	Date of Appointment
J. Shaw Gregory (special)	Apr., 1859
J. Shaw Gregory (agent)	June 26, 1860
John B. Hoffman	Apr. 15, 1861
Joel A. Potter	Mar. 6, 1865
Maj. W. H. Hugo	June 25, 1869
Henry C. Gregory	Oct. 18, 1870
Charles P. Birkett	Sept. 28, 1872
Arthur J. Carrier	Jan. 7, 1875
James Lawrence	Feb. 28, 1876
E. A. Howard	Apr. 3, 1877
Albert G. Boone	Dec. 3, 1877
William H. Whiteman	June 15, 1878
William Whiting	Mar. 17, 1880

POTAWATOMI AGENCY 1851-1880

The Potawatomi Agency, then usually spelled "Pottawatomie," was established under the Central Superintendency in 1851 as part of the general reorganization of that year. The agency was responsible for the Kansa (Kaw) Indians as well as the Potawatomi living in the present state of Kansas. The Potawatomi had been assigned to the Fort Leavenworth Agency since 1848, and Luke Lea, who was the Fort Leavenworth agent when that agency was discontinued in 1851, was appointed to the new Potawatomi Agency. For a few months in 1847 and 1848 there had been a subagency for the Potawatomi Indians, the correspondence relating to which is filed with that concerning the Fort Leavenworth Agency. Until 1847 the Potawatomi had been divided between the Osage River Subagency and the Council Bluffs Subagency. The Kansa had been attached to the Osage River Agency since 1847 and before that to the Fort Leavenworth Agency. In 1851 the Potawatomi had a reserve along the Kansas River west of the site of Topeka, and the Kansa lived on the Neosho River in the vicinity of Council Grove. In 1855 a separate Kansas Agency was established for the Kansa.

The Potawatomi Agency had no permanent headquarters for several years. At first the agent spent most of his time at Westport, Missouri (now part of Kansas City). In 1854 the agency was located at a place called Douglas about 50 miles west of Westport and 15 miles from the Potawatomi reserve. In 1857 the agent was at St. Mary's Mission on the reserve, and permanent buildings were built near the mission on the north side of the Kansas River.

Under the provisions of the treaties of 1861 and 1867 the Potawatomi were permitted either to become citizens and accept individual land allotments in Kansas or to move to Indian Territory. Except for the Prairie Band (those Indians who formerly had lived at Council Bluffs), most of the Indians accepted the terms and were henceforth known as Citizen Potawatomi. Most of the Citizen Potawatomi moved to Indian Territory and were later attached to the Sac and Fox Agency.

By 1871 the Potawatomi Agency was responsible only for the Prairie Band, which was assigned a reservation in Jackson County near Rossville, about 15 miles from the old agency buildings. Temporary quarters for the agency were rented about 12 miles from the reserve until 1873, when the agent moved onto the reserve. Until 1878, however, the agent usually gave his address as Rossville.

In 1874 the Kickapoo Agency for the Kickapoo Indians living north of the Potawatomi was consolidated with the Potawatomi Agency. The Potawatomi Agency was now the only agency in Kansas and was often called the Kansas Agency. It should not be confused with the Kansas Agency for the Kansa

Indians, which was discontinued in 1874, or with the Kansas Agency for the Delaware, Shawnee and other Indians, which operated from 1851 until 1855. For filing purposes the Bureau continued to use the name "Potawatomi." By 1876 the Potawatomi Agency was also responsible for the Chippewa and Munsee Indians who lived in Franklin County, Kansas and had not had an agent since the removal of the Sac and Fox Agency to Indian Territory in 1869. The Central Superintendency was discontinued in 1878 and thereafter the agent reported directly to the Bureau of Indian Affairs in Washington. In 1882 the Great Nemaha Agency was consolidated with the Potawatomi Agency to form the Potawatomi and Great Nemaha Agency.

Between 1864 and 1870 there was an agency in Wisconsin for stray Winnebago and Potawatomi Indians. Correspondence relating to this agency is filed with that relating to the Winnebago Agency. By 1877 the Sac and Fox Agency in Indian Territory was responsible for the Citizen Potawatomi and it also had charge of the Mexican Kickapoo who lived near the Sauk and Fox. Other Potawatomi Indians belonged to the Mackinac Agency in Michigan.

See also St. Louis and Central Superintendencies and Fort Leavenworth, Kansas, Osage River, Council Bluffs and Kickapoo Agents.

AGENTS

Name	Date of Appointment
Luke Lea	June 30, 1851
Francis W. Lea	July 26, 1851
John W. Whitfield	July 1, 1853
Richard C. S. Brown	Apr. 3, 1854
George W. Clarke	July 10, 1854
Isaac Winston	Nov. 29, 1856
William E. Murphy	Mar. 12, 1857
William W. Ross	Apr. 29, 1861
Luther R. Palmer	Sept. 20, 1864
Joel H. Morris	July 14, 1869
Mahlon H. Newlin	Jan. 23, 1873
Henry C. Linn	Aug. 2, 1878

PRAIRIE DU CHIEN AGENCY
1824-1842

The Prairie du Chien Agency was established in 1807 for the Indians in Louisiana Territory who lived on the waters of the Mississippi River above the Iowa River and for the Indians in Indiana Territory north of the Illinois River and west of a line running through a point on the river 20 miles above Peoria. The agency headquarters was at Prairie du Chien, on the east bank of the Mississippi River above the mouth of the Wisconsin River.

No specific tribes were assigned to the agency, but the Indians living within the limits of the agency included Winnebago, Chippewa, Sioux, Menominee and Sauk and Fox. The jurisdiction of the Prairie du Chien Agency was reduced with the establishment of new agencies, particularly the St. Peters Agency farther up the Missisippi, the Green Bay Agency and the Sac and Fox Agency at Rock Island. The Prairie du Chien Agency came to be responsible primarily for the Winnebago Indians, although frequent contacts with other tribes continued.

Until 1822 there was some confusion concerning the supervision of the agency. In 1811 the agent was informed that he should receive instructions from William Clark, the general Indian agent for Louisiana and from the Governors of Illinois and Louisiana. In 1812, when Louisiana became a state, the upper part of Louisiana Territory was organized as Missouri Territory, and in 1815 the agent was placed under the supervision of the Governor and *ex officio* Superintendent of Missouri, William Clark. The Prairie du Chien Agency was transferred in 1818 to the Illinois Superintendency, only to be returned to the Missouri Superintendency in 1820. When Missouri became a state in 1821, the Missouri Superintendency was automatically discontinued. The agent at Prairie du Chien was then directed to obey any instructions from the Governor and *ex officio* Superintendent of Michigan Territory that were not incompatible with instructions received directly from the War Department. In 1822 the Prairie du Chien Agency was assigned to the newly established St. Louis Superintendency, which continued to supervise the agency until the organization of Wisconsin Territory in 1836.

Until the Bureau of Indian Affairs was established in 1824, correspondence relating to the agency was transmitted directly to the Office of the Secretary of War. The filing of correspondence received by the Bureau relating to the Prairie du Chien and neighboring agencies is inconsistent. For the period from 1824 until after 1830 many letters are filed under the heading "Prairie du Chien" that actually relate to the Sac and Fox Agency at Rock Island. There are also letters filed under "Sac and Fox" that relate to the Prairie du Chien Agency. From 1826 there is also a "Winnebago" heading. Through 1829 the letters filed under this heading relate to the Winnebago Indians rather than to the affairs of any agency. For the years 1830-36 the letters filed under the heading "Winnebago" relate chiefly to the Fort Winnebago and Rock River Subagencies. Letters relating to these subagencies are also filed under "Prairie du Chien," "St. Louis," "Michigan" and, from 1836, "Wisconsin."

The Fort Winnebago Subagency, established under the Michigan Superintendency in 1828, was responsible for the Winnebago Indians living in the vicinity of the portage of the Wisconsin and Fox Rivers. For the Winnebago Indians living along the Rock River, the Rock River Subagency was established in 1831. It was assigned to the St. Louis Superintendency until 1832, when it was transferred to the Michigan Superintendency. With the establishment of these two subagencies, the Prairie du Chien Agency became responsible only for those Winnebago living in the area around Prairie du Chien.

There was a general reorganization in 1834. The jurisdiction of the Fort Winnebago Subagency was not changed, but the commanding officer at Fort Winnebago was designated to serve as acting subagent. The Rock River Subagency had been eliminated earlier in the year. The Prairie du Chien Agency was made responsible for the Indians living west of a north-south line running through the portage of the Wisconsin and Fox Rivers, with the exception of the Indians assigned to the Fort Winnebago Subagency. The Green Bay Agency was responsible for the Indians living east of that line, with the same exception. The Prairie du Chien Agency was bounded on the north, as before, by the St. Peters Agency, but Wabisha's band of Sioux was transferred from the St. Peters Agency to the Prairie du Chien Agency. To the west the jurisdiction of the agency extended as far as the Winnebago country. To the south the Prairie du Chien Agency included the Sauk and Fox and their country. The Sac and Fox Agency on Rock Island was eliminated. The Prairie du Chien Agency, however, was to be moved from Prairie du Chien to Rock Island, and the commanding officer of Fort Crawford at Prairie du Chien was to perform the duties of the Prairie du Chien Agency relating to the Winnebago and Sioux. Thus the Prairie du Chien Agency was to be immediately responsible only for the Sauk and Fox Indians.

The Prairie du Chien agent, Joseph Street, objected to these changes. On October 28, 1834 he obtained permission to return from Rock Island to Prairie du Chien until April 1, 1835. During this period the commanding officer at Fort Armstrong was to handle affairs at Rock Island. When Street returned to Rock Island, the commanding officer at Fort Crawford, Col. Zachary Taylor, was again to take charge at Prairie du Chien.

In 1836 the Prairie du Chien Agency and the Fort Winnebago Subagency were transferred to the new Wisconsin Superintendency. The Governor and *ex officio* Superintendent, Henry Dodge, was authorized to select the location for the Prairie du Chien Agency, and he gave Street permission to return to the Prairie du Chien. Street remained at Rock Island through the winter and in the spring of 1837 moved back to Prairie du Chien.

In 1837 a separate agency was again established for the Sauk and Fox. Prairie du Chien was reduced to a subagency and the Fort Winnebago Subagency was consolidated with it. The Prairie du Chien Subagency, therefore, had charge of all the Winnebago in Wisconsin and Wabisha's band of Sioux.

During 1840 the Winnebago were moved to the "Neutral Ground" in Iowa Territory. This was a 40-mile strip extending from the Mississippi to the Des Moines River, which had been set aside in 1825 as a buffer zone between the Sioux and the Sauk and Fox. By December, 1840 the Prairie du Chien Subagency had been moved to the Turkey River, and it was then transferred from the Wisconsin to the Iowa Superintendency. By this time Wabisha's band of Sioux was again attached to the St. Peters Agency.

The correspondence relating to the Winnebago Indians and their subagency for the year 1842 is filed under three agency headings as well as with the correspondence relating to the Iowa Superintendency. There are no letters filed under the heading "Winnebago" for the years 1837 through 1841, although some letters are filed under the separate "Winnebago Emigration" and "Winnebago Reserves" subheadings. In 1842 some letters relating to the subagency were filed under "Winnebago," a few letters were filed under the old "Prairie du Chien" heading and others were filed under "Turkey River." From 1843 through 1846 most of the correspondence was filed under "Turkey River," but a few letters in 1846 were filed under "Winnebago." Beginning in 1847 only the "Winnebago" heading was used. The heading "Prairie du Chien" was not used after 1842. For the years 1837-41 some letters are filed under the subheading "Prairie du Chien Emigration."

See also St. Louis, Michigan, Wisconsin and Iowa Superintendencies and Sac and Fox, Green Bay, St. Peters, Winnebago and Turkey River Agencies and Subagencies.

AGENTS AND SUBAGENTS

Prairie du Chien Agency

Name	Date of Appointment
John Campbell	Dec. 9, 1807
Nicholas Boilvin	Mar. 14, 1811; but had already been acting as agent for some time
Joseph M. Street	Aug. 8, 1827
Col. Zachary Taylor (acting)	Commanding officer at Fort Crawford. Acted as agent during periods when Street was stationed at Rock Island.

Prairie du Chien Subagency

(For later subagents see Turkey River and Fort Winnebago.)

Thomas A. B. Boyd	Mar. 31, 1837
David Lowry	June 5, 1839

Fort Winnebago Subagency

John H. Kinzie	Dec. 9, 1828
Robert A. McCabe	Sept. 10, 1833

Beginning in July, 1834 the commanding officer at Fort Winnebago was acting subagent. Lt. Col. Enos Cutler served during 1834 and part of 1835. He was succeeded by Bvt. Maj. N. Clark and later in the year by Maj. John Green, who served until the subagency was discontinued in 1837.

Rock River Subagency

Henry Gratiot	Mar. 7, 1831

QUAPAW AGENCY
1871-1880

The Quapaw Agency was established in 1871 for the several bands of Indians living on reserves east of the Neosho River in what is now the northeastern corner of Oklahoma. Previously the Indians living in this area and the Osage Indians living in southern Kansas had been assigned to the Neosho Agency. Since 1865, however, a special agent subordinate to the Neosho agent had been stationed on the Spring River in what became Eastern Shawnee country. This special agent had immediate responsibility for the Indians living in the Neosho River area, while the agent himself was chiefly concerned with the Osage Indians. The establishment of the Quapaw Agency, essentially a continuation of the special agency, relieved the Neosho agency (renamed the Osage Agency in 1874) of responsibility for Indians other than the Osage.

The Indians originally under the Neosho Agency were Quapaw, Seneca and Mixed Band of Seneca and Shawnee who had moved to the Neosho area during the 1830's. Under the terms of the treaty of February 23, 1867 the Shawnee separated from the Seneca and henceforth were known as Eastern Shawnee. The treaty also provided that the Ottawa and Confederated Peoria and Miami (Peoria, Kaskaskia, Wea, Piankeshaw, Miami and remnants of other tribes) of the Osage River Agency in Kansas and the Wyandot Indians then attached to the Delaware Agency in Kansas should settle on parts of the old Quapaw and Seneca reserves. The Quapaw Agency assumed responsibility for all of the Indians who moved as well as for the Quapaw, Seneca and Shawnee. In 1873, following the Modoc War, members of Captain Jack's band of Modoc were moved from Oregon and California to a section of the Shawnee reserve. During 1878 and 1879 members of Chief Joseph's band of Nez Percé Indians were attached to the Quapaw Agency before they moved to the Ponca Agency. There were also a few Potawatomi Indians and some members of the Black Bob band of Shawnee living in the Quapaw Agency area. In 1879 most of the Quapaw Indians joined the Osage Indians, who had moved from Kansas and were now living in Indian Territory.

The office of the Quapaw Agency remained at the headquarters of the former special agent on Spring River on the Shawnee reserve. The Quapaw Agency was under the Central Superintendency until the superintendency was discontinued in 1878; thereafter the agent reported directly to the Bureau of Indian Affairs in Washington. The agency remained in operation beyond 1880.

See also Central Superintendency and Neosho, Osage River, Delaware, Shawnee, Osage and Sac and Fox Agencies. For correspondence concerning the Modoc Indians before their removal to Indian Territory see Oregon Superintendency. For earlier correspondence concerning the Nez Percé Indians see Idaho Superintendcy; for later correspondence, see Ponca Agency.

AGENTS

Name	Date of Appointment
George W. Mitchell (special)	Originally appointed Apr. 8, 1864;
George W. Mitchell	Assigned to Quapaw Agency, Mar. 1, 1871
Hiram W. Jones (special)	Aug. 9, 1871
Hiram W. Jones (agent)	July 20, 1872
James M. Haworth (special)	In charge Apr. 19, 1879
Amos T. S. Kist	July 23, 1879
Daniel B. Dyer	June 25, 1880

RACCOON RIVER AGENCY
1843-1845

The Raccoon River Agency, at other times known as the Sac and Fox Agency, was the agency for the Sauk and Fox of the Mississippi. Under the terms of a treaty of October 11, 1842, the Sauk and Fox ceded all of their land west of the Mississippi. For three years, however, they were allowed to occupy the land west of the Painted or Red Rocks, on the White Breast Fork of the Des Moines River. The Indians moved to this area, and in 1843 the Sac and Fox Agency was moved from its previous location west of Fairfield, Iowa, to a place on the Des Moines River near the mouth of the Raccoon River (the site of the city of Des Moines). The agency remained here until the fall of 1845, when the Indians moved to the Osage River west of Missouri (now Kansas). The Sac and Fox Agency had been assigned to the Iowa Superintendency since 1838, but after the move to the Osage River was made, it was within the limits of the St. Louis Superintendency.

One letter for 1843 and most of the letters relating to the agency during 1844 and 1845 are filed under the heading "Raccoon River." Before and after these years the heading "Sac and Fox" was used, and some letters were filed under this name even during 1844 and 1845.

See also Iowa and St. Louis Superintendencies and Sac and Fox Agency.

AGENT

Name	Date of Appointment
John Beach	May 29, 1840

RED CLOUD AGENCY
1871-1880

The Red Cloud Agency was established in 1871 on the North Platte River near Fort Laramie in eastern Wyoming. It was primarily responsible for the Oglala

Sioux led by Chief Red Cloud but at times had charge of some Cheyenne and Arapaho as well as other bands of Sioux, including that of Chief Crazy Horse. These Indians were not assigned to any agency immediately before the establishment of the Red Cloud Agency, but at one time they had been under the Upper Platte Agency. Correspondence relating to them was filed under the "Upper Platte" heading through 1870.

In 1873 the Red Cloud Agency was moved to the White River near Camp Robinson in northwestern Nebraska; in 1877, to the Missouri River at the mouth of Medicine Creek, in what is now South Dakota; and, in 1878, to White Clay Creek in Dakota, just above the Nebraska border. James R. O'Beirne was special agent in charge of the removal and of the construction of buildings at the new agency site. Thereafter the agency was known as Pine Ridge Agency, but correspondence continued to be filed under "Red Cloud" through 1880. Some of the Indians did not move to the Missouri River location but stayed on White River in the charge of an acting agent until they went to White Clay Creek.

Except during the temporary re-establishment of the Dakota Superintendency in 1877-78, the Red Cloud agent was responsible directly to the Bureau of Indian Affairs in Washington. The Pine Ridge Agency continued in operation beyond 1880.

See also Dakota and Wyoming Superintendencies and Upper Platte, Spotted Tail and Cheyenne and Arapaho Agencies.

AGENTS

Name	Date of Appointment
Joseph W. Wham (special)	Feb. 15, 1871
Jared W. Daniels (special)	Oct. 31, 1871
Jared W. Daniels (agent)	Dec. 13, 1872
John J. Saville	July 12, 1873
James S. Hastings	Oct. 6, 1875
Lt. O. Elting (acting)	In charge ca. Aug. 7, 1876
Capt. Frank G. Smith (acting)	Sept. 26, 1876
Capt. Thomas F. Tobey (acting)	Oct. 25, 1876
Lt. C. A. Johnson (acting) In charge at the Red Cloud Agency in Nebraska until the Indians were moved to Dakota.	Jan. 11, 1877
James Irwin Assumed charge of the new Red Cloud Agency and later the Pine Ridge Agency.	Feb. 16, 1877

RED RIVER AGENCY
1824-1830

The Red River Agency was a continuation of an agency established at Natchitoches in 1804, usually known as the Natchitoches or the Lower Louisiana Agency. In 1820 the agent was given permission to move from Natchitoches, and the next year he reported that he had moved to Sulphur Fork on the Red River. It was after this change in location that the agency was called the Red River Agency.

The agency at Natchitoches had been responsible for the Indians in Louisiana west of the Mississippi River, and in 1819 responsibility for the Indians of the Upper Red River was added to the agency. In 1821 the Red River agent was made responsible for the Choctaw Indians who had moved west, but in 1825 a separate agency was established for these Indians. There were many small groups of Indians living in the Red River area, some of whom moved back and forth between the United States and Texas. The principal tribe was Caddo, but in 1824 the agent reported that there were also Biloxi, Apalachee, Pascagoula, Adai, Yatasi, Koasati, Delaware, Choctaw, Shawnee, Quapaw, Piankeshaw and Natchitoches Indians under his charge. In 1826 the Quapaw Indians of the Arkansas River moved to the Red River, but some of them soon returned to Arkansas, and in 1830 most of those remaining followed, although many returned to the Red River in 1833.

Sulphur Fork was located in Arkansas Territory rather than Louisiana, but the Red River Agency was never attached to the Arkansas Superintendency. Instead, the agent reported directly to the Office of the Secretary of War until 1824 and thereafter to the Bureau of Indian Affairs. In 1825 the agency was moved from Sulphur Fork about 25 miles down the Red River to Caddo Prairie.

After 1830 correspondence relating to the agency is filed under the heading "Caddo." This is a change in filing procedure only and reflects no change in the operations of the agency. There are some letters filed under the heading "Caddo" for the years 1824-30. Many of these letters relate to the Quapaw Indians.

See also Arkansas Superintendency and Caddo and Choctaw Agencies.

AGENTS

Name	*Date of Appointment*
John Sibley	Dec. 13, 1804
Thomas Gales	Aug. 20, 1814

John Jamison	Jan. 20, 1816
George Gray	Dec. 1, 1819
Thomas Griffith	Mar. 18, 1829
Jehiel Brooks	Notified Mar. 29, 1830

SAC AND FOX AGENCY
1824-1880

The name "Sac and Fox Agency" was not formally adopted until 1837, but an agency for the Sauk and Fox of the Mississippi was in operation at least as early as 1821. In 1806 Nicholas Boilvin was appointed subagent and stationed at the Sauk Villages on the Mississippi River above the mouth of the Des Moines River; he was soon transferred, however, to Prairie du Chien. In 1812 Thomas Forsyth was appointed subagent without any specific assignment. In 1818 he was promoted to agent for Missouri Territory, and by 1821 he was stationed at Fort Armstrong on Rock Island in the country of the Sauk and Fox of the Mississippi. When Missouri became a state in 1821 and the Missouri Superintendency was automatically discontinued, Forsyth was directed to follow any instructions from the Governor of Michigan Territory that were not incompatible with those received directly from the War Department. In 1822 Forsyth's agency was assigned to the new St. Louis Superintendency. Correspondence concerning the agency was transmitted directly to the Office of the Secretary of War until the Bureau of Indian Affairs was established in 1824.

Letters relating to both the agency on Rock Island for the Sauk and Fox and to the Prairie du Chien Agency farther up the Mississippi are filed under both "Sac and Fox" and "Prairie du Chien" from 1824 until 1837. Between 1829 and 1833 separate subagents were assigned to the vicinity of the Fox lead mines near Dubuque in present Iowa and in Galena, Illinois.

Under the reorganization plan of 1834 the agency for the Sauk and Fox of the Mississippi (then called the Rock Island Agency) was eliminated, and the Sauk and Fox were attached to the Prairie du Chien Agency, which previously had been responsible primarily for Winnebago Indians. Under the new organization the Prairie du Chien Agency, however, was to be moved from Prairie du Chien to

150

Rock Island and the commanding officer at Fort Crawford, Col. Zachary Taylor, was to take charge at Prairie du Chien, leaving the agent with immediate resposibility only for the Sauk and Fox. In practice, however, the agent alternated between Prairie du Chien and Rock Island. The commanding officer at Fort Armstrong took charge at Rock Island when the agent was away.

In 1836 the Prairie du Chien Agency was transferred from the St. Louis Superintendency to the new Wisconsin Superintendency. The reorganization of 1837 provided for a separate Sac and Fox Agency, but since by this time the Sauk and Fox were living in the area organized in 1838 as Iowa Territory the agency was moved in 1838 from Rock Island to a site near the Des Moines River about 17 miles west of Fairfield. The agency was also transferred from the Wisconsin Superintendency to the new Iowa Superintendency.

Under the provisions of a treaty of October 11, 1842, the Sauk and Fox of the Mississippi ceded all of their land west of the Mississippi River. For three years, however, they were allowed to occupy the area west of the Painted or Red Rocks on the White Breast Fork of the Des Moines River. In 1843, therefore, the agency was moved to a location on the Des Moines River near the mouth of the Raccoon River (the site of the city of Des Moines) and the agency was now usually called the Raccoon River Agency. Some letters relating to the agency were still filed under the heading "Sac and Fox," but one letter dated 1843 and most of the letters for 1844 and 1845 are filed under the heading "Raccoon River." Thereafter the heading "Sac and Fox" was used exclusively.

In 1845, under the terms of the 1842 treaty, the Sauk and Fox moved to a new reserve along the Osage River west of Missouri (in present Kansas). The agency was located on the Marais des Cygnes River about 65 miles southwest of Westport, Missouri (now part of Kansas City). The Sac and Fox Agency was then within the limits of the St. Louis Superintendency.

On December 8, 1847 the Sac and Fox agent was also placed in charge of the Kansa, Chippewa, Ottawa, Peoria, Kaskasia, Piankeshaw, Wea, Miami and New York Indians living west of Missouri. Previously the Kansa Indians had been assigned to the Fort Leavenworth Agency, and the other Indians had been assigned to the Osage River Subagency. The name of the Sac and Fox Agency was changed to the Osage River Agency. During the years 1848-50 a few letters were filed under the heading "Sac and Fox," but most of the correspondence relating to the agency is filed under the heading "Osage River."

In 1851 the Central Superintendency replaced the St. Louis Superintendency and there was a reorganization of the agencies. The Osage River Agency was divided, and a new Sac and Fox Agency was made responsible for the Sauk and Fox, Ottawa and Chippewa. Except for the Kansa, who were attached to the new Potawatomi Agency, the other Indians remained in the Osage River Agency.

In 1863 the Ottawa Agency was established for the Ottawa, Chippewa and some Munsee or "Christian" Indians who had left the Delaware reserve and joined the Chippewa in 1859. In 1864 the Chippewa and Munsee were transferred back to the Sac and Fox Agency.

The Sauk and Fox moved from Kansas in 1869 to a new reservation in central Indian Territory west of the Creek Nation. The Sac and Fox Agency was located near the junction of the Deep Fork and the Dry Fork of the Canadian River. The Chippewa and Munsee remained in Kansas. For several years no agent was responsible for them, but by 1876 they were attached to the Potawatomi Agency. The Sac and Fox Agency in Indian Territory was also responsible for the Absentee Shawnee living southwest of the Sauk and Fox and, after 1874, for the Mexican Kickapoo, who were being moved from Mexico to an area west of the Sauk and Fox. The Citizen Potawatomi, who also lived to the southwest of the Sauk and Fox, were not assigned to any agency for several years, but by 1877 the Sac and Fox agent had assumed responsibility for them. There were also stray bands of Potawatomi, Ottawa, Shawnee (chiefly members of Black Bob's band) and other Indians in the vicinity of the Sac and Fox Agency. After the Central Superintendency was discontinued in 1878, the agent reported directly to the Bureau of Indian Affairs in Washington.

Some Sauk and Fox of the Mississippi remained in Kansas, while others had returned to Iowa and purchased land along the Des Moines River in Tama County. An agent was established for those living on land in 1866, with headquarters at Toledo, and in 1879 the headquarters moved to Tama City. The agency was not assigned to any superintendency. Correspondence concerning the Sac and Fox Agency in Iowa as well as the agency in Kansas and Indian Territory is filed under the heading "Sac and Fox." Both agencies continued in operation beyond 1880. Some letters are filed under the subheadings "Sac and Fox Emigration," 1845-47, and "Sac and Fox Reserves," 1837-50.

Another important group of Sauk and Fox (in addition to the Sauk and Fox of the Mississippi) is the Sauk and Fox of the Missouri. These Indians were assigned to the Great Nemaha Agency on the Kansas-Nebraska border from 1837 until after 1880.

See also St. Louis, Wisconsin, Iowa and Central Superintendencies and Prairie du Chien, Raccoon River, Osage River, Fort Leavenworth, Potawatomi, Ottawa, Shawnee and Kickapoo Agencies.

AGENTS

Sac and Fox Agency at Rock Island

Name	*Date of Appointment*
Thomas Forsyth	Notified Apr. 22, 1818
Felix St. Vrain	Notified June 7, 1830
Marmaduke S. Davenport	Notified July 12, 1832

Prairie du Chien Agency

Joseph Street   Aug. 8, 1827

Sac and Fox-Raccoon River Agency

Joseph Street   Transferred from
                                                        Prairie du Chien
                                                        under regulations
                                                        of Apr. 13, 1837
John Beach   May 29, 1840
Solomon P. Sublette   Oct. 21, 1847

Osage River Agency

Solomon P. Sublette   Assigned Dec. 8,
                                                          1847
James S. Rains   May 18, 1848
Charles N. Handy   Mar. 30, 1849
John R. Chenault   Notified Oct. 12,
                                                          1850

Sac and Fox Agency in Kansas and Indian Territory

John R. Chenault   June 30, 1851
Burton A. James   Apr. 18, 1853
Francis Tymany   Jan. 21, 1858
Perry Fuller   Mar. 30, 1859
Clinton C. Hutchinson   Apr. 3, 1861
Henry W. Martin   Oct. 17, 1862
Albert Wiley   Mar. 18, 1867
Thomas Miller   June 22, 1869
John Hadley   Jan. 23, 1871
John H. Pickering   Dec. 9, 1872
Levi Woodward   Jan. 19, 1876
Joseph Hertford (acting)   June 9, 1879
John S. Shorb   July 23, 1879

Sac and Fox Agency in Iowa

Leander Clark (special)   June 30, 1866
Lt. Frank D. Garretty (special)   June 23, 1869
Leander Clark (special)   Sept. 15, 1870
A. R. Howbert   July 23, 1872
Thomas S. Free   Feb. 26, 1875
George L. Davenport   June 30, 1879

SAGINAW SUBAGENCY
1824-1850

The Saginaw Subagency was established in 1837 as the successor to the Detroit Subagency. Before 1834 there was usually a subagent stationed at Detroit as an assistant to the Territorial Governor of Michigan in his capacity as *ex officio* Superintendent of Indian Affairs. At times a subagent was assigned to the Saginaw Bay area north of Detroit. Under the reorganization plan of 1834 most of the subagencies under the Michigan Superintendency were eliminated. The Indians in the southern part of Michigan were assigned to a subagency to be located at or near Detroit. The Mackinac and Sault Ste. Marie Agency had charge of those Indians living farther north in Michigan.

In 1837 the Saginaw Subagency replaced the Detroit Subagency for the Indians in the lower part of Michigan. The only real change was that the subagency was supposed to be located at or near Saginaw rather than at Detroit. In practice, however, the Saginaw subagent usually stayed at Detroit rather than at the site chosen for the subagency near the entrance of the Saginaw River into Saginaw Bay. The Saginaw band of Chippewa lived in the Saginaw area. There were also Black River and Swan Creek Chippewa, Ottawa, Wyandot, Christian and remnants of other bands of Indians living in southern Michigan. The Ottawa of Maumee, Ohio were also considered Michigan Indians. Except for the first few years, however, the duties of the Saginaw subagent were restricted chiefly to the Saginaw Indians.

There are some letters filed under the heading "Saginaw" for the period before the subagency was established in 1837. Some of these relate to affairs at Saginaw, and a few pertain to the Detroit Subagency. There are also several letters that relate to a subagency for the Ottawa at Maumee, Ohio, which operated until 1836.

When the term of Subagent Henry Connor expired on March 4, 1839, he was not replaced. An acting subagent was designated to perform his duties. Saginaw continued to operate as an acting subagency until 1846. The duties of the Saginaw subagent were then added to those of the Mackinac agent. A few letters, most of them relating to the land of the Saginaw Indians, were filed under the heading "Saginaw" as late as 1850.

See also Michigan Superintendency and Mackinac Agency.

Name	*Date of Appointment*
Henry Connor	Appointed July 9, 1828 as subagent in Michigan Territory Assigned to the Saginaw Subagency under the regulations of Apr. 13, 1837
John Hulbert (acting)	Mar. 4, 1839
Andrew T. McReynolds (acting)	Oct. 21, 1843

ST. LOUIS SUPERINTENDENCY 1824-1851

The St. Louis Superintendency, also known as the District of St. Louis, was established in 1822. It succeeded the Missouri Superintendency, which was automatically abolished when Missouri became a state in 1821. William Clark, who had been Governor of Missouri and *ex officio* superintendent, became the first superintendent of the St. Louis Superintendency. The superintendency headquarters was located at St. Louis throughout the existence of the superintendency. Until the Bureau of Indian Affairs was established in 1824, correspondence concerning the superintendency was transmitted directly to the Office of the Secretary of War.

The area under the jurisdiction of the St. Louis Superintendency was changed several times. Originally the agencies on the Mississippi and Missouri Rivers were assigned to it. In 1834 the limits of the superintendency were defined as follows: "The superintendency at St. Louis will include all the Indians and Indian country west of the Mississippi River, and north of the Osage reservation, as far west as De Mun's Creek, and thence the said superintendency will be bounded on the south by the Santa Fe road, to where it crosses the Arkansa, and thence, by the Arkansa, to its source in the Rocky Mountains. And the said superintendency shall include all the Indians and Indian country west of the Rocky Mountains." The area south of the St. Louis Superintendency was assigned to the new Western Superintendency.

Wisconsin Territory was established in 1836 and originally included present Minnesota, Iowa and parts of the Dakotas. The agencies in this area were transferred from the St. Louis Superintendency to the new Wisconsin Superintendency.

In 1837 the boundaries of the St. Louis Superintendency were set as the northern line of the Osage reservation (in present southern Kansas) on the south and the Missouri River on the north. The upper Missouri River area and the Ottawa, Chippewa and Potawatomi then living in the Council Bluffs area in present Iowa were also assigned to the St. Louis Superintendency.

The southern boundary of the superintendency fluctuated because responsibility for the Osage Indians alternated between the St. Louis and Western Superintendencies. No changes were made in the north until 1846, when Iowa became a state and the Iowa Superintendency was discontinued. The agencies in the present states of Iowa and Minnesota (St. Peters and Winnebago), which had been assigned to the Wisconsin Superintendency from 1836 until 1838 and to the Iowa Superintendency from 1838 until 1846, were transferred to the St. Louis Superintendency. In 1849 these agencies, both in Minnesota, were transferred to the new Minnesota Superintendency. To the west the limits of the authority of the St. Louis Superintendency were indefinite. The Upper Missouri Agency had contacts with Indians living as far west as present Montana. Farther south the effective jurisdiction of the superintendency did not extend past central Kansas until after the Upper Platte Agency was established in 1846. After the Mexican Cession, new superintendencies were established in the Far West, but until 1851 the St. Louis Superintendency remained generally responsible for the area east of the Rocky Mountains.

There were many Indian tribes living within the limits of the St. Louis Superintendency, including Delaware, Shawnee, Kickapoo, Kansa (Kaw), Iowa, Potawatomi, Chippewa, Ottawa, Wea, Piankeshaw, Miami, Peoria, Kaskaskia, Oto, Missouri, Pawnee, Omaha, Ponca, Sauk and Fox, Osage, Munsee, Stockbridge, Wyandot, Winnebago, many bands of Sioux, Mandan, Arikara, Crow, Cheyenne, Arapaho, Kiowa, Comanche, Apache and Grosventre.

The Bureau maintained separate file headings for the correspondence relating to the individual agencies under the St. Louis Superintendency. Before about 1830, however, many important letters relating to individual agencies are filed with the superintendency correspondence. The information concerning the individual agencies given below is intended only to establish their relation with the St. Louis Superintendency. More information concerning each agency is provided in the sketch for the agency itself. For the agencies and subagencies for which there are no separate file headings, the heading under which relevant correspondence is filed has been noted.

The St. Louis Superintendency originally supervised the Upper Missouri, Sac and Fox, Prairie du Chien (Winnebago) and St. Peters (Sioux of the Mississippi) Agencies, an agency for the Osage, Delaware and Kickapoo Indians and the Kaskaskia Subagency.

The Upper Missouri Agency remained in the St. Louis Superintendency throughout the existence of the superintendency from 1822 to 1851. The Sac and Fox, Prairie du Chien and St. Peters Agencies were transferred to the Wisconsin Superintendency in 1836. The Sac and Fox Agency was again assigned to the St. Louis Superintendency when the Sauk and Fox of the Mississippi moved to the Osage River in 1845. Between 1846 and 1849 the St. Peters Agency (at times reduced to a subagency) was again in the St. Louis Superintendency.

In 1824 the agency for the Osage, Delaware and Kickapoo was divided into an agency for the Osage Indians and an agency for the Delaware, Kickapoo and other Indians living near them. The Osage Agency was reduced to a subagency and transferred to the new Western Superintendency in 1834. The Osage Subagency was assigned to the St. Louis Superintendency from 1843 to 1847 and again from 1849 to 1851. The agency for the Delaware, Kickapoo and other Indians came to be known as the Delaware and Shawnee Agency. In 1834 it became the Northern Agency and, in 1837, the Fort Leavenworth Agency. Correspondence relating to these three agencies is filed under the heading "Fort Leavenworth."

The Kaskaskia Subagency continued to operate until 1833. There is some correspondence concerning this agency filed under "Osage River."

Between 1822 and 1834 there were many subagencies in operation. Often these were short-lived, and many of the subagents were actually assistants to regular agents; some of these subagencies, however, are of particular significance.

The Peoria Subagency for the United Band of Ottawa, Chippewa and Potawatomi was transferred from the Michigan Superintendency in 1822. In 1832 it was consolidated with the Chicago Agency. Correspondence concerning this subagency is filed under "Chicago" and "Osage River."

The Sioux and Mandan Subagencies were established on the upper Missouri River in 1824. The Sioux Subagency was transferred to the Wisconsin Superintendency in 1836, but in 1837 the Upper Missouri Agency was moved to the site of the Sioux Subagency and the subagency was discontinued. The Mandan Subagency was abolished in 1838 and its functions also were absorbed by the Upper Missouri Agency. Some of the correspondence relating to the Sioux and Mandan Subagencies is filed under "St. Louis," but most is filed with the correspondence relating to the Upper Missouri Agency.

The Ioway Subagency for the Iowa (and at times the Sauk and Fox of the Missouri) operated from 1825 until 1837, when it was replaced by the Great Nemaha Agency. In 1836 it was transferred to the Wisconsin Superintendency.

The Kansas Subagency for the Kansa Indians was established in 1825. It was made a full agency in 1832, but in 1834 it was abolished and the Kansa were assigned to the Northern Agency. The correspondence relating to the Kansas Subagency and Agency is filed under "St. Louis" and "Fort Leavenworth."

157

The Rock River Subagency (Winnebago Indians) was established under the St. Louis Superintendency in 1831 but transferred to the Michigan Superintendency in 1832. Most of the correspondence concerning this agency is filed under "Winnebago."

In the reorganization of 1834 the following changes were made in the St. Louis Superintendency. The Osage Agency was transferred to the Western Superintendency. The two agencies operating in the Kansas River area, the Delaware and Shawnee Agency and the Kansas Agency were discontinued. The Northern Agency was established for the Delaware, Kansa and Kickapoo. The Shawnee, Ottawa and other Indians in that area were assigned to a subagency. The following year, however, the subagency was discontinued and the Northern Agency also took charge of these Indians. The correspondence relating to both the Northern Agency and the subagency is filed under the heading "Fort Leavenworth." The several subagencies attached to agencies were discontinued. In 1834, therefore, the St. Louis Superintendency was responsible for the Upper Missouri, Sac and Fox, St. Peters, Prairie du Chien and Northern Agencies; the Ioway, Sioux and Mandan Subagencies; and the short-lived subagency for the Shawnee, Ottawa and other Indians living west of Missouri.

In 1835 the Crow Wing Subagency was established for the Chippewa of the Mississippi, but in 1836 this subagency was transferred to the Wisconsin Superintendency along with the Sac and Fox, St. Peters and Prairie du Chien Agencies and the Sioux and Ioway Subagencies.

In 1837 there was another general reorganization of the Indian field service. The Council Bluffs Agency was established for the Oto, Missouri, Omaha and Pawnee Indians living west of the Missouri River in present Nebraska. The Council Bluffs Subagency was established for the United Band of Ottawa, Chippewa and Potawatomi who had moved to the east side of the Missouri River in present Iowa. The Upper Missouri Agency was moved farther up the river to the site of the now discontinued Sioux Subagency. The Northern Agency was replaced by the Fort Leavenworth Agency, which was responsible only for the Delaware, Shawnee, Kansa, Kickapoo and, after 1839, Munsee and Stockbridge Indians. The Osage River Subagency was established for the other Indians previously assigned to the Northern Agency. The Iowa Subagency was replaced by the Great Nemaha Subagency, which was assigned to the St. Louis Superintendency rather than to the Wisconsin Superintendency. The St. Louis Superintendency, therefore, was then responsible for the Upper Missouri, Council Bluffs and Fort Leavenworth Agencies and the Mandan (discontinued in 1838), Council Bluffs, Great Nemaha and Osage River Subagencies.

As has been noted, from 1843 to 1847 and from 1849 to 1851 the Osage Subagency was assigned to the St. Louis Superintendency rather than to the Western Superintendency. In 1843 the Wyandot Subagency was established for the Wyandot Indians who had recently emigrated from Ohio. In 1845 the Sac and Fox Agency was moved from the Raccoon River in Iowa to the Osage River and thereafter remained in the St. Louis Superintendency. In 1847 the Sac and

Fox Agency was consolidated with the Osage River Subagency to form the Osage River Agency. At the same time the Council Bluffs Subagency was discontinued. The Ottawa and Chippewa were assigned to the Osage River Agency. The Potawatomi of Council Bluffs and the Osage River were united and they had their own subagent for a few motnhs, but early in 1848 they were assigned to the Fort Leavenworth Agency. The Kansa Indians were transferred from the Fort Leavenworth Agency to the Osage River Agency.

Several changes were made in 1846. The Upper Platte Agency was established for the upper areas of the Arkansas and Platte Rivers. Iowa became a state, the Iowa Superintendency was discontinued and the St. Peters Agency and Winnebago (Turkey River) Subagency were transferred to the St. Louis Superintendency. In 1849 they were transferred again to the new Minnesota Superintendency.

After 1839, when the use of military disbursing officers was discontinued, the St. Louis superintendent made those disbursements that the *ex officio* superintendents were not authorized to handle. This practice was followed for the Iowa, Wisconsin and Minnesota Superintendencies and for a time for the new superintendencies and agencies in the Far West.

In 1851 the St. Louis Superintendency was replaced by the Central Superintendency. There was also a reorganization of the agencies. Assigned to the Central Superintendency were the Upper Missouri, Council Bluffs, Great Nemaha (Iowa, Sauk and Fox of the Missouri and Kickapoo Indians), Potawatomi (Potawatomi and Kansa Indians), Kansas (Delaware, Shawnee, Wyandot, Stockbridge and Munsee), Sac and Fox (Sauk and Fox of the Mississippi, Ottawa and Chippewa) and Upper Platte Agencies.

For the years 1837-41 there are some letters filed under the subheading "St. Louis Emigration."

See also Central, Wisconsin, Iowa, Michigan, Western and Minnesota Superintendencies and Upper Missouri, Sac and Fox, St. Peters, Prairie du Chien, Ioway, Fort Leavenworth, Osage, Crow Wing, Council Bluffs, Great Nemaha, Osage River, Raccoon River, Turkey River, Winnebago, Chicago, Wyandot, Upper Platte, Potawatomi and Kansas Agencies and Subagencies. There are a few field records of the St. Louis Superintendency among the records of the Bureau of Indian Affairs in the National Archives.

SUPERINTENDENTS

Name	*Date of Appointment*
William Clark	Notified May 28, 1822
Joshua Pilcher	Mar. 4, 1839
David D. Mitchell	Sept. 13, 1841
Thomas H. Harvey	Oct. 3, 1843
David D. Mitchell	Mar. 30, 1849

159

ST. PETERS AGENCY
1824-1870

The St. Peters Agency was established in 1819. Originally no specific tribes nor geographic areas were assigned to the agency, but in general the agency assumed responsiblity for the Indians living in present Minnesota and part of Iowa. Previously this area had been within the limits of the Prairie du Chien Agency. The principal Indian tribes for which the agent was responsible were various bands of Sioux and Chippewa. By 1827 the St. Peters Agency was responsible primarily only for the Sioux and the Sault Ste. Marie Agency was responsible for the Chippewa. The Sioux belonging to the St. Peters Agency were known collectively as the Sioux of the Mississippi to distinguish them from other Sioux living in the Missouri River region who were assigned to the Upper Missouri Agency. There were four main bands of Sioux of the Mississippi: Mdewakanton, Wahpekute, Sisseton and Wahpeton. The St. Peters Agency also had some contact with the Yankton and Assiniboin Sioux, but these Indians were more closely associated with the Upper Missouri Agency.

The St. Peters Agency was located at the mouth of the St. Peters (now known as the Minnesota) River, near the site of Minneapolis. The Indians, however, inhabited a wide area in present Minnesota and Iowa.

In 1819 the agent was instructed to report directly to the War Department. In 1821 he was directed to follow instructions from the Governor of Michigan Territory that were not incompatible with those received from the War Department. In 1822 the agency was assigned to the new St. Louis Superintendency. Until the Bureau of Indian Affairs was established in 1824, correspondence relating to the St. Peters Agency was transmitted directly to the Office of the Secretary of War.

Under the reorganization plan of 1834 the St. Peters Agency was given responsibility for the Sioux living on the waters of the Mississippi and its tributaries and the waters of the Red River. The Sioux of Wabisha's band (a group of Mdewakanton) were transferred to the Prairie du Chien Agency. By 1841, however, these Indians were again attached to the St. Peters Agency. Geographically, the St. Peters Agency included the area west of the Mackinac and Sault Ste. Marie Agency and north of the Green Bay and Prairie du Chien Agencies.

With the establishment of new territories and the advancement of territories to statehood the St. Peters Agency changed superintendencies several times. In 1836 it was transferred from the St. Louis Superintendency to the new Wisconsin Superintendency and in 1838 it was transferred to the Iowa Superintendency. When Iowa became a state in 1846, the St. Peters Agency was left in unorganized territory and was transferred back to the St. Louis Superintendency. In 1849 it was assigned to the Minnesota Superintendency and, in 1856, to the Northern Superintendency. From 1848 until 1851 the agency was reduced to a subagency.

By treaties negotiated in 1851 with the Mdewakanton and Wahpekute and with the Sisseton and Wahpeton the Indians ceded their land in Minnesota and Iowa except for reserves along the Minnesota (formerly St. Peters) River in western Minnesota. Most of the Indians moved during 1853, and by 1854 the St. Peters Agency was located near the mouth of the Redwood River on the reserve for the Mdewakanton and Wahpekute (or Lower) Sioux. Permanent agency buildings were finished in 1858 on both the lower reserve and at Yellow Medicine on the reserve for the Sisseton and Wahpeton. The agent divided his time between the two locations and the two places were known, respectively, as the Lower Sioux Agency and the Upper Sioux Agency. For filing purposes, however, the name "St. Peters" was retained by the Bureau.

After an uprising of the Sioux Indians in Minnesota in 1862 many of the Sioux and Winnebago were moved the following year to an area on the Missouri River in Dakota Territory near the mouth of Crow Creek. The St. Peters agent remained in Minnesota, and the Winnebago agent was placed in charge of both tribes at Crow Creek until 1865. By that time the Winnebago had moved to Nebraska, and the successor to the St. Peters agent was assigned to the Sioux Indians at Crow Creek. At the same time the agency for the Sioux was transferred from the Northern Superintendency to the Dakota Superintendency. In 1866 the Sioux Indians at Crow Creek, now known as Santee Sioux, moved again to a reservation in northeastern Nebraska near the mouth of the Niobrara River. After this move the agency was again within the normal limits of the Northern Superintendency. During the next few years the agency and Indians were moved several times to different points on the Missouri River and the agency was finally located about 12 miles below the mouth of the Niobrara. The agency was now usually known as the Santee Sioux or Santee Agency, but the name "St. Peters" was used by the Bureau for filing purposes until 1871, when "Santee Sioux" began to be used.

Under the heading "St. Peters" there is also correspondence concerning the Indians who remained in Minnesota, chiefly Sisseton and Wahpeton. Under the provisions of a treaty of 1867 these Indians agreed to settle on reservations in Dakota. The Sisseton Agency was established for them in 1867, but in 1871 this agency was divided by the establishment of the Devil's Lake Agency.

For the years 1839-49 there are some letters filed under the subheading "St. Peters Reserves."

See also St. Louis, Michigan, Wisconsin, Iowa, Minnesota, Northern and Dakota Superintendencies and Santee Sioux, Upper Missouri, Prairie du Chien, Mackinac, Sault Ste. Marie, Winnebago, Sisseton and Devil's Lake Agencies.

AGENTS

Name	Date of Appointment
Lawrence Taliaferro	Mar. 27, 1819
Amos J. Bruce	Jan. 1, 1840
Richard G. Murphy (subagent)	May 5, 1848
Nathaniel McClean (subagent)	Nov. 7, 1849
Nathaniel McClean (agent)	June 30, 1851
Richard G. Murphy	Apr. 18, 1853
Charles E. Flandrau	Aug. 13, 1856
Joseph R. Brown	Sept. 11, 1857
Thomas J. Galbraith	Mar. 23, 1861
St. A. D. Balcombe (Winnebago agent also assigned to Sioux at Crow Creek)	Dec. 18, 1863
James M. Stone	Mar. 21, 1865
Asa M. Janney	Apr. 22, 1869

SANDY LAKE SUBAGENCY 1850-1851

The Sandy Lake Subagency was established in 1851 under the Minnesota Superintendency, with the removal of the La Pointe Subagency of Wisconsin to Sandy Lake, Minnesota. The "La Pointe" title was revived in 1855 for correspondence concerning the Chippewa Indians who continued to live in Wisconsin and Minnesota along Lake Superior. The Sandy Lake Subagency was responsible for the Chippewa of Lake Superior transferred from La Pointe and for the Chippewa of the Mississippi who previously had been attached to the Winnebago Agency. On June 30, 1851 Sandy Lake was made a full agency and renamed the Chippewa Agency.

See also Minnesota Superintendency and Winnebago, Chippewa, La Pointe and Mackinac Agencies.

Name	Date of Appointment
John S. Watrous	Apr. 20, 1850

SANTA FE AGENCY
1849-1851

The Santa Fe Agency was established in 1849 for the Indians who lived in the vicinity of Santa Fe, New Mexico. These Indians included Navajo, Apache, Ute and Pueblo, as well as other tribes. After the Territory of New Mexico was organized in 1850, the Santa Fe Agency was replaced by the New Mexico Superintendency. Three letters dated 1851, however, were filed under "Santa Fe."

See also New Mexico Superintendency.

AGENT

Name	Date of Appointment
James S. Calhoun	Mar. 30, 1849

SANTEE SIOUX AGENCY
1871-1876

"Santee Sioux" was the name used for filing purposes by the Bureau after 1871 to replace the name "St. Peters." The St. Peters Agency, however, established in 1819, had been commonly known as the Santee Sioux or Santee Agency since 1866. In that year the agency and some of the Santee Sioux (formerly known as Sioux of the Mississippi) were moved from Dakota and Minnesota to northeastern Nebraska. After several changes in location, the agency headquarters was permanently located on the west side of the Missouri River about 12 miles below the mouth of the Niobrara River.

After 1878, in addition to the Santee Sioux, there were a few Ponca Indians attached to the agency. In 1879 the Flandreau Agency at Flandreau, Dakota, established in 1873 for a group of Santee Sioux who had left the Santee Sioux Agency, was consolidated with the Santee Sioux Agency.

The Santee Sioux Agency was assigned to the Northern Superintendency until June 30, 1876, when the superintendency was discontinued. Thereafter the agent reported directly to the Bureau of Indian Affairs in Washington. After July 1, 1876 correspondence relating to the Santee Sioux Agency and other agencies in Nebraska was filed under the heading "Nebraska."

In April, 1877, because the Senate failed to confirm the appointment of an agent, the Santee Sioux Agency was temporarily under the jurisdiction of the Yankton agent. The following year an agent was appointed and the Santee Sioux Agency continued in operation beyond 1880.

See also Northern and Dakota Superintendencies and St. Peters, Flandreau and Nebraska Agencies.

AGENTS

Name	*Date of Appointment*
Asa M. Janney	Apr. 22, 1869
Joseph Webster	June 19, 1871
Charles H. Searing	Aug. 27, 1875
John G. Gasmann	In charge Apr. 25,
(Yankton agent also in charge of the	1877
Santee Sioux Agency)	
John W. Douglas	Mar. 28, 1878
(Yankton agent also in charge of the	
Santee Sioux Agency)	
Isaiah Lightner	Apr. 25, 1877
(farmer-in-charge)	
Isaiah Lightner (agent)	Apr. 24, 1878

SAULT STE. MARIE AGENCY
1824-1852

The Sault Ste. Marie Agency was established in 1822. The agency was located on the Upper Peninsula of Michigan near the *sault* or falls of the St. Mary's River. No specific tribes or geographical limits were assigned to the agency originally, but it assumed charge of the Chippewa and Ottawa Indians living in the upper part of Michigan and in present Wisconsin and Minnesota. The St. Peters Agency on the Mississippi River also claimed jurisdiction over some of the Chippewa Indians, but in 1827 the Chippewa were definitely assigned to the Sault Ste. Marie Agency. Other Chippewa and Ottawa Indians belonged to the Mackinac Agency to the south of the Sault Ste. Marie in Michigan and to the Chicago Agency.

The Sault Ste. Marie Agency was responsible to the Michigan Superintendency. Until 1834 there were usually one or two subagents subordinate to the Sault Ste. Marie agent, including for a time one stationed at La Pointe. Until the Bureau of Indian Affairs was established in 1824, correspondence relating to the agency was transmitted directly to the Office of the Secretary of War.

In 1832 the Mackinac and Sault Ste. Marie Agencies were consolidated. The agent remained at Sault Ste. Marie until 1833, when he moved to Mackinac. Under the regulations adopted in 1834 the area assigned to the Mackinac and Sault Ste. Marie Agency included the northern part of the Lower Peninsula, the islands of Lake Huron, the Upper Peninsula, the country of Lake Superior and the country of the Chippewa of the Upper Mississippi. The commanding officer of Fort Brady at Sault Ste. Marie was put in charge of the Indians in that immediate vicinity.

In 1835 the Crow Wing Subagency was established for the Chippewa of the Mississippi, and in 1836 the La Pointe Subagency was established for the Chippewa of Lake Superior who lived in the newly established Territory of Wisconsin.

In 1837 a separate subagency was established at Sault Ste. Marie and it was assigned the area of the Upper Peninsula to the eastern boundary of Wisconsin. When the Michigan Superintendency was discontinued in 1851, the Indians and agencies in Michigan were assigned to the new Northern Superintendency. In practice, however, the Sault Ste. Marie subagent had little contact with the Northern Superintendency and he usually reported to the Bureau either directly or through the Mackinac Agency. The Sault Ste. Marie Subagency was discontinued on June 30, 1852, and its duties were transferred to the Mackinac Agency.

*See also Michigan, Wisconsin, Minnesota, St. Louis and Northern Superin-
tendencies and Mackinac, St. Peters, Crow Wing, La Pointe, Chicago, Sandy
Lake, Chippewa and Saginaw Agencies and Subagencies. There are field records
of the Sault Ste. Marie Agency and Subagency with the records of the Michigan
Superintendency. Some of these have been reproduced by the National Archives
and Records Service as part of Microfilm Publication 1.*

AGENTS

Name	*Date of Appointment*
Henry R. Schoolcraft	Notified May 29, 1822
Bvt. Maj. W. V. Cobbs (acting) (Assigned to the immediate vicinity of Sault Ste. Marie. Schoolcraft was in charge of the combined Mackinac and Sault Ste. Marie Agency)	July 23, 1834
James Ord (subagent)	June 27, 1837
David Aitken (subagent)	Jan. 29, 1850

SCHOOLS
1824-1873

The correspondence concerning schools relates to the establishment and operation of missionary, tribal and Government day and boarding schools for Indians.
A few letters concerning land reserved for school purposes are filed separately
under the subheading "Schools Reserves," but most correspondence of this
nature is with the main "Schools" file or with the records concerning individual
agencies and superintendencies.

As early as 1819 Congress authorized a "Civilization Fund" of $10,000 a year,
which was used primarily to aid missionary societies in operating schools for
Indians. Even earlier, stipulations of various treaties provided for funds to be
used for educational purposes. Gradually Government-operated schools, chiefly
manual labor schools, were opened on reservations. Until after 1880 these
schools were under the supervision of the individual Indian agents. In 1879

Congress made the first general appropriation for Indian education. The first nonreservation boarding school for Indians was established at Carlisle, Pennsylvania in 1879.

After a Medical and Educational Division was established in the Bureau of Indian Affairs in 1873, records concerning schools were maintained in this Division, and the "Schools" classification was discontinued. Few records of the Medical and Educational Division, however, have been preserved.

See also the correspondence concerning individual superintendencies and agencies.

SEMINOLE AGENCY
1824-1876

The Seminole Agency was established under the Florida Superintendency in 1822. In 1821 a subagent had been appointed for the Indians of Florida, and in the same year a temporary agent was appointed to serve during the absence of the Governor. The subagency was continued after the appointment of a regular agent, the subagent usually acting as assistant to the agent. A second subagency was established in 1826 for the Indians living along the Apalachicola River (see Apalachicola Subagency).

The Florida or Seminole Agency had no permanent headquarters until 1825, when it was located on the Seminole Reservation in central Florida. Correspondence concerning the agency was transmitted directly to the Office of the Secretary of War until the Bureau of Indian Affairs was established in 1824.

The Florida Superintendency and the subagencies were abolished on June 30, 1834 in expectation of the removal of the Indians to Indian Territory. On November 20, 1834 the Seminole agent was made Superintendent of Emigration; he served in that capacity until his death on December 28, 1835. His duties were assumed by Army officers, except for a few months in 1849 when a subagent was assigned to the Seminole Indians in Florida. Correspondence concerning the Seminole in Florida was filed under both "Florida" and "Seminole" until 1850, when the Florida classification was discontinued. Later correspondence was filed under "Seminole."

The Seminole who emigrated to the Indian Territory were under the general supervision of the Western Superintendency. In 1837 they were attached to the

Creek Agency, but in 1842 a subagency for the western Seminole was established on the Deep Fork of the Canadian River. In 1845 the agency was moved to the Little River. In 1851 the Southern Superintendency replaced the Western Superintendency.

The Seminole Subagency was made a full agency in 1855 and, after many of the Seminole were removed from Florida in 1858, a new agency headquarters was built about 60 miles farther west. During the Civil War, when Confederate troops occupied Indian Territory, those Seminole who remained loyal to the United States went to Kansas and the agency was moved to Neosho Falls. In 1867 the agency was moved to Wewoka, Indian Territory.

After the Southern Superintendency was discontinued in 1870, the Central superintendent took over those duties of the superintendent that were required by the terms of treaties, such as the investigation of certain claims. For most purposes the agent now reported directly to the Bureau of Indian Affairs in Washington. In 1874 the Seminole, Choctaw and Creek Agencies were consolidated with the Cherokee Agency to form the Union Agency. Some correspondence, however, was filed under the heading "Seminole" until 1876. Some correspondence concerning the removal of the Seminole from Florida between 1827 and 1859 is filed under the subheading "Seminole Emigration."

See also Florida, Western, Southern and Central Superintendencies, Creek and Union Agencies and Apalachicola Subagency.

AGENTS AND SUBAGENTS

Seminole Agency in Florida

Name	*Date of Appointment*
Gad Humphrey.	May 8, 1822
John Phagan	June 10, 1830
Wiley Thompson	Aug. 29, 1833

Seminole Subagency in West

John McKee	Jan. 19, 1842
Thomas S. Judge	Oct. 29, 1842
Marcellus DuVal	July 11, 1845
Bryant H. Smithson	Apr. 26, 1853
Josiah W. Washbourne	Apr. 20, 1854

Seminole Agency in West

Josiah W. Washbourne	June 8, 1855
Samuel Rutherford	Nov. 5, 1857
William P. Davis	July 13, 1861 (but did not serve)

George C. Snow   Jan. 7, 1862
George A. Reyonolds   Mar. 18, 1865
Capt. T. A. Baldwin   June 23, 1869
Henry Breiner   Oct. 24, 1870

SENECA AGENCY IN NEW YORK
1824-1832

The Seneca Agency is the same as that named Six Nations. The agency, established in 1792, was responsible for the Seneca and other Indians living in western New York. The agency headquarters was at Canandaigua until 1829, at Medina from 1829 until 1832, and thereafter at Buffalo. Most of the correspondence relating to the agency is filed under the heading "Six Nations." The letters filed under "Seneca" for the most part relate specificially to the Seneca Indians. For a more detailed history and a list of agents see Six Nations Agency. Other Seneca Indians were assigned during this period to the Piqua-Ohio Agency.

See Cherokee Agency for correspondence concerning Seneca who had moved west of the Mississippi River.

SHAWNEE AGENCY
1855-1876

The Shawnee Agency was established in 1855 for the Shawnee and Wyandot Indians who lived in eastern Kansas. The Shawnee lived on a reserve south of the Kansas River, which had been granted to them by a treaty in 1825 but was greatly reduced in area by another treaty in 1854. The treaty of 1854 also provided for the allotment of tribal land to individual Indians. The Wyandot had

169

purchased their tract from the Delaware Indians in 1843. A treaty of 1855 provided for individual land holdings.

The Shawnee Agency was under the supervision of the Central Superintendency. The buildings of the former Kansas Agency on the Shawnee reserve were designated for the use of the Shawnee Agency, but the first agent made his headquarters at Westport, Missouri. In 1861 the agency headquarters was moved from Westport to De Soto, Kansas, but until 1863 the agent usually reported from Lexington, Kansas. In 1869 the agency office was moved from De Soto to Shawnee and later in the same year to Olathe.

In 1863 the Wyandot Indians were transferred to the Delaware Agency, leaving the Shawnee Agency responsible only for the Shawnee Indians. In 1871 the Shawnee agent was made responsible for settling the affairs of the recently discontinued Osage River Agency and was put in charge of the Miami Indians who had not yet moved to the Quapaw Agency in Indian Territory.

By 1871 most of the Kansas Shawnee had joined the Cherokee Nation in Indian Territory and were attached to the Cherokee Agency. Others, chiefly members of the Black Bob band, had joined other groups of Shawnee at the Quapaw and Sac and Fox Agencies. Therefore the Shawnee Agency was discontinued on December 31, 1871. Some correspondence, however, mainly concerning the settlement of the affairs of the Shawnee in Kansas, was filed under "Shawnee" until 1876.

As early as 1821 an agent was assigned to the various tribes living in the Kansas River area. Between 1824 and 1834 there was an agency for the Shawnee, Delaware and other Indians that was usually called the Delaware and Shawnee Agency. In 1834 a subagency was established for the Shawnee, Ottawa and other Indians and it was consolidated with the Northern Agency in 1835. The correspondence concerning these agencies is filed under "Fort Leavenworth" and "St. Louis." from 1837 until 1851 the Shawnee were attached to the Fort Leavenworth Agency. There was a subagency for the Wyandot in operation from 1843 until 1851. As part of the general reorganization of 1851, both the Fort Leavenworth Agency and the Wyandot Subagency were discontinued, and the Shawnee, Wyandot and other Indians living along the Kansas River were assigned to the Kansas Agency. In 1855 the Kansas Agency was divided into the Shawnee Agency and the Delaware Agency.

There were two other important groups of Shawnee. The Eastern Shawnee, a part of the Mixed Band of Seneca and Shawnee until 1867, had moved from Ohio and settled in northeastern Indian Territory as early as 1832. They were assigned to the Neosho Agency from 1837 until 1871, when they were assigned to the Quapaw Agency. Other bands of Shawnee were known as Absentee Shawnee. Some of them had settled on Creek, Choctaw and Cherokee land in 1836 and 1839. Others lived in Texas until their removal to the Wichita Agency in 1859. During the Civil War many of the Absentee Shawnee took refuge in Kansas. After the war they were united under the Sac and Fox Agency in Indian Territory.

See also Central and St. Louis Superintendencies; Kansas, Delaware, Cherokee, Neosho, Quapaw, Sac and Fox, Osage River, Fort Leavenworth, Choctaw, Creek, Texas and Wichita Agencies; and Wyandot Subagency.

AGENTS

Name	Date of Appointment
Robert C. Miller	Mar. 3, 1855
William Gay	Dec. 27, 1855
Anselim Arnold	July 15, 1856
Benjamin J. Newsom	June 3, 1858
James B. Abbott	Apr. 25, 1861
H. L. Taylor	Oct. 5, 1866
Reuben L. Roberts	Apr. 22, 1869

SISSETON AGENCY
1867-1880

Under the provisions of a treaty of February 19, 1867, the Sisseton Agency was established in 1867 for the Sisseton and Wahpeton Sioux who had been granted reservations in the Lake Traverse and Devil's Lake areas of Dakota Territory. Earlier correspondence concerning these Indians is filed with the correspondence concerning the St. Peters Agency. In 1871 the Devil's Lake Agency was established for the Indians at Devil's Lake.

Although it was located in Dakota Territory, the Sisseton Agency was not assigned to the Dakota Superintendency. For a time during 1869 and 1870 the agent reported through the office of H. B. Whipple, Episcopal bishop at Fairbault, Minnesota, who had been placed in charge of some of the funds allocated for the Sisseton and Wahpeton Indians.

The headquarters of the Sisseton Agency was on the Lake Traverse Reservation, but until 1869 the agent often stayed at St. Paul, Minnesota. The agency continued in operation beyond 1880.

See also Dakota Superintendency and St. Peters, Santee Sioux and Devil's Lake Agencies.

Name	Date of Appointment
Benjamin Thompson	May 25, 1867
Jared W. Daniels	Apr. 9, 1869
Moses N. Adams	Nov. 1, 1871
John G. Hamilton	Mar. 22, 1875
Edward H. C. Hooper	July 12, 1877
Charles Crissey	Mar. 3, 1879

SIX NATIONS AGENCY 1824-1834

An agent, Israel Chapin, was appointed for the Iroquois Indians of New York as early as 1792. His successors were given various titles, but in effect the Six Nations Agency remained in operation thereafter. The term "Six Nations" refers to the principal Iroquois tribes: Seneca, Onondaga, Cayuga, Tuscarora, Oneida and Mohawk. This name for the agency was not entirely accurate. Most of the Indians were Seneca, and the agency was sometimes known as the Seneca Agency. Almost all the Mohawk were living in Canada, but the Saint Regis band of Iroquois, not affiliated with any of the Six Nations, was assigned to the agency. Also the Stockbridge, Munsee and Brotherton Indians (all Algonquin rather than Iroquois) were under the supervision of the Six Nations Agency until most of them, as well as the Oneida, moved to Green Bay in what became Wisconsin. Most of the Indians of the Six Nations Agency were living on reserves in western New York.

In 1818 the Six Nations Agency was reduced to a subagency. Until the Bureau of Indian Affairs was established in 1824, the subagent corresponded directly with the Office of the Secretary of War. The subagency was not subordinate to any superintendency. Subagent Jasper Parrish lived at Canandaigua, New York. His successor, Justus Ingersoll, appointed in 1829 and usually designated as a superintendent, lived at Medina. When Ingersoll was released in 1832, his duties were turned over to Subagent James Stryker. Stryker had been appointed in 1830 as subagent under the Green Bay agent for the Indians who had moved from New York to Green Bay but he had been authorized to remain temporarily at Buffalo, New York. After he was put in charge of the Indians of the Six

Nations, Stryker continued to reside at Buffalo. He was instructed, however, to report to the Governor of Michigan Territory, who served as *ex officio* superintendent of Indian affairs. In the regulations adopted by the Bureau in 1834, the subagency was designated as the New York Subagency, and it was made responsible for all the Indians living in New York. The subagent was instructed to report directly to the Bureau of Indian Affairs in Washington rather than through the Governor of Michigan. At the beginning of 1835 the heading "Six Nations" was abandoned and replaced by "New York."

There are some letters dated between 1824 and 1832, relating to the Seneca Indians in New York, filed under the heading "Seneca" instead of "Six Nations." This was a filing practice; there was no separate agency for the Seneca. There are also letters relating to the removal of Indians from New York, which are filed under the subheading "New York Emigration" as early as 1829 even though the main New York heading does not begin until 1835.

See also Michigan Superintendency and Seneca, New York and Green Bay Agencies. For correspondence concerning the Seneca Indians in Ohio during this period see Piqua and Ohio Agencies; for correspondence concerning Seneca living west of the Mississippi River see Cherokee Agency.

AGENTS

Name	*Date of Appointment*
Israel Chapin	Apr. 23, 1792
Callender Irvine	July 8, 1802
Erastus Granger	Jan. 30, 1804
Jasper Parrish (subagent)	Appointed Feb. 15, 1803, to serve under the agent; put in charge May 8, 1818.
Justus Ingersoll (superintendent)	July 31, 1829
James Stryker (subagent)	Appointed Mar. 16, 1830 as subagent under Green Bay Agency; put in charge of Six Nations Agency, Apr. 1, 1832.

SOUTHERN SUPERINTENDENCY 1851-1871

As part of the general organization of the Indian field service of 1851, the Southern Superintendency was established to replace the Western Superintendency. The new superintendency was responsible for the Cherokee, Creek, Chickasaw, Seminole, Quapaw, Seneca and Mixed Band of Seneca and Shawnee living in Indian Territory and for the Osage Indians of southern Kansas. The superintendency had supervision over the Cherokee, Creek, Choctaw and Chickasaw Agencies and the Seminole Subagency, all of which had been assigned to the Western Superintendency. To these were added the new Neosho Agency, formed by the consolidation of the Neosho Subagency (for the Quapaw, Seneca and Seneca and Shawnee Indians) and the Osage Subagency.

The Chickasaw Agency was consolidated with the Choctaw Agency in 1855, and the Seminole Subagency was made a full agency. The Neosho Agency was transferred to the Central Superintendency in 1867.

In 1857 the Wichita Agency was established under the Southern Superintendency for the Wichita and Kichai Indians. In 1859 Caddo, Anadarko, Waco, Tonkawa, Hainai, Kichai, Tawakoni, Delaware, Shawnee and Comanche Indians were moved from Texas to the Wichita Agency in Indian Territory. The Wichita Agency was consolidated with the Kiowa Agency of the Central Superintendency in 1869. The following year the Wichita Agency was re-established as a separate agency, but it remained under the Central Superintendency. By 1870 the Southern Superintendency had supervision over only the Cherokee, Creek, Choctaw (and Chickasaw) and Seminole Agencies. Correspondence concerning the individual agencies is usually filed under the name of that agency rather than with the superintendency correspondence. The office of the Southern Superintendency was originally at Van Buren, Arkansas. In 1853 it was moved to Fort Smith, Arkansas.

At the beginning of the Civil War the Indian Territory was occupied by Confederate troops. The superintendent and some of the agents of the Southern Superintendency accepted similar positions under the Confederacy. Those Indians who remained loyal to the United States fled to Kansas, and temporary headquarters for the several agencies were established in that state. A new superintendent, unable to reach Fort Smith, also established his headquarters in Kansas. Humboldt, the first headquarters, was burned by Confederate troops, and during most of the war the superintendent remained at Leavenworth. For a time he had a second office at Lawrence, Kansas.

The Indians began to return to Indian Territory in 1864. The superintendency office was re-established at Fort Smith in 1866, but in 1868 it was moved to the intended location of the Creek Agency on the Deep Fork of the Canadian River about 50 miles west of Fort Gibson.

In 1869 Congress appropriated money for only two superintendencies east of the Rocky Mountains, and it was decided to close the Southern Superintendency on July 1, 1869. The treaties with the various tribes, however, stipulated the services of a superintendent in certain matters, such as the investigation of claims, and on June 30 an Army officer was detailed to act as superintendent. The superintendent was to act only in conformity with the treaty stipulations and as specially directed by the Bureau. On other matters the agents were to be responsible directly to the Bureau of Indian Affairs in Washington. This arrangement was continued until August, 1870, when the Southern Superintendency was completely abolished and the Central Superintendency was placed in charge of the Creek, Cherokee, Choctaw and Seminole Agencies. It was originally intended that the Central Superintendency should exercise full supervisory control over these agencies and that the agents should report through the superintendent. On December 21, 1870, however, the instructions were modified so that the superintendent was to handle only the treaty stipulations. Otherwise the agents were to be responsible directly to the Bureau of Indian Affairs in Washington.

See also Western and Central Superintendencies and Cherokee, Creek, Choctaw, Chickasaw, Seminole, Neosho, Wichita, Texas and Kiowa Agencies. There are also field records of the Southern Superintendency among the records of the Bureau of Indian Affairs in the National Archives. They have been reproduced by the National Archives and Records Service as part of Microfilm Publication 640.

SUPERINTENDENTS

Name	*Date of Appointment*
John Drennen	Mar. 12, 1851
Thomas S. Drew	Apr. 8, 1853
Charles W. Dean	Mar. 3, 1855
Elias Rector	Mar. 17, 1857
William G. Coffin	May. 3, 1861
Elijah Sells	Apr. 28, 1865
William Byers	Sept. 20, 1866
James Wortham	Mar. 27, 1867
L. Newton Robinson	June 17, 1868
Bvt. Maj. Gen. W. B. Hazen	June 30, 1869

SPOTTED TAIL AGENCY
1875-1880

The Spotted Tail Agency was successor to the Whetstone Agency, which in 1869 had replaced the Upper Platte Agency to supervise the band of Brulé Sioux led by Spotted Tail. Other bands of Sioux, including Sans Arcs, Oglala, Hunkpapa and Miniconjou, also belonged to the Spotted Tail Agency.

On December 22, 1874, when the Whetstone Agency was renamed the Spotted Tail Agency, it was located on the White River near the Nebraska-Dakota border. In 1875 the Spotted Tail Agency was moved about twelve miles to the head of Beaver Creek in northwestern Nebraska. In 1877 the agency was moved to the site of the old Ponca Agency on the Missouri River about 60 miles above Yankton. For a short time agents were stationed at both locations. In 1878 the agency was moved to Rosebud Creek near its junction with the South Fork of the White River. Thereafter the agency was called the Rosebud Agency, but the Bureau of Indian Affairs continued to file correspondence under "Spotted Tail" through 1880. James R. O'Beirne was special agent in charge of the removal and of the construction of buildings at the new agency.

The Spotted Tail Agency was under the supervision of the Dakota Superintendency from March, 1877 until June, 1878, the time during which the superintendency was temporarily re-established, but the agent continued to report directly to the Bureau of Indian Affairs in Washington. The Rosebud Agency continued in operation beyond 1880.

See also Dakota Superintendency and Upper Platte, Whetstone and Red Cloud Agencies.

AGENTS

Name	*Date of Appointment*
Edwin A. Howard	Mar. 24, 1873
Lt. M. C. Foot (acting)	Began service Aug. 10, 1876
Lt. A. C. Paul (acting)	Oct. 27, 1876
Lt. Horace Neide (acting)	Nov. 30, 1876
Lt. J. M. Lee (acting)	Stationed at the Spotted Tail Agency on Beaver Creek Jan. 11, 1877; assumed charge of the new agency Dec. 31, 1877

James Lawrence	Stationed at the new agency site on the Missouri River Mar. 29, 1877
William J. Pollock (Special Agent at Large)	July 1, 1878
Cicero Newell	Apr. 3, 1879
John Cook	Feb. 2, 1880

STANDING ROCK AGENCY 1875-1880

The Standing Rock Agency, on the west bank of the Missouri River at Standing Rock near Fort Yates, Dakota Territory, succeeded the Grand River Agency established in 1869. It was renamed Standing Rock Agency on December 22, 1874. By then it had charge of bands of Upper and Lower Yanktonai, Hunkpapa and Blackfeet Sioux.

During the temporary re-establishment of the Dakota Superintendency from March, 1877 until June, 1878 the Standing Rock Agency was under the supervision of that superintendency, but the agent continued to report directly to the Bureau of Indian Affairs in Washington. The Standing Rock Agency continued to operate beyond 1880.

See also Dakota Superintendency and Grand River Agency.

AGENTS

Name	*Date of Appointment*
Edmond Palmer	May 19, 1873
John Burke	Feb. 26, 1875
Capt. R. E. Johnston (acting) (Continued to serve under the supervision of Carlin)	Aug. 30, 1876
Lt. Col. W. P. Carlin	Sept. 8, 1876
William T. Hughes	Oct. 20, 1876
Leverett M. Kelley	Aug. 30, 1878
Joseph A. Stephan	Sept. 26, 1878

STOCKS
1836-1873

The correspondence filed under the heading "Stocks" relates to securities held in trust for Indians. Under the provisions of various treaties and by acts of Congress, trust funds were established for different groups of Indians. These funds were administered by the Secretary of War until 1849 and thereafter by the Secretary of the Interior, acting through the Bureau of Indian Affairs. In 1876 Congress transferred custody of the securities and authority to make purchases and sales to the Treasurer of the United States, but the Secretary of the Interior continued to control the investments. The principal for the funds was obtained from the proceeds of land sales, Government payments under treaty provisions and other sources. Actually the money was usually invested in Federal and state bonds rather than in stocks. Interest and dividends from the investments could be distributed among the Indians or used for some special purpose, such as the maintenance of schools.

The correspondence filed under the heading "Stocks" relates chiefly to the purchase and sale of securities, the collection of interest and dividends and the status of various funds. Correspondence relating to the use of proceeds by the Indians is ordinarily found with the correspondence relating to the agency or superintendency with which the Indians were affiliated. Much of the correspondence is from bankers. For the later years the correspondence consists largely of communications from the Secretary of the Interior, often transmitting copies of his correspondence on the subject of the trust funds. Before 1836 and after 1873 and even during the years when the "Stocks" heading was in use, there is correspondence relating to the trust funds under the heading "Miscellaneous." There are other records relating to trust funds among the records of the Finance Division of the Bureau.

TEXAS AGENCY
1847-1859

The Texas Agency was established with the appointment of Robert S. Neighbors as special agent on March 20, 1847. Previously the Bureau of Indian Affairs had not been active in Texas. The special agent was responsible for all the Indians in the state. These included Comanche, Caddo, Anadarko, Waco, Tonkawa, Hainai (Ioni), Kichai, Tawakoni, Delaware, Shawnee, Lipan, Apache, Wichita and other Indians, some of whom were considered intruders and not residents of Texas. Because the Indians in Texas were nomadic, the special agent had no permanent headquarters and spent much of his time traveling.

In 1850 Congress authorized the appointment of three special agents in Texas. The appointed agents informally assigned themselves districts. In 1852 one of the agents was designated as supervising agent, with duties similar to those of a superintendent. In 1859 a full Texas Superintendency, with a superintendent and two agents, was established.

Until 1855 the assignment of agents remained informal. One agent was usually assigned to the Indians living along the Brazos River, and the name Brazos Agency came to be applied to his agency.

Two reservations were established in 1855 on land granted for that purpose by the state of Texas. An agent was assigned to each of the reservations, with the supervising agent in general charge. The Brazos Agency was responsible for the Caddo, Anadarko, Tonkawa, Tawakoni, Kichai, Delaware and Shawnee Indians who settled on one reservation located on the main fork of the Brazos River near Fort Belknap in Young County. The Comanche Agency was responsible for the Southern Band of Comanche who settled on a reservation on the Clear Fork of the Brazos River about 35 miles southwest of Belknap.

In 1859 the Indians of both reservations were moved to the Wichita Agency in Indian Territory. Superintendent Neighbors was killed following the removal and was not replaced. On March 20, 1860 the agent of the Brazos Agency was notified that his services had been terminated. In July the agent of the former Comanche Agency was appointed agent of the Wichita Agency. Correspondence after 1859 concerning the settlement of affairs in Texas is filed under "Wichita."

AGENTS

Name	Date of Appointment
Robert S. Neighbors	Mar. 20, 1847
John H. Rollins	Aug. 11, 1849

After November 1850 there were three agents in Texas. The incumbents are listed in three columns in order to show the succession of appointments.

Name and Date	*Name and Date*	*Name and Date*
John A. Rogers Nov. 2, 1850	John H. Rollins Nov. 5, 1850	Jesse Stem Nov. 5, 1850
Horace Capron Mar. 10, 1852	George Thomas Howard Jan. 9, 1852 (supervising agent)	
Robert S. Neighbors May 9, 1853 (supervising agent)		George W. Hill May 9, 1853
Robert S. Neighbors Mar. 1, 1859 (superintendent)		
	Comanche Agency	*Brazos Agency*
	John R. Baylor July 2, 1855	Shapely R. Ross July 7, 1855
	Mathew Leeper Mar. 13, 1857	

TURKEY RIVER SUBAGENCY
1842-1846

The Turkey River Subagency, successor to the Prairie du Chien Subagency, was responsible for the Winnebago Indians living in the "Neutral Ground" in Iowa Territory. This area was a 40-mile strip, running west from the Mississippi River to the Des Moines River, which had been established in 1825 as a buffer zone between the Sioux and the Sauk and Fox. Actually by December, 1840 the Winnebago Indians had moved into this area, and the subagency had been moved from Prairie du Chien to a site on the Turkey River. The agency remained there until 1848. The Bureau adopted the heading "Turkey River" in 1842 for filing purposes but discontinued its use after 1846. These changes in filing practices do not reflect any changes in the operations of the subagency. Until 1842 most correspondence relating to the subagency was filed under the heading "Prairie du Chien." Some letters dated 1842 were filed under "Winnebago." Three letters dated 1846 and all the later correspondence relating to the subagency were filed under Winnebago.

The subagency was transferred from the Wisconsin Superintendency to the Iowa Superintendency in 1841 following the removal of the agency from Prairie du Chien. When Iowa became a state in 1846, the subagency was transferred to the St. Louis Superintendency.

See also Wisconsin, Iowa and St. Louis Superintendencies and Prairie du Chien and Winnebago Agencies.

SUBAGENTS

Name	Date of Appointment
David Lowry	June 5, 1839
James McGregor	July 5, 1844
Jonathan E. Fletcher	June 2, 1845

UNION AGENCY
1875-1880

The Union Agency was established by the consolidation of four separate agencies in Indian Territory, responsible, respectively, for the Cherokee, Creek, Choctaw and Seminole Indians and known by the names of these tribes. The Chickasaw Indians had been attached to the Choctaw Agency since 1855. These five tribes were known collectively as the "Five Civilized Tribes." Living with the Cherokee were Delaware and Shawnee Indians who had moved from Kansas. There were also remnants of other tribes living among the Five Tribes.

The Creek, Choctaw and Seminole Agencies were consolidated with the Cherokee Agency on June 30, 1874. George P. Ingalls, appointed on July 3, 1874, was designated as agent for the Consolidated Agencies of the Cherokees, Creeks, Choctaws, Chickasaws and Seminoles. On December 22, 1874 the name was changed to Union Agency. The Bureau began filing correspondence under this name at the beginning of 1875. Until then the names of the four predecessor agencies had been used, and some correspondence was filed under these names until 1876 (1880 for "Cherokee").

The Union Agency headquarters was at Muskogee in the eastern part of the Creek Nation. The agent ordinarily reported directly to the Bureau of Indian Affairs in Washington. Until the Central Superintendency was abolished in 1878, however, the superintendent had occasional duties concerning the Indians of the Union Agency. These duties related to carrying out the provisions of treaties that required the services of a superintendent, such as the investigation of certain claims, or they were imposed by special instructions from the Bureau.

The Union Agency was abolished on June 30, 1878. It was re-established in August, 1879 and continued to operate beyond 1880.

See also Central Superintendency and Cherokee, Creek, Choctaw, Seminole, Chickasaw, Delaware and Shawnee Agencies. There are a few field records of the Union Agency among the records of the Bureau of Indian Affairs in the National Archives.

AGENTS

Name	*Date of Appointment*
John B. Jones	Appointed to Cherokee Agency, Dec. 9, 1870. Took charge of merged agencies, July 1, 1874
George W. Ingalls	July 3, 1874
Maj. J. J. Upham (acting)	Began service, Jan. 2, 1876
Sylvester W. Marston	Apr. 27, 1876
John Q. Tufts	Aug. 1, 1879

UPPER ARKANSAS AGENCY
1855-1874

The Upper Arkansas Agency was established in 1855 for the Indians living along the upper part of the Arkansas River in what is now eastern Colorado and western Kansas. The Indians living in this area previously had been assigned to the Upper Platte Agency. The Upper Arkansas Agency was responsible principally for the Southern Cheyenne and Arapaho. Originally the agency was also responsible for Kiowa, Comanche and Apache (Kiowa-Apache) Indians, and, after 1862, for some Caddo Indians who left Texas because of the Civil War. In 1864 the Kiowa Agency was established for the Indians other then the Cheyenne and Arapaho who were previously assigned to the Upper Arkansas Agency. From 1865 to 1867, however, the Apache were affiliated with the Cheyenne. The affairs of the Upper Arkansas and Kiowa Agencies remained closely connected until the Indians were moved to Indian Territory.

The Upper Arkansas Agency was assigned to the Central Superintendency until 1861, when it was transferred to the new Colorado Superintendency. Between 1855 and 1861 the agent usually stayed at Bent's Fort on the Arkansas River in Colorado. By the Treaty of Fort Wise of 1861 the Cheyenne and Arapaho ceded their claim to all land except a reservation in southeastern Colorado. During 1861 and 1862 the agent stayed at Fort Wise and thereafter at Fort Lyon. Construction of permanent buildings for the agency on the reservation on the Arkansas River near Fort Lyon was begun, but the project was abandoned because of unsettled conditions made worse by the "Chivington massacre" of a group of Cheyenne at Sand Creek in 1864.

Because the Cheyenne and Arapaho remained nomadic and warlike for several years, the administrative position of the Upper Arkansas Agency was uncertain. By 1866 it had been reassigned to the Central Superintendency. Also in 1866, after a short stay at Fort Zarah, Kansas, the agency headquarters was moved to Fort Larned, Kansas. By a treaty negotiated at Medicine Lodge Creek in 1867, the Cheyenne and Arapaho agreed to move to Indian Territory, but war continued until the following year. In 1869, by an Executive order, a reservation for the Cheyenne and Arapaho was established on the North Fork of the Canadian River.

Agent Darlington, appointed in 1869, first made his headquarters at Camp Supply in Indian Territory and the following year established the permanent headquarters for the Upper Arkansas Agency on the reservation at the site of Darlington. Some Apache who were already living on the reservation were attached to the agency, and beginning in 1874 some Northern Cheyenne were moved to the reservation.

By this time the agency was often called the Cheyenne and Arapahoe Agency rather than the Upper Arkansas Agency. On December 22, 1874 the name change was made official. From 1875 correspondence was filed under the new name.

See also Central and Colorado Superintendencies and Upper Platte, Kiowa, Texas and Cheyenne and Arapahoe Agencies.

AGENTS

Name	Date of Appointment
John W. Whitfield	Mar. 3, 1855
Robert C. Miller	Dec. 27, 1855
William W. Bent	Apr. 27, 1859
Albert G. Boone	Oct. 17, 1860
Samuel G. Colley	July 26, 1861
Ichabod C. Taylor	Aug. 3, 1865
Edward W. Wynkoop	Sept. 20, 1866
Brinton Darlington	Apr. 22, 1869
John D. Miles	Assigned temporarily June 1, 1872; permanent appointment Jan. 23, 1873

UPPER MISSOURI AGENCY
1824-1874

The Upper Missouri Agency was established in 1819. Until 1821 the agency was under the supervision of the Governor of Missouri Territory in his capacity as *ex officio* superintendent of Indian affairs. Beginning in 1822 it was under the St. Louis Superintendency. Until the Bureau of Indian Affairs was established in 1824, correspondence concerning the agency was transmitted directly to the Office of the Secretary of War.

The Upper Missouri agent was not assigned responsibility for any specific Indian tribes but rather for a vaguely defined region along the Missouri River. The Indians living in this area included Pawnee, Oto, Missouri, Omaha, Ponca, Cheyenne, Cree, Crow, Mandan, Arikara, Grosventre, Blackfeet, Assiniboin and several bands of Sioux. In 1824 two subagencies were established in the Upper Missouri area. The Sioux Subagency was located in the vicinity of the Great (or Big) Bend of the Missouri River in the central part of what is now South Dakota. The Mandan Subagency—responsible for the Mandan, Arikara, Grosventre, Cree, Crow and Assiniboin Indians—was located at the Mandan Villages on the Missouri River above the site of Bismarck, North Dakota. The authority exercised by the Upper Missouri Agency over these subagencies varied. Correspondence concerning them is filed under both "Upper Missouri" and "St. Louis." In 1830 the Ioway Subagency for the Iowa and Sauk and Fox of the Missouri was designated as being within the Upper Missouri Agency, but this assignment does not appear to have been carried into practice. In 1834 the Sauk and Fox of the Missouri were transferred to the Prairie du Chien-Sac and Fox Agency and in 1835 to the Upper Missouri Agency.

The Upper Missouri Agency was originally located at Council Bluffs in the present state of Iowa. When the troops were removed from Council Bluffs in 1827, the agency was moved temporarily to Fort Leavenworth. In 1832 the agency was located at Bellevue about 20 miles below Council Bluffs on the other side of the river in the present state of Nebraska. In 1835 the agency was moved again to Fort Leavenworth.

In 1836 the Sioux Subagency, which by this time was virtually independent of the Upper Missouri Agency, was transferred to the new Wisconsin Superintendency. In 1837 the Sioux Subagency, now a full agency under the St. Louis Superintendency, was made responsible for the Sioux, Ponca and Cheyenne Indians of the upper Missouri. Thereafter it was this agency that was known as the Upper Missouri Agency. The old Upper Missouri Agency became the Council Bluffs Agency and was responsible primarily for the Oto, Missouri, Pawnee and Omaha Indians. The subagency at the Mandan Villages continued to operate until 1838, when its functions were absorbed by the Upper Missouri Agency. Most of the Mandan and many of the other Indians previously assigned to the subagency had died of smallpox.

Between 1839 and 1842 there was no agent appointed for the Upper Missouri Agency, and from 1841 to 1843 no correspondence was filed under the heading "Upper Missouri." After the agency was reactivated in 1842, it had no fixed location, and the agent was expected to make frequent trips up and down the Missouri River visiting the several tribes in his charge. In 1849 the agency was reduced to a subagency. In 1851 it was again made a full agency under the Central Superintendency, which had replaced the St. Louis Superintendency. In 1861 the Upper Missouri Agency was transferred to the new Dakota Superintendency. After the Dakota Superintendency was discontinued in 1870, the Upper Missouri agent reported directly to the Bureau of Indian Affairs in Washington.

In 1866 a permanent location for the agency office was selected near Crow Creek below the Great Bend of the Missouri. This area had just been abandoned by the Santee Sioux of the St. Peters Agency who had moved to Nebraska. By this time the jurisdiction of the Upper Missouri Agency was restricted principally to the Lower Yanktonai Sioux at Crow Creek and the Lower Brulé who lived a few miles farther down the Missouri River. Until 1868 some Two Kettle (Oohenonpa) Sioux lived at the agency.

After 1866 the Upper Missouri Agency was commonly called the Crow Creek Agency, and on December 22, 1874 the change in name was made official. Beginning in 1875 correspondence relating to the agency was filed under the new name. Some correspondence, however, had been filed under "Crow Creek" as early as 1871. For the years 1837-49 there is some correspondence, relating mainly to lands reserved for Sioux Indians, filed under the subheading "Upper Missouri Reserves."

The creation of new agencies resulted in a reduction in the jurisdiction of the Upper Missouri Agency. The Upper Platte Agency, established in 1846, assumed responsibility for the Cheyenne and some of the wandering Sioux bands, as well as Arapaho, Kiowa, Comanche and other Indians. The Blackfeet Agency was established in 1855 and took charge of many of the Blackfeet (Siksika), Piegan, Blood (Kainah) and Grosventre Indians. After 1859 the Yankton Agency had charge of the Yankton Sioux. Also in 1859 a separate agency was established for the Ponca Indians who had been without an agency for several years.

In 1864 the Upper Missouri Agency was divided. A new agent was assigned to the Assiniboin, Mandan, Grosventre, Arikara and Crow Indians living around Fort Berthold and Fort Union in the present state of North Dakota and in eastern Montana, leaving the incumbent agent in charge of the Sioux Indians not assigned to other agencies. The correspondence relating to both of these agencies was filed under "Upper Missouri" until 1867, after which correspondence concerning the new agency was filed under "Fort Berthold."

Between 1865 and 1868 a series of treaties was negotiated with many of the Sioux and other Indians who roamed the upper Missouri and Platte regions. New agencies were established for the Indians who agreed to move onto reserves established under these treaties. Established in 1869 were the Grand River Agency, principally for Yanktonai, Hunkpapa, Cuthead (Pabaska) and Blackfeet Sioux; the Whetstone Agency, for Chief Spotted Tail's band of Brulé Sioux; and the Cheyenne River Agency, for Miniconjou, Sans Arcs, Two Kettle (Oohenonpa) and Blackfeet Sioux. The Red Cloud Agency for the Oglala Sioux was established in 1871.

See also St. Louis, Central, Wisconsin and Dakota Superintendencies, Council Bluffs, St. Peters, Upper Platte, Blackfeet, Yankton, Ponca, Fort Berthold, Cheyenne River, Whetstone, Grand River, Red Cloud and Crow Creek Agencies and Ioway Subagency.

AGENTS

Upper Missouri Agency

Name	*Date of Appointment*
Benjamin O'Fallon	Mar. 8, 1819
John Dougherty	Jan. 22, 1827
Joshua Pilcher	Mar. 8, 1837
Andrew Dripps	Aug. 31, 1842
Thomas P. Moore	Mar. 31, 1846
Gideon C. Matlock	Mar. 3, 1847

Upper Missouri Agency (cont.)

Samuel A. Hatten (subagent)	Apr. 12, 1849
James H. Norwood	Aug. 2, 1851
Robert B. Lambdin	Nov. 10, 1852
Alfred J. Vaughn	Apr. 18, 1853
Alexander H. Redfield	May 23, 1857
Bernard S. Schoonover	Mar. 29, 1859
Samuel N. Latta	Aug. 3, 1861
Mahlon Wilkinson	Mar. 2, 1864
Appointed in addition to Latta	
(Fort Berthold Agency)	
Joseph R. Hanson	Mar. 21, 1866
Capt. W. H. French	June 25, 1869
Henry F. Livingston	Oct. 18, 1870

Sioux Subagency

George Kennerly	June 7, 1824
Andrew S. Hughes	Apr. 2, 1828
Jonathan Bean	Transferred from Ioway Subagency, Sept. 5, 1828
Joshua Pilcher	Notified Mar. 5, 1835

Mandan Subagency

Peter Wilson	June 7, 1824
John F. A. Sandford	June 30, 1826
William N. Fulkerson	Notified Mar. 5, 1835

UPPER PLATTE AGENCY
1846-1870

The Upper Platte Agency was established in 1846 with Thomas Fitzpatrick as agent. The agency originally included the upper Arkansas River area as well as the upper Platte, and within its jurisdiction there were large parts of present Kansas, Colorado, Nebraska and Wyoming. The principal Indian tribes living in this area were Cheyenne, Arapaho, Kiowa, Comanche, Apache (Kiowa-Apache) and several bands of Sioux. Other tribes came in occasionally. For the most part these Indians had never been under Bureau control, although the Upper Missouri Agency—which lay farther north—had contacts with them and, at least nominally, they were under the jurisdiction of the St. Louis Superintendency.

The Indians of the Upper Platte Agency were nomadic, and for many years the agent had no permanent headquarters. Agent Fitzpatrick spent much of his time along the Arkansas River and used Bent's Fort (near present La Junta, Colorado) as a base. In 1855 a separate Upper Arkansas Agency was established. The new agency assumed responsibility for the Southern Cheyenne and Arapaho, Kiowa, Comanche and Apache, which left the Northern Cheyenne and Arapaho and the Sioux, principally Oglala and Brulé, with the Upper Platte Agency. Fort Laramie was the principal outpost in the area, and at various times the agent remained in its vicinity. From 1857 until 1861 the agency headquarters was on Deer Creek about 110 miles west of Fort Laramie. In 1861 the agent moved nearer to Fort Laramie, and in 1863 agency buildings were built on the North Platte River about 25 miles east of Fort Laramie. In 1867 the agent established himself in North Platte, Nebraska. Special agents were sent occasionally to the Fort Laramie region. In December, 1868 the Upper Platte Agency was moved to the mouth of Whetstone Creek on the Missouri River, 18 miles from Fort Randall in Dakota Territory.

The Upper Platte Agency was assigned to the St. Louis Superintendency until 1851, when the Central Superintendency replaced the St. Louis Superintendency. In 1865 the agency was transferred to the Northern Superintendency, and in June, 1869 it was transferred to the Dakota Superintendency and renamed the Whetstone Agency. Although the Whetstone Agency was responsible principally for the band of Brulé led by Chief Spotted Tail, there were also other Brulé and Oglala and Miniconjou Sioux under its jurisdiction. The Grand River and Cheyenne River Agencies were also established in June, 1869. The Grand River Agency was located at the junction of the Grand River with the Missouri River in the present state of North Dakota and was responsible for Yanktonai, Hunkpapa, Cuthead (Pabaska) and Blackfeet Sioux. The Cheyenne River Agency was located on the west bank of the Missouri below the mouth of the Big Cheyenne River about six miles from Fort Sully in the present state of

South Dakota and was responsible for Miniconjou, Sans Arcs, Two Kettle (Oohenonpa) and Blackfeet Sioux. Correspondence concerning all three of these agencies was filed under the "Upper Platte" heading during 1869 and 1870. There is also correspondence concerning the Oglala Sioux led by Red Cloud and the Cheyenne and Arapaho who were then living in the vicinity of Fort Laramie and were not under the control of any agency. In 1871 separate file headings were established for each of the three agencies. In the same year the Red Cloud Agency was established near Fort Laramie for the Sioux, Cheyenne and Arapaho Indians there. The "Upper Platte" heading was discontinued at the beginning of 1871.

See also St. Louis, Central, Northern, Dakota and Wyoming Superintendencies and Upper Missouri, Upper Arkansas, Whetstone, Cheyenne River, Grand River, Red Cloud, Kiowa and Cheyenne and Arapaho Agencies.

AGENTS

Upper Platte Agency

Name	*Date of Appointment*
Thomas Fitzpatrick	Aug. 3, 1846
John W. Whitfield	Apr. 3, 1854
Thomas S. Twiss	Mar. 3, 1855
Joseph A. Cody	May 14, 1861
John Loree	Apr. 14, 1862
Vital Jerrott	Mar. 3, 1865
Mathewson T. Patrick	Aug. 3, 1866

Whetstone Agency, 1869-70

Capt. DeWitt C. Poole	June 14, 1869
John M. Washburn	Oct. 18, 1870

Cheyenne River Agency, 1869-70

Bvt. Maj. George M. Randall (special)	June 14, 1869
J. Lee Engelbert (special)	Oct. 19, 1870
Percival B. Spear (special)	Dec. 16, 1870

Grand River Agency, 1869-70

Bvt. Maj. J. A. Hearn (special)	June 14, 1869
William F. Cady (special)	Sept. 30, 1870

For complete lists of agents of the Whetstone, Cheyenne River and Grand River Agencies, see the sketches for these agencies.

UTAH SUPERINTENDENCY
1849-1880

The Utah Superintendency (preceded by the Salt Lake Agency from March, 1849 until the Territory of Utah was organized in September, 1850) was established at Salt Lake City to supervise the Ute, Paiute, Shoshoni, Bannock, Pahvant and other Indians who lived in the Great Basin area between the Rocky and Sierra Nevada Mountains. The Territorial Governor acted as *ex officio* superintendent until 1857, when a full-time superintendent was appointed.

By 1855 there were for Utah two agencies and some subagents. One agency was established in 1851 and the other in 1855. The agents did not have specific assignments, but one usually made his headquarters at Salt Lake City and the other at Provo. Gradually three permanent agencies were established: Spanish Fork-Uintah Valley (Ute Indians), Fort Bridger (Shoshoni and Bannock) and Carson Valley (Paiute and Washo).

The jurisdiction of the Utah Superintendency was reduced with the creation of the new Territories and Superintendencies of Nevada and Colorado in 1861 and of Wyoming in 1868. In 1862 and 1866 additional parts of Utah were transferred to Nevada. By 1869 only the Uintah Valley Agency was left in Utah. The Utah Superintendency was abolished in 1870, and thereafter the agents reported directly to the Bureau of Indian Affairs in Washington. Until the change of filing systems in 1881, however, correspondence relating to the Uintah Valley Agency was filed under the heading "Utah."

See also California, Nevada, Wyoming, Colorado, New Mexico and Arizona Superintendencies. There are also field records of the Utah Superintendency among the records of the Bureau of Indian Affairs in the National Archives.

SPANISH FORK-UINTAH VALLEY AGENCY

This agency was a continuation of the agency established in 1851. Until 1859 the agent usually stayed at Salt Lake City. In that year the agency was moved to the Spanish Fork Reservation for the Ute Indians, and in 1865 it was moved to Uintah Valley. The Uintah Valley Agency continued to operate beyond 1880.

FORT BRIDGER AGENCY

The Fort Bridger Agency was a continuation of the agency that was located at Provo in 1855. It was moved to Fort Bridger in 1861 and given jurisdiction over the Shoshoni and Bannock Indians. In 1869 the agency was transferred to the Wyoming Superintendency.

CARSON VALLEY AGENCY

The Carson Valley Agency was established in 1858 for the Paiute and Washo Indians in the western part of the Territory. In 1861 the agency was transferred to the Nevada Superintendency.

SPECIAL AGENTS AND COMMISSIONS

During 1871 and 1872 George Dodge acted as special agent for the Western, Northwestern and Goship Shoshoni Indians. In 1873 John W. Powell and George W. Ingalls were sent as special commissioners to negotiate with the Ute Indians.

AGENTS OF THE SALT LAKE AGENCY

Name	Date of Appointment
John Wilson	Mar. 30, 1849
Edward Cooper	Aug. 30, 1850

SUPERINTENDENTS

Brigham Young (Governor and *Ex Officio* Superintendent)	Sept. 28, 1850
Jacob Forney	Aug. 27, 1857
Benjamin Davies	June 21, 1860
Henry Martin	May 1, 1861
James D. Doty	Sept. 23, 1861
Thomas A. Marshall	Appointed July 27, 1863, but did not serve
Orsamus H. Irish	Feb. 2, 1864
Franklin H. Head	Mar. 21, 1866
Bvt. Col. J. E. Tourtellotte	June 10, 1869

AGENTS

Spanish Fork-Uintah Valley Agency

At Salt Lake City

Jacob H. Holeman	Mar. 12, 1851
Edward A. Bedell	Apr. 18, 1853
Garland Hurt	Aug. 4, 1854

At Spanish Fork

Andrew Humphries	Jan. 19, 1859
Frederick W. Hatch	July 16, 1861
Lathrop B. Kinney	June 7, 1864

At Uintah Valley

Lathrop B. Kinney	June 7, 1864 for the Spanish Fork Agency
Dudley W. Rhodes	July 13, 1866
Pardon Dodds	Feb. 10, 1868
Lt. George Graffam	June 25, 1869
John J. Critchlow	Oct. 21, 1870

Fort Bridger Agency

At Provo

George W. Armstrong	June 8, 1855
Columbus L. Craig	Jan. 6, 1858
Robert B. Jarvis	Oct. 14, 1858
William H. Rogers	Aug. 19, 1859
William L. Brown	Appointed Apr. 29, 1861, but did not serve

At Fort Bridger

Luther Mann	July 30, 1861

Carson Valley Agency

Frederick Dodge	June 12, 1858

WASHINGTON SUPERINTENDENCY 1853-1880

The Washington Superintendency was established in 1853, the year Washington Territory was organized. Previously the Washington area had been included in the Oregon Superintendency. Washington originally included the area north of the Columbia River and the 36th parallel and west of the Continental Divide. When Oregon became a state in 1859, the eastern part of the former Territory of Oregon was transferred to Washington Territory, which included all of present Idaho and parts of Montana and Wyoming. With the organization of Idaho Territory in 1863, Washington was reduced to the boundaries of the present state. Between 1857 and 1861 the Oregon and Washington Superintendencies were combined. The correspondence relating to the consolidated superintendency is filed with that for the Oregon Superintendency.

There were many groups of Indians in Washington, including Makah, Skokomish, Yakima, Colville, Puyallup, Tulalip, Nisqualli, Nez Percé, Flathead, Spokan, Pend d'Oreille, Cayuse, Paloos, Wallawalla, Quinaielt, Blackfeet, Chehalis, Chilkat, Chinook, Clackamas, Clallam, Lake, Klikitat, Coeur d'Alène, Cowlitz, Dwamish, Lummi, Muckleshoot, Quileute, Quaitso (Queet), Squaxon and Swinomish.

The superintendency headquarters was located at Olympia, the territorial capital, except while Oregon and Washington Superintendencies were combined from 1857 to 1861, when headquarters was at Salem and Portland in Oregon. Before the consolidation the Territorial Governor served as *ex officio* superintendent; thereafter there was a full-time superintendent. After the Washington Superintendency was abolished in 1874, the agents reported directly to the Bureau of Indian Affairs in Washington, D.C. Until the change of filing systems in 1881, however, correspondence relating to the separate agencies in Washington was filed under the heading "Washington" rather than under the names of the individual agencies.

The first agents in Washington were usually assigned by the superintendent on a geographic basis. After a series of treaties negotiated between 1854 and 1856, the Indians who had agreed to a particular treaty often were assigned to one agency. The agencies in Washington were Puget Sound District, Columbia River District, Flathead (Eastern District), Nez Percé (Washington East of the Cascades), Yakima, Puyallup (Nisqually), Tulalip, Skokomish (Sklallam), Neah Bay, Umatilla, Quinaielt and Colville. There were also numerous special agencies, subagencies and local agencies.

See also Oregon, Idaho and Montana Superintendencies and Blackfeet Agency. There are also field records of the Washington Superintendency among the records of the Bureau of Indian Affairs in the National Archives, many of which have been reproduced by the National Archives and Records Service as Microfilm Publication 5. The introduction prepared for this microcopy by James R. Masterson gives a more detailed administrative history of the Washington Superintendency. Part of this introduction has been published under the title, "Research Suggestions, The Records of the Washington Superintendency of Indian Affairs, 1853-74," Pacific Northwest Quarterly, *XXXVII (1946), 31-57.*

PUGET SOUND DISTRICT AGENCY

The Puget Sound District Agency, established in 1851 under the Oregon Superintendency, was located at Steilacoom and was responsible for all of the Indians in the Puget Sound area. It was transferred to the new Washington Superintendency in 1853, after which the agent made his headquarters at Olympia.

On December 1, 1856 the Indians at the head of Puget Sound who had agreed to the Treaty of Medicine Creek were placed under the supervision of Special Agent Wesley Gosnell. From time to time other groups of Indians were assigned to special agents, subagents or local agents who were either under the Puget Sound agent or responsible directly to the superintendent. During 1861 and 1862 the Puyallup, Tulalip, Neah Bay, Skokomish and Quinaielt Agencies were formed from the Puget Sound District, and the Puget Sound Agency ceased to exist.

COLUMBIA RIVER (SOUTHERN) DISTRICT AGENCY

The Columbia River or Southern District Agency was established in 1854 for the Indians living on the Washington side of the Columbia River and south of the Skookumchuck and Chehalis Rivers. The agency headquarters, usually at Vancouver, was moved to the White Salmon Reservation in 1858. In 1859 the agency was moved to Fort Simcoe on the Yakima Reservation and thereafter it was called the Yakima Agency.

FLATHEAD (EASTERN DISTRICT) AGENCY

The Flathead Agency, known briefly as the Eastern District Agency, was established in 1854 for the Indians living between the Cascade and Bitter Root Mountains, particularly the Flatheads, Kutenai and Upper Pend d'Oreille. The agency was located at the junction of the Flathead and Jocko Rivers. The Flathead Agency was discontinued after the Oregon and Washington Superintendencies were consolidated and the agent was designated agent for Washington East of the Cascades. A special agent or subagent was assigned to the Flatheads until 1861, when they were again given a full agent. The Flathead Agency was transferred to the Idaho Superintendency in 1863.

NEZ PERCÉ
(WASHINGTON EAST OF THE CASCADES) AGENCY

Subagents were assigned to the Nez Percé and neighboring tribes as early as 1855. When the Flathead Agency was discontinued in 1857, its agent was stationed at The Dalles and assigned to Washington East of the Cascade Mountains. He was made responsible particularly for the Nez Percé, Flathead and Coeur d'Alène Indians. The following year the agency was moved to the Walla Walla Valley and was responsible chiefly for the Nez Percé, Cayuse and Paloos, and, at times, for Spokan and Coeur d'Alène Indians. After 1861 the agent usually stayed at Lapwai on the Nez Percé Reservation in present Idaho and the agency was usually called the Nez Percé Agency. From 1862 until the agency was transferred to the Idaho Superintendency in 1863, a subagent was in charge.

YAKIMA AGENCY

The Yakima Agency (usually spelled "Yakama" at the time), established in 1859, was the successor to the Columbia River District Agency. It was located at Fort Simcoe on the Yakima Reservation and it continued in operation beyond 1880.

PUYALLUP AGENCY

The Puyallup Agency was the outgrowth of the special agency established on December 1, 1856, for the various bands of Indians living around the head of Puget Sound who had agreed to the Treaty of Medicine Creek in 1854. It was definitely established as a distinct agency by 1861. Principally, it had charge of the Indians living on the Puyallup, Nisqually and Squaxin Reservations, although sometimes other reservations—notably Chehalis—were included in its jurisdiction. The agency was originally located on the Squaxin Reservation on Squaxin Island, but the agent spent much of his time at Olympia, and in effect this became the agency headquarters.

Between 1865 and 1869 one agent was assigned to both the Puyallup and Tulalip Agencies. From 1869 until the Washington Superintendency was discontinued in 1874, the Indians on the reservations established under the Treaty of Medicine Creek were under the immediate control of the superintendent. The Puyallup Agency, now sometimes called the Nisqually Agency, was reactivated in 1874, and the agent established himself at Olympia. The agency had charge of the Indians living on the Puyallup, Nisqually, Squaxin, Muckleshoot, Shoalwater Bay and Chehalis Reservations. In 1882 the Puyallup Agency was consolidated with the Skokomish Agency and briefly that same year with the Tulalip Agency.

TULALIP AGENCY

The Tulalip Agency was established in 1861 for the bands of Indians who had agreed to the Treaty of Point Elliot (1855), mainly those Indians living on the eastern side of Puget Sound. It had charge of the Indians living on the Tulalip, Port Madison, Swimonish (Perry's Island) and Lummi Reservations. Although the Muckleshoot Reservation was also established under the Treaty of Point Elliot, most of the time it was under the jurisdiction of the Puyallup Agency. The Tulalip agent usually made his headquarters on the Tulalip Reservation.

From 1865 to 1869 there was one agent for both the Tulalip and Puyallup Agencies. The Tulalip Agency continued in operation beyond 1880, except for a brief consolidation with the Puyallup and Skokomish Agencies in 1882.

NEAH BAY AGENCY

The Neah Bay Agency for the Makah and Quileute Indians living on the Makah Reservation was established at Neah Bay in 1861. It remained in operation beyond 1880.

SKOKOMISH (SKLALLAM) AGENCY

The Skokomish Agency, also known as the Sklallam Agency, for the Skokomish, Clallam (Sklallam) and other Indians who were parties to the Treaty of Point No Point in 1855 was established as a subagency in 1862. A full agent was assigned to the agency in 1868. The agency was located on the Skokomish Reservation at the confluence of Hood's Canal and the Skokomish River. In 1882 it was consolidated with the Puyallup Agency and, temporarily, with the Tulalip Agency.

UMATILLA AGENCY

The Umatilla Agency for the Umatilla, Cayuse and Wallawalla Indians living on the Umatilla Reservation in northeastern Oregon was under the Oregon Superintendency except for a few months in 1861 and 1862, when it was placed under the Washington Superintendency.

QUINAIELT AGENCY

The Quinaielt Subagency was established in 1861 for the Quinaielt and Quileute Indians who had agreed to the Treaty of Olympia in 1856. In 1863 the agency was moved about ten miles from its original site on the Quinaielt Reservation to the mouth of the Quinaielt River. After 1874 Quinaielt was a special agency rather than a subagency; in 1878 it was made a full agency. The Quinaielt Agency continued in operation beyond 1880.

COLVILLE AGENCY

The Colville Agency at Fort Colville for the Colville, Lake, Spokan, Coeur d'Alène and other Indians living on the Colville Reservation and the Coeur d'Alène Reservation in Idaho was established as a special agency in 1872. In 1875 it was made a regular agency. It continued in operation beyond 1880.

GOVERNOR AND *EX OFFICIO* SUPERINTENDENT

Name	*Date of Appointment*
Isaac I. Stevens	Mar. 17, 1853

SUPERINTENDENTS
Oregon and Washington

James W. Nesmith	Mar. 12, 1857
Edward R. Geary	Mar. 22, 1859

Washington

William W. Miller	Feb. 21, 1861
Bion F. Kendall	July 16, 1861
Calvin H. Hale	Mar. 6, 1862
William H. Waterman	May 21, 1864
Thomas J. McKenny	Sept. 25, 1866
Bvt. Col. Samuel Ross	June 10, 1869
Thomas J. McKenny	Reinstated Oct. 22, 1870
Robert H. Milroy	June 6, 1872

AGENTS
Puget Sound District Agency

Edmund A. Starling	July 10, 1851
Joseph M. Garrison	Mar. 22, 1853
Michael T. Simmons (special)	Mar. 9, 1854
Michael T. Simmons (agent)	Feb. 27, 1856
Wesley B. Gosnell	Nov. 21, 1860 Relieved Simmons Apr. 15, 1861. *See Puyallup.*

Puget Sound District Agency (cont.)

George A. Paige   Feb. 21, 1861. Appointed in addition to Gosnell. Jurisdiction varied. Both served until 1862.

Columbia River (Southern) District

William H. Tappan (special)   May 1, 1854
William H. Tappan (subagent)   Sept. 4, 1854
John Cain   Jan. 5, 1855
Richard H. Lansdale   Transferred from Washington East of Cascades, Apr. 1, 1858

Flathead (Eastern District) Agency

Thomas Adams (special)   Jan. 1, 1854
Richard H. Lansdale   Aug. 4, 1854
John Owen (special)   Oct. 13, 1856
John Owen (subagent)   Notified Nov. 17, 1858

John Owen (agent)   Feb. 21, 1861
Charles Hutchins   Transferred from Nez Percé Agency, Sept. 30, 1862

Nez Percé (Washington East of Cascades) Agency

At The Dalles

Richard H. Lansdale   Transferred from Flathead Agency, June 2, 1857

At Walla Walla and Lapwai

Andrew J. Cain   Aug. 19, 1858
Charles Hutchins   June 13, 1861
John W. Anderson (subagent)   Aug. 23, 1862

Yakima Agency

Richard H. Lansdale   Moved from Columbia River District June 2, 1859

Yakima Agency (cont.)

Ashley A. Bancroft   May 14, 1861
James H. Wilbur   June 4, 1864
Lt. James M. Smith   June 22, 1869
James H. Wilbur   Reinstated Apr. 22,
             1870

Puyallup Agency

Wesley B. Gosnell (special) Dec. 1, 1856
Wesley B. Gosnell (subagent) Nov. 16, 1858
Wesley B. Gosnell (agent)   Nov. 21, 1860 (for
             Puget Sound Dis-
             trict)

Ezra Baker   July 16, 1861
Alfred R. Elder   May 9, 1863
Henry C. Hale (subagent)   June 1, 1868 (Puyal-
             lup and Tulalip)
             (No agent Aug., 1896-
             July, 1874)

Hiram Gibson   July 11, 1874
Robert H. Milroy   Aug. 27, 1875

Tulalip Agency

Benjamin F. Shaw   Feb. 21, 1861
Samuel D. Howe   Jan. 22, 1862
Alfred R. Elder   Appointed to Puyal-
             lup Agency May 9,
             1863. Also assigned
             to Tulalip Sept.
             30, 1865.

Henry C. Hale (subagent)   June 1, 1868 (Puyal-
             lup and Tulalip)

Lt. George D. Hill (subagent) July 8, 1869
Eugene D. Chirouse (subagent) Feb. 20, 1871
Edmond Mallet (special)   July 24, 1876
Alfred Marion (special)   Nov. 1, 1877
John O'Keane   Nov. 25, 1878

Neah Bay Agency

Henry A. Webster   July 16, 1861
Bvt. Capt. Joseph H. Hays June 11, 1869
Elkanah M. Gibson   Apr. 12, 1871
Charles A. Huntington   Jan. 23, 1874

Neah Bay Agency (cont.)

Lt. George D. Hill (acting)	Sept. 23, 1877
Charles Willoughby	Feb. 6, 1878

Skokomish (Sklallam) Agency

Franklin C. Purdy (subagent)	July 15, 1862
John T. Knox (subagent)	June 1, 1864
Charles S. King	Mar. 16, 1868
Lt. Joseph M. Kelley	June 22, 1869
Charles S. King	Reinstated Oct. 1, 1870
Edwin Eells	Apr. 17, 1871

Umatilla Agency

William H. Barnhart	July 16, 1861

Quinaielt Agency

Subagents

John W. Anderson	Aug. 12, 1861
Giles Ford	July 1, 1862
Joseph Hill	Dec. 31, 1864
Henry Winsor	June 8, 1868
Bvt. Maj. Thomas H. Hay	July 15, 1869
Gordon A. Henry	Dec. 12, 1870

Special Agents

Gordon A. Henry	July 15, 1874
Oliver Wood	Feb. 6, 1878

Agents

Oliver Wood	July 1, 1878

Colville Agency

John A. Simms (special)	July 1, 1872
John A. Simms (agent)	Feb. 10, 1875

WESTERN SUPERINTENDENCY 1832-1851

The Western Superintendency was established in 1834 in accordance with an act of Congress of June 30, 1834 (4 Stat. 735). The jurisdiction of the superintendency extended west of the Mississippi River to the Rocky Mountains and south from the borders of the St. Louis Superintendency (the northern boundary of the land of the Osage Indians). The principal tribes originally in the superintendency were Choctaw, Cherokee, Creek, Osage, Seneca and Mixed Band of Seneca and Shawnee. Quapaw, Seminole and Chickasaw Indians moved in within a few years. On occasion the Western superintendent had some responsibility relating to Caddo, Kiowa, Comanche and other Indians.

The correspondence filed under the name of the superintendency for the years between 1832 and 1834 relates principally to the activities of a commission consisting of Montford Stokes, John F. Schermerhorn and Henry L. Ellsworth, who were appointed to negotiate with the various tribes in the West.

The Western Superintendency was an acting superintendency with the extra duties of the superintendent detailed to the agent for the Choctaw Indians. The superintendency headquarters was at the Choctaw Agency near Fort Coffee in the eastern part of present Oklahoma. Originally there was only one agency in the superintendency. Designated as the Southern Agency, it was really a continuation of the agency established in 1831 for the Choctaw Indians living west of the Mississippi, and after 1837 it was again known as the Choctaw Agency. There was also a Northern Agency, but this agency was in the St. Louis Superintendency. Three subagencies assigned to the Western Superintendency were responsible, respectively, for the Creek, Cherokee and Osage Indians. The Cherokee Subagency was also responsible for the Seneca and Mixed Band of Seneca and Shawnee, and the Osage Agency was responsible for the Quapaw Indians.

The Western Superintendency was reorganized in 1837. In addition to the Choctaw (formerly Southern) Agency, full agencies were established for the Cherokee and the Creek Indians. The Seminole Indians were attached to the Creek Agency. The Neosho Subagency was established for the Quapaw, Seneca and Seneca and Shawnee Indians, leaving the Osage Subagency responsible only for the Osage Indians. In 1839 the Chickasaw Agency was established for the Chickasaw Indians who had moved west onto Choctaw land. A separate subagency was established for the Seminole in 1842. The Osage Subagency was transferred to the St. Louis Superintendency in 1843, it was returned to the Western Superintendency in 1847, and it was transferred again to the St. Louis Superintendency in 1849. In 1851 the Western Superintendency was replaced by the Southern Superintendency.

Separate file headings were maintained by the Bureau for the individual agencies in the Western Superintendency. One should consult both the superintendency and the agency headings, however, to find all the correspondence relating to an agency. Some correspondence for the years 1836-42 is filed under the subheading "Western Superintendency Emigration." It relates to the removal of Indians to the jurisdiction of the Western Superintendency. Many other letters on this subject are with the general correspondence relating to the superintendency and with the correspondence relating to the individual agencies.

See also St. Louis and Southern Superintendencies and Choctaw, Cherokee, Creek, Chickasaw, Osage, Neosho, Seminole, Caddo and Fort Leavenworth Agencies. There are also field records of the Western Superintendency among the records of the Bureau of Indian Affairs in the National Archives, which have been reproduced by the National Archives and Records Service as part of Microfilm Publication 640.

SUPERINTENDENTS

Name	*Date of Appointment*
Francis W. Armstrong	June 30, 1834
William Armstrong	Sept. 8, 1835
Samuel M. Rutherford	July 10, 1847
John Drennen	May 29, 1849

WHETSTONE AGENCY
1871-1874

The Whetstone Agency succeeded the Upper Platte Agency, which in December, 1868 was moved from the Platte River area to the mouth of Whetstone Creek on the Missouri River (about 18 miles from Fort Randall in present South Dakota). In June, 1869 the agency was transferred from the Northern Superintendency to the Dakota Superintendency and renamed the Whetstone Agency. Through 1870, however, correspondence was filed under the heading "Upper Platte." The Whetstone Agency was responsible primarily for the band of Brulé Sioux led by Spotted Tail, but other bands of Sioux, including Brulé, Oglala and Miniconjou, also lived near the agency.

In June, 1871 the Whetstone Agency was moved to Big White Clay Creek, a tributary of the White River. In November it was moved to the White River near the Dakota-Nebraska boundary, where it remained until 1875.

On December 22, 1874 the name of the Whetstone Agency was changed to Spotted Tail Agency. Beginning in 1875 correspondence was filed under the new name.

See also Dakota Superintendency and Upper Platte, Spotted Tail and Red Cloud Agencies.

AGENTS

Name	*Date of Appointment*
Capt. DeWitt C. Poole	June 14, 1869
John M. Washburn	Oct. 18, 1870
D. R. Risley	Nov. 23, 1871
Edwin A. Howard	Mar. 24, 1873

WICHITA AGENCY
1857-1878

The Wichita Agency was established in 1857 under the Southern Superintendency for the Wichita and other Indians who were to live in the Leased District. The Leased District was an area in Indian Territory, between the 98th and 100th meridians, which the United States had leased from the Choctaw and Chickasaw in 1855 for the settlement of various tribes. Wichita and Kichai (Keechi) Indians were already living in the Leased District, but in 1858 they were driven by Comanche Indians farther east to the Fort Arbuckle area. They returned to the Leased District in 1859. In the same year Caddo, Anadarko, Waco, Tonkawa, Hainai (Ioni), Kichai, Tawakoni, Delaware and Shawnee Indians were moved from the Brazos Agency in Texas and Penateka Comanche were moved from the Comanche Agency in Texas into the Leased District. Between 1873 and 1875 some Pawnee who had moved from Nebraska were at the Wichita Agency before moving to their new reservation in Indian Territory.

From 1857 until 1859 the Wichita Agency had no permanent headquarters, but the agent usually stayed at Fort Arbuckle. During this period correspondence concerning the Wichita and Texas Agencies is closely related. It is necessary to consult the headings for both agencies for correspondence relating to either of them. The heading "Texas" was discontinued in 1859, and correspondence concerning the settlement of affairs in Texas is filed with the correspondence relating to the Wichita Agency.

With the removal of the Indians to the Leased District in 1859, the agency was permanently located near the site of Fort Cobb on the Washita River. During the Civil War the Indian Territory was occupied by Confederate troops. The Wichita agent remained at his post as agent for the Confederate government, but in 1862 most of the Indians fled to Kansas. When agents appointed for the Wichita Agency by the United States in 1861 and 1862 were unable to reach the agency, temporary headquarters were established in Kansas. The agent usually stayed at Towanda in Butler County, east of the site of Wichita.

In 1867 the agent and the Indians, except for the Shawnee who joined other groups of Absentee Shawnee under the Sac and Fox Agency, returned to the Leased District and the agency was relocated near the site of Anadarko. During 1869 and 1870 the Wichita Agency was consolidated with the Kiowa Agency at Fort Sill, also in the Leased District. The Kiowa Agency was then under the Central Superintendency and when the Wichita Agency was re-established in 1870, it was also assigned to the Central Superintendency, where it remained until the closing of the superintendency in 1878. Thereafter the agent reported directly to the Bureau of Indian Affairs in Washington. On September 1, 1878 the Wichita Agency was again consolidated with the Kiowa Agency, although the headquarters of the Kiowa Agency was soon moved to Anadarko. The Kiowa Agency remained in operation beyond 1880.

See also Southern and Central Superintendencies and Texas, Kiowa, Shawnee and Sac and Fox Agencies. There are with the records of the Southern Superintendency some field records of the Wichita Agency, including some for the period of Confederate control. They have been reproduced by the National Archives and Records Service as part of Microfilm Publication 640.

AGENTS

Name	*Date of Appointment*
Alexander H. McKisick	Mar. 12, 1857
Samuel A. Blain	July 6, 1858
Mathew Leeper	July 26, 1860
John J. Humphries	Apr. 19, 1861
Edwin H. Carruth	Mar. 6, 1862
Milo Gookins	July 22, 1864
Henry Shanklin	Apr. 26, 1866
Laurie Tatum	Kiowa agent put in charge of the Wichita Agency, May 19, 1869

Jonathan Richards   July 21, 1870
Andrew C. Williams   Jan. 19, 1876

WINNEBAGO AGENCY
1826-1876

The heading "Winnebago" was not used regularly for the correspondence relating to the principal agency for the Winnebago Indians until 1847. The correspondence dated before 1830 relates to Winnebago Indians rather than to the affairs of any one agency. The letters from 1830 to 1836 relate primarily to two subagencies for the Winnebago Indians that operated independently of the main agency at Prairie du Chien.

The first of these subagencies, the Fort Winnebago Subagency, was established in 1828 for the Winnebago Indians living in the vicinity of the portage of the Fox and Wisconsin Rivers. This subagency was assigned to the Michigan Superintendency until Wisconsin Territory was established in 1836, when it was transferred to the Wisconsin Superintendency. After 1834 the commanding officer at Fort Winnebago acted as subagent. The Fort Winnebago Subagency was consolidated with the Prairie du Chien Subagency in 1837.

The second of the subagencies, the Rock River Subagency, was established in 1831 at Sugar Creek for the Winnebago Indians living along Rock River. It was assigned to the St. Louis Superintendency until 1832, when it was transferred to the Michigan Superintendency. The Rock River Subagency was discontinued in 1834. After 1837 the Prairie du Chien Subagency was responsible for all the Winnebago Indians.

Much of the correspondence relating to the Fort Winnebago and Rock River Subagencies is filed under the heading "Prairie du Chien" rather than under "Winnebago," and some is filed under the names of the supervising superintendencies, St. Louis, Michigan and Wisconsin. Between 1837 and 1841 the "Winnebago" heading was not used, although a few letters for this period are filed under the subheadings "Winnebago Emigration" and "Winnebago Reserves." Letters dated 1842 concerning the subagency for the Winnebago are filed under three different headings: "Prairie du Chien," "Winnebago" and

"Turkey River." The subagency had been moved from Prairie du Chien, Wisconsin to the Turkey River in Iowa and was assigned to the Iowa Superintendency. From 1843 through 1845 only the heading "Turkey River" was used, except for some letters filed under "Winnebago Emigration" and "Winnebago Reserves." The "Prairie du Chien" heading was discontinued permanently. For 1846 there were three letters filed under "Winnebago," with the remaining correspondence filed under "Turkey River." From 1847 only the heading "Winnebago" was used. When Iowa became a state in 1846, the Winnebago or Turkey River Subagency was transferred from the discontinued Iowa Superintendency to the St. Louis Superintendency. The subagency remained at Turkey River, however, and the change in file designation did not reflect any changes in the operation of the agency.

In 1848 the Winnebago did move to a new home in central Minnesota west of the Mississippi River and north of the Watab River. The subagency accordingly was moved to a site on the Long Prairie River. During the same year the agency at St. Peters for the Sioux of the Mississippi was reduced to a subagency and the Winnebago Subagency was made a full agency. Technically this was a change in the location of the St. Peters Agency and the Winnebago Agency was sometimes called the St. Peters or Upper Mississippi Agency; however, for filing purposes "Winnebago" was used. In addition to the Winnebago the agency was made responsible for the Chippewa of the Mississippi and those Sioux living in the vicinity of the agency who were not attached to the St. Peters Subagency. The agent apparently had little contact with any Sioux. In 1850 the La Pointe Agency for the Chippewa of Lake Superior was moved to Sandy Lake, Minnesota, where it also assumed charge of the Chippewa of the Mississippi. In 1851 the Sandy Lake Subagency became the Chippewa Agency. Instructions for the new agent appointed to the Winnebago Agency in 1850 related only to the Winnebago Indians, and in the reorganization of 1851 only Winnebago Indians were assigned to the Winnebago Agency.

When Minnesota Territory was organized in 1849, the Winnebago Agency was transferred from the St. Louis Superintendency to the new Minnesota Superintendency. In 1856 the Minnesota Superintendency was discontinued, and the agency was transferred to the Northern Superintendency.

In 1855 the Winnebago moved south from the Watab and Long Prairie Rivers to a new reserve in the Blue Earth River area south of Mankato, Minnesota. The agency was moved from the Long Prairie River to a site on the Le Sueur River about ten miles from Mankato.

As a result of an uprising of the Sioux Indians of the St. Peters Agency, many of the Sioux and Winnebago Indians were moved in 1863 from Minnesota to adjacent reserves on the Missouri River near the mouth of Crow Creek in Dakota Territory. The Winnebago agent was placed in charge of both the Winnebago and Sioux Indians at Crow Creek. The agency remained responsible to the Northern Superintendency rather than to the Dakota Superintendency. Much of the correspondence for the next several years related to the disposal of Winnebago land in Minnesota and to Indians who had gone to Wisconsin and Iowa to avoid moving to Dakota. In 1864 a special agency was established for stray bands of Winnebago and Potawatomi in Wisconsin. The agency was located at Plover in Portage County until 1869. In that year it was moved, first to Necedah and then to New Lisbon, both in Juneau County. The special agency was abolished in 1870. Correspondence concerning this agency is filed with that relating to the main Winnebago Agency.

The Winnebago Indians did not like the Crow Creek area, and many of them soon abandoned it. Some of them stayed temporarily at the Great Nemaha Agency, but most of them settled on the Omaha reserve west of the Missouri River in eastern Nebraska. The Winnebago secured a strip in the northern part of the Omaha reserve, and in 1865 the Winnebago Agency was moved from Crow Creek to the new reservation in Nebraska. A separate agent was appointed for the Sioux Indians remaining at Crow Creek.

The Northern Superintendency was discontinued on June 30, 1876, and thereafter the Winnebago agent reported directly to the Bureau of Indian Affairs in Washington. From July 1, 1876, correspondence relating to the Winnebago Agency and other agencies in Nebraska was filed under the heading "Nebraska." In 1879 the Omaha and Winnebago Agencies were consolidated to form the Omaha and Winnebago Agency. This agency remained in operation beyond 1880.

See also St. Louis, Michigan, Wisconsin, Iowa, Minnesota, Northern and Dakota Superintendencies and Prairie du Chien, Turkey River, St. Peters, La Pointe, Sandy Lake, Chippewa, Omaha, Great Nemaha and Nebraska Agencies and Subagencies.

AGENTS AND SUBAGENTS

Fort Winnebago Subagency

Name	*Date of Appointment*
John H. Kinzie	Dec. 9, 1828
Robert A. McCabe	Sept 10, 1833

Beginning in July, 1834 the commanding officer at Fort Winnebago was acting subagent. Lt. Col. Enos Cutler served during 1834 and part of 1835. He was succeeded by Bvt. Maj. N. Clark and, later in the year, by Maj. John Green, who served until the subagency was discontinued in 1837.

Rock River Subagency

Henry Gratiot	Mar. 7, 1831

Prairie du Chien—Turkey River Subagency

(See Prairie du Chien for earlier agents.)

Thomas A. B. Boyd	Mar. 31, 1837
David Lowry	June 5, 1839
James McGregor	July 5, 1844
Jonathan E. Fletcher	June 2, 1845

Winnebago Agency

Jonathan E. Fletcher	May 18, 1848
Abram M. Fridley	Notified Nov. 11, 1850
Jonathan E. Fletcher	Apr. 18, 1853
Charles H. Mix	June 14, 1858
St. A. D. Balcombe	Mar. 27, 1861
Charles Mathewson	Sept. 7, 1865
George W. Wilkinson	Mar. 3, 1869
Howard White	June 9, 1869
Taylor Bradley	Sept. 1, 1873
Howard White	Sept. 4, 1875

Special Agency for Stray Winnebago and Potawatomi Indians in Wisconsin

Oliver H. Lamoreaux	Notified July 8, 1864
John T. Kingston	Apr. 14, 1869
Capt. David A. Griffith	June 23, 1869

WISCONSIN SUPERINTENDENCY 1836-1848

The Wisconsin Superintendency was established in 1836, the year Wisconsin Territory was organized from the western part of Michigan Territory. Wisconsin originally included the present states of Iowa and Minnesota and much of the Dakotas. When Iowa Territory was organized in 1838, Wisconsin was reduced to the boundaries of the present state and that part of Minnesota east of the Mississippi River. The Territorial Governor served as *ex officio* superintendent throughout the existence of the Wisconsin Superintendency. His first headquarters was at Elk Grove, but in October, 1836 he moved to Belmont and in 1837 to Mineral Point. These cities are all in the southwestern part of present Wisconsin. After 1841 the Governor stayed at Madison.

Sauk and Fox, Winnebago, Chippewa, Menominee, Oneida, Stockbridge, Munsee, Iowa and other Indians lived in Wisconsin Territory. The Prairie du Chien (Winnebago and Sauk and Fox Indians), St. Peters (Sioux of the Mississippi) and Green Bay (Menominee and other Indians) Agencies and the Sioux, Ioway, Fort Winnebago and Crow Wing (Chippewa of the Mississippi) Subagencies were assigned originally to the Wisconsin Superintendency. The Green Bay Agency and the Fort Winnebago Subagency previously had been assigned to the Michigan Superintendency. The other agencies and subagenices had been assigned to the St. Louis Superintendency.

In November, 1836 the superintendent established a subagency at La Pointe for the Chippewa of Lake Superior, previously assigned to the Mackinac and Sault Ste. Marie Agency. The subagent was not formally commissioned until the following year.

The Green Bay Agency was discontinued on December 31, 1836, and the commanding officer at Fort Howard was designated to take charge of the agency business. In March, 1837 a subagent was appointed for the Menominee and other Indians at Green Bay.

Under the regulations adopted in 1834, the old Sac and Fox Agency at Rock Island was discontinued. The Prairie du Chien Agency, however, was moved from Prairie du Chien to Rock Island. The commanding officer at Fort Crawford was designated to take immediate responsibility for the Indians (Winnebago and Sioux) in the vicinity of Prairie du Chien. In practice, however, the agent alternated between Prairie du Chien and Rock Island. In 1837 a separate Sac and Fox Agency was established again, Prairie du Chien was reduced to a subagency, and the Fort Winnebago Subagency was consolidated with it.

Other changes in the Wisconsin Superintendency were made in 1837. The Ioway Subagency was replaced by the Great Nemaha Subagency, which was assigned to the St. Louis Superintendency. The Sioux Subagency was discontinued, and the Upper Missouri Agency was moved to the location of the Sioux Subagency. Both the Upper Missouri Agency and the Council Bluffs Subagency, established for the United Band of Ottawa, Chippewa and Potawatomi, were located in Wisconsin Territory but were assigned to the St. Louis Superintendency.

With the organization of Iowa Territory in 1838 the Sac and Fox and St. Peters Agencies were transferred to the Iowa Superintendency. The Prairie du Chien Subagency was moved to Iowa in 1840 and was transferred to the Iowa Superintendency the next year.

The Crow Wing Subagency was discontinued in 1839 and the Indians were assigned to the La Pointe Subagency. By 1841, therefore, the Wisconsin Superintendency had charge of only the Green Bay Subagency for the Menominee, Oneida, Stockbridge and Munsee Indians and of the La Pointe Subagency for the Chippewa in Wisconsin.

Most of the correspondence relating to the individual agencies and subagencies in Wisconsin is filed under agency names rather than with the correspondence relating to the superintendency.

The Wisconsin Superintendency was discontinued in 1848 when Wisconsin became a state. Thereafter the two subagents reported directly to the Bureau of Indian Affairs in Washington.

See also St. Louis, Michigan and Iowa Superintendencies and Prairie du Chien, Winnebago, St. Peters, Sac and Fox, Crow Wing, Green Bay, Ioway, La Pointe, Upper Missouri (includes Sioux Subagency correspondence), Council Bluffs, Mackinac and Sault Ste. Marie Agencies and Subagencies. There are also some field records of the Wisconsin Superintendency among the records of the Bureau of Indian Affairs in the National Archives.

GOVERNORS AND *EX OFFICIO* SUPERINTENDENTS

Name	*Date of Appointment*
Henry Dodge	Apr. 30, 1836
James Duane Doty	Apr. 15, 1841
Nathaniel P. Tallmadge	June 21, 1844
Henry Dodge	Apr. 8, 1845

WYANDOT SUBAGENCY 1839-1863, 1870-1872

The Wyandot Subagency was established in 1843 for the Wyandot Indians who had just emigrated from Ohio to the present state of Kansas. Before their removal these Indians had been assigned to the Ohio Subagency, which also had often been called the Wyandot Subagency. The Indians settled on a tract at the junction of the Kansas and Missouri Rivers, which they had purchased from the Delaware Indians. The headquarters of the Wyandot Subagency was at the site of

Wyandot City, now part of Kansas City. The subagency was under the St. Louis Superintendency.

The Wyandot Subagency was discontinued in 1851. From 1851 to 1855 the Wyandot in Kansas were assigned to the Kansas Agency, from 1855 to 1863 to the Shawnee Agency, and from 1863 to 1869 to the Delaware Agency. During these years correspondence concerning these Indians was filed under the name of the appropriate agency. By 1870 most of the Wyandot had moved to the Seneca Reservation in Indian Territory. They were attached to the Neosho Agency until 1871 and thereafter to the Quapaw Agency. Between 1870 and 1872, however, some correspondence concerning the settlement of Wyandot affairs in Kansas and even some concerning the Wyandot in Indian Territory was filed under the heading "Wyandot."

There is some correspondence filed under the subheading "Wyandot Emigration" for the years 1839-51. Most of the correspondence concerning this subject is among the general correspondence relating to the Ohio and Wyandot Subagencies. There is a "Wyandot Reserves" subheading for the years 1845-63, with correspondence relating to Wyandot lands in both Ohio and Kansas.

See also St. Louis and Central Superintendencies and Piqua, Ohio, Kansas, Delaware, Neosho and Quapaw Agencies.

SUBAGENTS

Name	Date of Appointment
Jonathan Phillips	Oct. 21, 1843
Richard Hewitt	Apr. 24, 1845
Thomas Mosely, Jr.	May 29, 1849

WYOMING SUPERINTENDENCY 1869-1880

The Wyoming Superintendency was established in 1868, the year Wyoming Territory was organized from parts of Dakota, Idaho and Utah Territories. Territorial officials, however, were not appointed until April, 1869. Most of Wyoming was part of Oregon Territory from 1848-59, of Washington Territory from 1859-63, of Idaho Territory from 1863-64 and of Dakota Territory from

1864-68. The only Indian agency in Wyoming in 1868, however, had been assigned to the Utah Superintendency. The principal Indians under Bureau control in Wyoming were Eastern Shoshoni. There were also Bannock, Arapaho, Cheyenne and Sioux in Wyoming during the years 1869-80.

The territorial governor at Cheyenne served as *ex officio* superintendent. The Wyoming Superintendency itself had a very brief existence, being discontinued in November, 1870. Thereafter the agents reported directly to the Bureau of Indians Affairs in Washington. Correspondence relating to the Shoshone and Bannock Agency, for most of the period the only agency in Wyoming, was filed under the heading "Wyoming" until the change of filing systems in 1881.

The correspondence filed under the heading "Wyoming" relates principally to the affairs of the Shoshone and Bannock Agency and, in the earlier years, to roving bands of Cheyenne, Arapaho and Sioux that were not under Bureau supervision. The Red Cloud Agency was located at Fort Laramie from 1871 to 1873, but most of the correspondence concerning this agency is filed under the name of the agency. The Red Cloud Agency was more closely associated with Dakota than with Wyoming.

The Shoshone and Bannock Agency was a continuation of the Fort Bridger Agency of the Utah Superintendency. The agency was located at Fort Bridger in 1861 and was given responsibility for the Eastern bands of Shoshoni and Bannock. In 1868 the Indians agreed by treaty to settle on a reservation in the Wind River area of northwestern Wyoming. The agency was moved to the reservation in 1870 with temporary headquarters in the Popo Agie Valley at Camp Brown. In 1871 permanent agency buildings were located about 15 miles farther north in the Little Wind River Valley.

The Bannock Indians did not settle permanently on the Wind River Reservation, and in 1872, except for a few who had joined the Shoshoni, they moved to the Fort Hall Reservation in Idaho. The agency, however, continued to be called the "Shoshone and Bannock Agency" more frequently than simply the "Shoshone Agency." In 1878 some Northern Arapaho and a few Cheyenne, who had previously been attached to the Red Cloud Agency, settled on the Wind River Reservation.

See also Oregon, Washington, Idaho, Utah, Montana, Dakota, Nevada and Colorado Superintendencies and Red Cloud Agency. There are also some field records of the Wyoming Superintendency among the records of the Bureau of Indian Affairs in the National Archives.

GOVERNOR AND *EX OFFICIO* SUPERINTENDENT

Name	*Date of Appointment*
John A. Campbell	Apr. 7, 1869

AGENTS

Shoshone and Bannock Agency

Luther Mann	July 30, 1861, for Fort Bridger Agency
Capt. J. H. Patterson (special)	June 29, 1869
Lt. G. W. Fleming (special)	Nov. 9, 1869
J. W. Wham (special)	July 20, 1870
James Irwin	Mar. 6, 1871
James I. Patten	Mar. 29, 1877
Charles Hatton	Dec. 17, 1879

YANKTON AGENCY
1859-1876

The Yankton Agency (often spelled "Yancton") was established in 1859 for the Yankton Sioux. The agency was located on the Missouri River near Greenwood in the present state of South Dakota.

Originally the Yankton Agency was assigned to the Central Superintendency, but it was transferred to the new Dakota Superintendency in 1861. After the Dakota Superintendency was abolished in 1870, the agent reported directly to the Bureau of Indian Affairs in Washington. The Yankton Agency was assigned to the revived Dakota Superintendency of 1877-78. The Yankton agent was put in charge of the Santee Sioux Agency from April, 1877 until June, 1878. The Yankton Agency continued in operation beyond 1880, but after July 1, 1876 the heading "Dakota" was used for its correspondence.

See also Central and Dakota Superintendencies and Santee Sioux Agency.

AGENTS

Name	*Date of Appointment*
Alexander H. Redfield	Mar. 9, 1859
Walter A. Burleigh	Mar. 28, 1861
Patrick Henry Conger	Mar. 23, 1865

AGENTS (cont.)

Capt. William J. Broatch	June 25, 1869
Maj. J. M. Goodhue	Apr. 23, 1870
Samuel D. Webster	Oct. 18, 1870
Frederick G. Holmes	Oct. 10, 1871
John G. Gasmann	Feb. 23, 1872
John W. Douglas	Mar. 28, 1876
Robert S. Gardner (special)	On duty May 16, 1879
William D. E. Andrus	June 30, 1879

TRIBAL INDEX

This index lists the tribes and more important bands of Indians under the supervision of the Office of Indian Affairs between 1824 and 1880. The HEADING column indicates the historical sketches which should be consulted for information about each tribe. Correspondence concerning the tribe may be found in Microcopy 234 under the same headings.

Agencies with primary responsibility for a tribe are listed first and are followed by agencies with responsibility for some part of the tribe and by superintendencies having supervisory control over the responsible agencies. For Indians assigned to agencies for which no sketch has been prepared—and for which there is no file heading in Microcopy 234—only the names of superintendencies are given.

Where a tribe was assigned to an agency for a specific period of time, that period is noted in the HEADING column, although no attempt has been made to establish exact dates. Where no date is shown it indicates that no specific assignment of the tribe to the agency was made, although the agency did have administrative responsibility for the tribe owing to the tribe's location. This index does not list every jurisdiction having contact with members of a tribe, but only jurisdictions with actual administrative responsibility.

215

TRIBE	HEADING	PAGE
Arapaho (cont.)	Colorado Superintendency	46
	Northern Superintendency	118
	Wyoming Superintendency	211
Arickaree. *See* Arikara		
Arikara	1824-66, Upper Missouri Agency	184
	1867-80, Fort Berthold Agency	63
	St. Louis Superintendency	155
	Central Superintendency	28
	Dakota Superintendency	57
Assiniboin	1824-66, Upper Missouri Agency	184
	1867-70, Fort Berthold Agency	63
	1864-80, Montana Superintendency	99
	St. Peters Agency	160
	St. Louis Superintendency	155
	Central Superintendency	28
	Minnesota Superintendency	97
	Dakota Superintendency	57

B

TRIBE	HEADING	PAGE
Bannock	Oregon Superintendency	123
	Utah Superintendency	190
	Idaho Superintendency	74
	Montana Superintendency	99
	Wyoming Superintendency	211
Biloxi	Red River Agency	149
	Caddo Agency	18
Blackfeet	1855-69, Blackfeet Agency	17
	1864-80, Montana Superintendency	99
	Washington Superintendency	193
	Central Superintendency	28
	Dakota Superintendency	57
	Idaho Superintendency	74
Blackfeet Sioux	Upper Missouri Agency	184
	Upper Platte Agency	188
	Cheyenne River Agency	36
	Grand River Agency	68
	Standing Rock Agency	177
	St. Louis Superintendency	155
	Central Superintendency	28
	Dakota Superintendency	57
Blood	1855-59, Blackfeet Agency	17
	1869-80, Montana Superintendency	99
	Washington Superintendency	193
	Central Superintendency	28
	Dakota Superintendency	57
	Idaho Superintendency	74
Boise Shoshoni	Idaho Superintendency	74
Brotherton	Six Nations Agency	172
	Green Bay Agency	71
	Michigan Superintendency	94
	Wisconsin Superintendency	208

216

TRIBE	HEADING	PAGE
Choctaw (cont.)	1824-25, Red River Agency	149
	1829-31, Cherokee Agency, West	32
	Arkansas Superintendency	15
	Western Superintendency	201
	Southern Superintendency	174
	Central Superintendency	28
"Christian". *See* Stockbridge *and* Munsee		
Clackamas	Oregon Superintendency	123
	Washington Superintendency	193
Clallam	Washington Superintendency	193
	Oregon Superintendency	123
Coeur d'Alène	Oregon Superintendency	123
	Washington Superintendency	193
Colville	Washington Superintendency	193
Comanche	1846-55, Upper Platte Agency	188
	1855-64, Upper Arkansas Agency	182
	1864-80, Kiowa Agency	85
	St. Louis Superintendency	155
	Central Superintendency	28
	Colorado Superintendency	46
—Texas or Penateka band	1847-59, Texas Agency	179
	1859-78, Wichita Agency	203
	1878-80, Kiowa Agency	85
	Western Superintendency	201
	Southern Superintendency	174
	Central Superintendency	28
Concow	California Superintendency	19
Confederated Peoria and Miami. *See also* individual tribes	1871-80, Quapaw Agency	145
	Central Superintendency	28
Cowlitz	Washington Superintendency	193
	Oregon Superintendency	123
Coyotero Apache	to 1877, New Mexico Superintendency	110
	1877-80, Arizona Superintendency	11
Cree	Upper Missouri Agency	184
	St. Louis Superintendency	155
Creek	1824-76, Creek Agency	52
	1875-80, Union Agency	181
	Western Superintendency	201
	Southern Superintendency	174
	Central Superintendency	28
Crow	1824-66, Upper Missouri Agency	184
	1867-70, Fort Berthold Agency	63
	1864-80, Montana Superintendency	99
	St. Louis Superintendency	155
	Central Superintendency	28
	Dakota Superintendency	57
Cuthead Sioux	Upper Missouri Agency	184

220

TRIBE	HEADING	PAGE
Grosventre (cont.)	1864-80, Montana Superintendency	99
	St. Louis Superintendency	155
	Central Superintendency	28
	Washington Superintendency	193
	Dakota Superintendency	57
	Idaho Superintendency	74

H

TRIBE	HEADING	PAGE
Hainai	1847-59, Texas Agency	179
	1859-, Wichita Agency	203
	Southern Superintendency	174
	Central Superintendency	28
Hualapai. *See* Walapai		
Havasupai	Arizona Superintendency	11
Hoopa	California Superintendency	19
Hopi	Arizona Superintendency	11
	New Mexico Superintendency	110
Hunkpapa Sioux	Upper Missouri Agency	184
	Upper Platte Agency	188
	Spotted Tail Agency	176
	Grand River Agency	68
	Standing Rock Agency	177
	Dakota Superintendency	57
Hupa	California Superintendency	19

I

TRIBE	HEADING	PAGE
Ioni. *See* Hainai		
Iowa	1825-37, Ioway Subagency	81
	1837-76, Great Nemaha Agency	69
	1876-80, Nebraska Agencies	103
	St. Louis Superintendency	155
	Wisconsin Superintendency	208
	Central Superintendency	28
	Northern Superintendency	118
Iroquois. *See also* individual tribes	1824-34, Six Nations Agency	172
	1835-80, New York Agency	169
	1935-80, New York Agency	117
	1832-34, Michigan Superintendency	94

J

TRIBE	HEADING	PAGE
Jicarilla Apache	New Mexico Superintendency	110
Joshua	Oregon Superintendency	123

K

TRIBE	HEADING	PAGE
Kainah. *See* Blood		
Kalapuya	Oregon Superintendency	123

221

TRIBE	HEADING	PAGE
Kansa		
—in Kansas	1824-47, Fort Leavenworth Agency	64
	1847-51, Osage River Agency	132
	1851-55, Potawatomi Agency	140
	1855-76, Kansas Agency	83
	St. Louis Superintendency	155
	Central Superintendency	28
—in Indian Territory	1874, Neosho Agency	106
	1874-80, Osage Agency	130
	Central Superintendency	28
Kaskaskia		
—in Kansas	Fort Leavenworth Agency	64
	Osage River Agency	132
	St. Louis Superintendency	155
	Central Superintendency	28
—in Indian Territory	1867-71, Neosho Agency	106
	1871-80, Quapaw Agency	145
	Central Superintendency	28
Kaw. *See* Kansa		
Kawia	California Superintendency	19
Keechi. *See* Kichai		
Kern River	California Superintendency	19
Kianamaras	California Superintendency	19
Kichai	1847-59, Texas Agency	179
	1857-78, Wichita Agency	203
	1878-80, Kiowa Agency	85
	Southern Superintendency	174
	Central Superintendency	28
Kickapoo		
—in Kansas	1824-51, Fort Leavenworth Agency	64
	1851-55, Great Nemaha Agency	69
	1855-76, Kickapoo Agency	84
	1874-80, Potawatomi Agency	140
	St. Louis Superintendency	155
	Central Superintendency	28
—Mexican	1873-75, Kickapoo Agency	84
	1874-80, Sac and Fox Agency	150
	Central Superintendency	28
Kings River	California Superintendency	19
Kiowa	1846-55, Upper Platte Agency	188
	1856-64, Upper Arkansas Agency	182
	1864-80, Kiowa Agency	85
	Western Superintendency	201
	St. Louis Superintendency	155
	Central Superintendency	28
	Colorado Superintendency	46
Kiowa Apache	1846-55, Upper Platte Agency	188
	1855-67, Upper Arkansas Agency	182
	1864-80, Kiowa Agency	85

TRIBE	HEADING	PAGE
Kiowa Apache (cont.)	Cheyenne and Arapahoe Agency	36
	St. Louis Superintendency	155
	Central Superintendency	28
	Colorado Superintendency	46
Klamath		
—of California	California Superintendency	19
—of Oregon	Oregon Superintendency	123
Klikitat	Washington Superintendency	193
	Oregon Superintendency	123
Koasati	Red River Agency	149
	Caddo Agency	18
Konkau	California Superintendency	19
Kutenai	1864-80, Montana Superintendency	99
	Washington Superintendency	193
	Oregon Superintendency	123
	Idaho Superintendency	74
Kwatami	Oregon Superintendency	123

L

TRIBE	HEADING	PAGE
Lake	Washington Superintendency	193
	Oregon Superintendency	123
Lake Winnebigoshish Chippewa	Chippewa Agency	41
	Minnesota Superintendency	97
	Northern Superintendency	118
Lipan	1847-59, Texas Agency	179
	1876-80, Central Superintendency	28
Little Lake Valley	California Superintendency	19
Lower Brulé. *See also* Brulé		
Sioux	to 1874, Upper Missouri Agency	184
	1874-75, Crow Creek Agency	55
	1875-76, Lower Brulé Agency	89
	1861-80, Dakota Superintendency	57
Lummi	Washington Superintendency	193
	Oregon Superintendency	123

M

TRIBE	HEADING	PAGE
Makah	Washington Superintendency	193
	Oregon Superintendency	123
Mandan	1824-66, Upper Missouri Agency	184
	1867-80, Fort Berthold Agency	63
	St. Louis Superintendency	155
	Minnesota Superintendency	97
	Central Superintendency	28
	Dakota Superintendency	57
Maricopa	Pima Agency	137
	New Mexico Superintendency	110
	Arizona Superintendency	11
Mattole	California Superintendency	19

TRIBE	HEADING	PAGE
Mdewakanton Sioux. *See also* Sioux of the Missouri and Santee Sioux	St. Peters Agency	160
	St. Louis Superintendency	155
	Wisconsin Superintendency	208
	Iowa Superintendency	80
	Minnesota Superintendency	97
	Northern Superintendency	118
Menominee	Green Bay Agency	71
	Michigan Superintendency	94
	Wisconsin Superintendency	208
	Northern Superintendency	118
Mescalero Apache	New Mexico Superintendency	110
Mexican Kickapoo. *See* Kickapoo		
Miami		
—in Ohio	Fort Wayne Agency	67
	Indiana Agency	78
	Miami Subagency	92
	Michigan Superintendency	94
—in Kansas	to 1871, Osage River Agency	132
	1871, Shawnee Agency	169
	St. Louis Superintendency	155
	Central Superintendency	28
—in Indian Territory	1871-80, Quapaw Agency	145
	Central Superintendency	28
Mimbreño Apache	to 1877, New Mexico Superintendency	110
	1877-80, Arizona Superintendency	11
Miniconjou Sioux	Upper Missouri Agency	184
	Upper Platte Agency	188
	Whetstone Agency	202
	Spotted Tail Agency	176
	Cheyenne River Agency	36
	Dakota Superintendency	57
Mission	California Superintendency	19
Missouri	1824-37, Upper Missouri Agency	184
	1837-56, Council Bluffs Agency	51
	1856-76, Otoe Agency	133
	1876-80, Nebraska Agencies	103
	St. Louis Superintendency	155
	Central Superintendency	28
	Northern Superintendency	118
Mixed Band of Seneca and Shawnee. *See also* Seneca and Shawnee Tribes		
—in Ohio	Piqua Agency	138
	Ohio Agency	120
	Michigan Superintendency	94
—in Indian Territory	1834-36, Cherokee Agency, West	32
	1836-37, Cherokee Agency	32

TRIBE	HEADING	PAGE
Noi-sas	California Superintendency	19
Nomelaki	California Superintendency	19
Nuimok	California Superintendency	19

O

TRIBE	HEADING	PAGE
Oglala Sioux	Upper Missouri Agency	184
	Upper Platte Agency	188
	Red Cloud Agency	147
	Whetstone Agency	202
	Spotted Tail Agency	176
	Grand River Agency	68
	Central Superintendency	28
	Northern Superintendency	118
	Wyoming Superintendency	211
	Dakota Superintendency	57
Omaha	1824-37, Upper Missouri Agency	184
	1837-56, Council Bluffs Agency	51
	1856-76, Omaha Agency	122
	1876-80, Nebraska Agencies	103
	St. Louis Superintendency	155
	Central Superintendency	28
	Northern Superintendency	118
Oneida		
—in New York	1824-34, Six Nations Agency	172
	1835-80, New York Agency	117
	1832-34, Michigan Superintendency	94
—in Wisconsin	Green Bay Agency	71
	Michigan Superintendency	94
	Wisconsin Superintendency	208
	Northern Superintendency	118
Onondaga	1824-34, Six Nations Agency	172
	1835-80, New York Agency	117
	1832-34, Michigan Superintendency	94
Oohenonpa. *See* Two Kettle Sioux		
Osage	1824-51, Osage Agency	130
	1851-74, Neosho Agency	106
	1874-80, Osage Agency	130
	St. Louis Superintendency	155
	Western Superintendency	201
	Southern Superintendency	174
	Central Superintendency	28
Oto	1824-37, Upper Missouri Agency	184
	1837-56, Council Bluffs Agency	51
	1856-76, Otoe Agency	133
	1876-80, Nebraska Agencies	103
	St. Louis Superintendency	155
	Central Superintendency	28
	Northern Superintendency	118

227

TRIBE	HEADING	PAGE
Pend d'Oreille (cont.)	Montana Superintendency	99
Peoria		
−in Kansas	Fort Leavenworth Agency	64
	Osage River Agency	132
	St. Louis Superintendency	155
	Central Superintendency	28
−in Indian Territory	1867-71, Neosho Agency	106
	1871-80, Quapaw Agency	145
	Central Superintendency	28
Piankeshaw	Red River Agency	149
−in Kansas	Fort Leavenworth Agency	64
	Osage River Agency	132
	St. Louis Agency	155
	Central Agency	28
−in Indian Territory	1867-71, Neosho Agency	106
	1871-80, Quapaw Agency	145
	Central Superintendency	28
Piegan	1855-69, Blackfeet Agency	17
	1864-80, Montana Superintendency	99
	Washington Superintendency	193
	Central Superintendency	28
	Dakota Superintendency	57
	Idaho Superintendency	74
Pillager Chippewa	Chippewa Agency	41
	Minnesota Superintendency	97
	Northern Superintendency	118
Pima	Pima Agency	137
	New Mexico Superintendency	110
	Arizona Superintendency	11
Pit River	California Superintendency	19
Piute. *See* Paiute		
Pomo	California Superintendency	19
Ponca	1824-59, Upper Missouri Agency	184
	1859-80, Ponca Agency	139
	1878-80, Santee Sioux Agency	163
	St. Louis Superintendency	155
	Central Superintendency	28
	Dakota Superintendency	57
Potawatomi		
−in East	Fort Wayne Agency	67
	Indiana Agency	78
	Green Bay Agency	71
	Chicago Agency	37
	Mackinac Agency	90
	Michigan Superintendency	94
	Northern Superintendency	118
	1864-70, Winnebago Agency	205
−in Iowa	1837-47, Council Bluffs Agency	51
	St. Louis Superintendency	155

228

TRIBE	HEADING	PAGE
Salan Pomo	California Superintendency	19
Sans Arc Sioux	Upper Missouri Agency	184
	Upper Platte Agency	188
	Spotted Tail Agency	176
	Grand River Agency	68
	Cheyenne River Agency	36
	Dakota Superintendency	57
Santee Sioux. *See also* Sioux of the Mississippi	to 1870, St. Peters Agency	160
	1871-76, Santee Sioux Agency	163
	1876-80, Nebraska Agencies	103
	1873-76, Flandreau Agency	61
	Winnebago Agency	205
	Yankton Agency	213
	Dakota Superintendency	57
	Northern Superintendency	118
	Montana Superintendency	99
Sauk and Fox of the Mississippi	1824-80, Sac and Fox Agency	150
	1843-45, Raccoon River Agency	145
	1847-51, Osage River Agency	132
	Prairie du Chien Agency	142
	St. Louis Superintendency	155
	Wisconsin Superintendency	208
	Iowa Superintendency	80
	Central Superintendency	28
Sauk and Fox of the Missouri	1829-34, Ioway Subagency	81
	1835-37, Upper Missouri Agency	184
	1837-76, Great Nemaha Agency	69
	1876-80, Nebraska Agencies	103
	St. Louis Superintendency	155
	Central Superintendency	28
	Northern Superintendency	118
Seminole	1824-76, Seminole Agency	167
	1875-80, Union Agency	181
	Apalachicola Subagency	10
	1837-42, Creek Agency	52
	Florida Superintendency	62
	Western Superintendency	201
	Southern Superintendency	174
	Central Superintendency	28
Seneca. *See also* Mixed Band of Seneca and Shawnee (prior to 1867)		
—in New York	1824-34, Six Nations Agency	172
	1824-32, Seneca Agency in New York	169
	1835-80, New York Agency	117
	1832-34, Michigan Superintendency	94
—in Ohio	Piqua Agency	138
	Ohio Agency	120
	Michigan Superintendency	94

230

TRIBE	HEADING	PAGE
Seneca (cont.)		
—in Indian Territory	1831-36, Cherokee Agency, West	32
	1836-37, Cherokee Agency	32
	1837-71, Neosho Agency	106
	1871-80, Quapaw Agency	145
	Western Superintendency	201
	Southern Superintendency	174
	Central Superintendency	28
Shasta	Oregon Superintendency	123
Shawnee		
—in Ohio	Piqua Agency	138
	Ohio Agency	120
	Michigan Superintendency	94
—in Kansas	1824-51, Fort Leavenworth Agency	64
	1851-55, Kansas Agency	83
	1855-76, Shawnee Agency	169
	St. Louis Superintendency	155
	Central Superintendency	28
—Kansas Shawnee in Indian Territory	1869-74, Cherokee Agency	32
	1875-80, Union Agency	181
	Southern Superintendency	174
	Central Superintendency	28
—Eastern Shawnee. See also Mixed Band of Seneca and Shawnee (prior to 1867)	1867-71, Neosho Agency	106
	1871-80, Quapaw Agency	145
	Central Superintendency	28
—Absentee Shawnee	Red River Agency	149
	Caddo Agency	18
	1847-59, Texas Agency	179
	1859-67, Wichita Agency	203
	ca. 1869-80, Sac and Fox Agency	150
	Southern Superintendency	174
	Central Superintendency	28
Sheepeater. See Tukyuarika		
Shoshoni. See also individual bands	Utah Superintendency	190
	Oregon Superintendency	123
	Nevada Superintendency	108
	Idaho Superintendency	74
	Montana Superintendency	99
	Wyoming Superintendency	211
Siksika. See Blackfeet		
Sioux of the Mississippi. See also Sisseton, Wahpeton, Wahpekute, Mdewakanton and Santee Sioux	St. Peters Agency	160
	Prairie du Chien Agency	142

TRIBE	HEADING	PAGE
Sioux of the Mississippi (cont.)	Winnebago Agency	205
	St. Louis Superintendency	155
	Wisconsin Superintendency	208
	Iowa Superintendency	80
	Minnesota Superintendency	97
	Northern Superintendency	118
	Dakota Superintendency	57
Sioux (of Missouri and Platte Rivers). *See also* individual bands	Upper Missouri Agency	184
	Upper Platte Agency	188
	Yankton Agency	213
	Upper Arkansas Agency	182
	Whetstone Agency	202
	Spotted Tail Agency	176
	Red Cloud Agency	147
	Cheyenne River Agency	36
	Grand River Agency	68
	Standing Rock Agency	177
	Crow Creek Agency	55
	Lower Brulé Agency	89
	St. Louis Superintendency	155
	Central Superintendency	28
	Dakota Superintendency	57
	Montana Superintendency	99
	Northern Superintendency	118
	Wyoming Superintendency	211
Sisseton Sioux. *See also* Sioux of the Mississippi and Santee Sioux	St. Peters Agency	160
	Sisseton Agency	171
	Devil's Lake Agency	61
	St. Louis Superintendency	155
	Wisconsin Superintendency	208
	Iowa Superintendency	80
	Minnesota Superintendency	97
	Northern Superintendency	118
	Dakota Superintendency	57
Sixes	Oregon Superintendency	123
Sklallam	Washington Superintendency	193
	Oregon Superintendency	123
Skokomish	Washington Superintendency	193
	Oregon Superintendency	123
Snake. *See* Shoshoni		
Spokan	Oregon Superintendency	123
	Washington Superintendency	193
Squaxon	Washington Superintendency	193
	Oregon Superintendency	123

TRIBE	HEADING	PAGE
Stockbridge. *See also* Munsee (after 1859)		
—in New York	Six Nations Agency	172
—in Wisconsin	Green Bay Agency	71
	Michigan Superintendency	94
	Wisconsin Superintendency	208
	Northern Superintendency	118
—in Kansas	1839-51, Fort Leavenworth Agency	64
	1851-55, Kansas Agency	83
	1855-59, Delaware Agency	59
	St. Louis Superintendency	155
	Central Superintendency	28
Swinomish	Washington Superintendency	193
	Oregon Superintendency	123

T

TRIBE	HEADING	PAGE
Tabaquache Ute	to 1861, New Mexico Superintendency	110
	1861-80, Colorado Superintendency	46
Taensa	Caddo Agency	18
Tawakoni	1847-59, Texas Agency	179
	1859-78, Wichita Agency	203
	1878-80, Kiowa Agency	85
	Southern Superintendency	174
	Central Superintendency	28
Tejon	California Superintendency	19
Tenino	Oregon Superintendency	123
Tonkawa	1847-59, Texas Agency	179
	1859-, Wichita Agency	203
	Southern Superintendency	174
	Central Superintendency	28
—in Texas	1876-80, Central Superintendency	28
Tubatulabal	California Superintendency	19
Tukuarika	Idaho Superintendency	81
	Montana Superintendency	99
Tulalip	Washington Superintendency	193
	Oregon Superintendency	123
Tule (Tulareños)	California Superintendency	19
Tuscarora	1824-34, Six Nations Agency	172
	1835-80, New York Agency	117
	1832-34, Michigan Superintendency	94
Two Kettle Sioux	Upper Missouri Agency	184
	Upper Platte Agency	188
	Grand River Agency	68
	Cheyenne River Agency	36
	Dakota Superintendency	57

235

TRIBE	HEADING	PAGE
Wyandot (cont.)		
—in Kansas (cont.)	1870-72, Wyandot	210
	St. Louis Superintendency	155
	Central Superintendency	28
—in Indian Territory	1867-71, Neosho Agency	106
	1871-80, Quapaw Agency	145
	Central Superintendency	28

Y

TRIBE	HEADING	PAGE
Yakima	Washington Superintendency	193
	Oregon Superintendency	123
Yamel	Oregon Superintendency	123
Yampa Ute	Colorado Superintendency	46
Yankton Sioux	to 1859, Upper Missouri Agency	184
	1859-76, Yankton Agency	213
	1861-80, Dakota Superintendency	57
	St. Peters Agency	160
	St. Louis Agency	155
	Central Superintendency	28
	Minnesota Superintendency	97
Yanktonai Sioux	Upper Missouri Agency	184
	Upper Platte Agency	188
	Crow Creek Agency	55
	Grand River Agency	68
	Standing Rock Agency	177
	Dakota Superintendency	57
	Montana Superintendency	99
Yatasi	Red River Agency	149
Yavapai	Arizona Superintendency	11
Yokaia	California Superintendency	19
Yuki	California Superintendency	19
Yuma	Arizona Superintendency	11
	California Superintendency	19
Yupu	California Superintendency	19

JURISDICTIONAL INDEX

This index lists, for the period 1824 to 1880, the names and dates of operation of Indian superintendencies and agencies, and the file headings under which correspondence concerning them may be found in Microcopy 234. Each File Heading is also the name of a historical sketch in this volume. As the historical sketches were originally written for file headings rather than jurisdictions, it is necessary for the user interested in a particular agency or superintendency to consult all the sketches listed for that jurisdiction. The years during which correspondence was filed under a particular heading do not necessarily coincide with the dates of operation of the agency or superintendency of the same name.

It has been impossible to include the name of every subagency and special agency. Probably the most significant omissions are the agencies and subagencies established during the early years of a superintendency, when agents were moved about without permanent assignments to a particular tribe or locality. For information concerning such agencies, see superintendency headings.

This index also lists the reel numbers in Microcopy 234 which contain the correspondence for the file heading and years of filing noted in the adjoining columns. That is to say, the reel numbers shown are not necessarily *all* the reels for the particular heading, but only those reels covering the jurisdiction in question.

The reel numbers have been provided to facilitate the acquisition and use of individual reels from among the 962 in Microcopy 234.

JURISDICTION AND YEARS OF OPERATION	YEARS OF FILING	FILE HEADING	REEL NO.	PAGE
A				
Abiquiu Agency, 1854-78	1854-78	New Mexico	547-575	110
Alaska Agency, 1873-74	1873-74	Alaska	1	9
Apache Agency. *See* Southern Apache Agency				
Apalachicola Subagency, 1826-34	1826-42	Apalachicola	2	10
Arizona Superintendency, 1863-73	1863-80	Arizona	3-28	11
Arkansas Superintendency, 1819-34				
1819-34	1824-34	Arkansas	29	15

JURISDICTION AND YEARS OF OPERATION	YEARS OF FILING	FILE HEADING	REEL NO.	PAGE
B				
Blackfeet Agency, 1855-80	1855-69	Blackfeet	30	17
	1869-80	Montana	489-518	99
Brazos Agency, 1855-60	1855-59	Texas	860-861	179
	1860	Wichita	928	203
C				
Caddo Agency, 1821-34	1824-30	Red River	727	149
	1824-42	Caddo	31	18
California Superintendency, 1852-60, 1864-73	1849-80	California	32-52	19
Camp Apache Agency, 1872-75	1872-75	Arizona	5-15	11
Camp Grant Agency, 1871-73	1871-73	Arizona	4-9	11
Carson Valley Agency, 1858-61	1858-61	Utah	898-900	190
Central Superintendency, 1851-78	1851-80	Central	55-70	28
Cherokee Agency: East, 1801-39	1824-36	Cherokee	71-76	32
West, 1813-74	1824-36	Cherokee	77-79	32
	1836-80	Cherokee	71-118	32
Cheyenne and Arapahoe Agency 1875-80	1875-80	Cheyenne and Arapahoe	119-126	36
Cheyenne River Agency, 1869-80	1869-70	Upper Platte	894-895	188
	1871-80	Cheyenne River	127-131	36
Chicago Agency, 1805-34	1824-47	Chicago	132-134	37
Chickasaw Agency, 1800-55	1824-70	Chickasaw	135-148	40
Chippewa Agency, 1851-80	1851-80	Chippewa	149-168	41
Chiricahua Agency, 1872-76	1872-76	Arizona	5-17	11
Choctaw Agency: East, 1792-1832 West, 1825-74	1824-76	Choctaw	169-196	44
Choctaw and Chickasaw Agency, 1856-74	1856-76	Choctaw	174-196	44
Cimarron Agency, 1862-76	1862-76	New Mexico	551-556	110
Colorado River Agency, 1864-80	1864-80	Arizona	3-28	11
Colorado Superintendency, 1861-70	1861-80	Colorado	197-214	46
Columbia River District Agency, 1854-59	1854-57	Washington	907	193
	1857-59	Oregon	610-611	123
Colville Agency, 1872-80	1872-80	Washington	912-920	193
Comanche Agency, 1855-60	1855-69	Texas	860-861	179
	1860	Wichita	928	203
Conejos Agency, 1860-69	1860-61	New Mexico	550	110
	1861-69	Colorado	197-200	46
Consolidated Agencies of the Cherokees, Creeks, Choctaws, Chickasaws and Seminoles, 1874	1874	Cherokee	107	32
	1874	Creek	235	52
	1874	Choctaw	181	44
	1874	Seminole	805	167

JURISDICTION AND YEARS OF OPERATION	YEARS OF FILING	FILE HEADING	REEL NO.	PAGE
Council Bluffs Agency, 1837-56	1836-57	Council Bluffs	215-218	51
Council Bluffs Subagency, 1837-47	1837-47	Council Bluffs	215-217	51
Country West of the Rocky Mountains, 1842-46	1842-46	Oregon	607	123
Creek Agency: East, 1792-1836 West, 1826-74	1824-76	Creek	219-248	52
Crow Agency, 1869-80	1869-80	Montana	489-518	99
Crow Creek Agency, 1874-80	1871-76	Crow Creek	249	55
	1876-80	Dakota	256-273	57
Crow Wing Subagency, 1835-39	1835-40	Crow Wing	249	56

D

JURISDICTION AND YEARS OF OPERATION	YEARS OF FILING	FILE HEADING	REEL NO.	PAGE
Dakota Superintendency, 1861-70, 1877-78	1861-80	Dakota	250-273	57
Dalles Agency. See Warm Springs Agency				
Delaware Agency, 1855-69	1855-73	Delaware	274-280	59
Delaware and Shawnee Agency, 1824-34	1824-34	Fort Leavenworth	300	64
	1824-34	St. Louis	747-750	155
Denver Special Agency, 1871-75	1871-75	Colorado	201-205	46
Detroit Subagency, 1824-37	1824-37	Michigan	419-421	94
	1824-37	Saginaw	745	154
Devil's Lake Agency, 1871-80	1871-80	Devil's Lake	281-284	61

E

JURISDICTION AND YEARS OF OPERATION	YEARS OF FILING	FILE HEADING	REEL NO.	PAGE
Eastern District Agency (Washington). See Flathead Agency				
Eastern Oregon Agency. See Warm Springs Agency				

F

JURISDICTION AND YEARS OF OPERATION	YEARS OF FILING	FILE HEADING	REEL NO.	PAGE
Flandreau Agency, 1873-79	1873-76	Flandreau	285	61
	1876-79	Nebraska	519-527	103
Flathead Agency, 1854-80	1854-57	Washington	907	193
	1857-61	Oregon	610-612	123
	1861-63	Washington	907-908	193
	1863-66	Idaho	337	74
	1864-80	Montana	488-518	99
Florida Agency. See Seminole Agency				
Florida Superintendency, 1822-34	1824-53	Florida	286-291	62
Fort Belknap Agency, 1873-76, 1878-80	1873-80	Montana	494-518	99
Fort Berthold Agency, 1864-80	1864-66	Upper Missouri	885-886	184
	1867-80	Fort Berthold	292-299	63
Fort Bridger Agency, 1861-69	1861-69	Utah	900-902	190

JURISDICTION AND YEARS OF OPERATION	YEARS OF FILING	FILE HEADING	REEL NO.	PAGE
Kiowa, Comanche and Wichita Agency. *See* Kiowa Agency				
Klamath Agency (California), 1856-60	1856-60	California	35-37	19
Klamath Agency (Oregon), 1862-80	1862-80	Oregon	613-630	123

L

La Pointe Agency, 1836-50, 1858-80	1831-50	La Pointe	387-390	87
	1855-80	La Pointe	391-400	87
Leech Lake Agency, 1874-79	1874-79	Chippewa	161-167	41
Lemhi Agency, 1873-80	1873-80	Idaho	337-353	74
	1873-80	Montana	494-518	99
Los Pinos Agency, 1869-80	1869-80	Colorado	200-214	46
Lower Brulé Agency, 1875-80	1875-76	Lower Brulé	401	89
	1876-80	Dakota	256-273	57
Lower Sioux Agency. *See* St. Peters Agency				
Lower (Ute) Agency. *See* Los Pinos Agency				

M

Mackinac Agency, 1815-80	1824-27	Michigan	419	94
	1828-80	Mackinac	402-415	90
Mackinac and Sault Ste. Marie Agency. *See* Mackinac Agency *and* Sault Ste. Marie Agency				
Malheur Agency, 1873-82	1873-80	Oregon	618-630	123
Mandan Subagency, 1824-38	1824-38	Upper Missouri	883-884	184
	1824-38	St. Louis	747-751	155
Mendocino Subagency, 1855-60	1855-60	California	34-37	19
Mescalero Agency, 1861-80	1861-80	New Mexico	550-582	110
Miami Subagency, 1838-47	1824-53	Miami	416-418	92
	1838-50	Indiana	356-361	78
Michigan Agency. *See* Mackinac Agency				
Michigan Superintendency, 1805-51	1824-51	Michigan	419-427	94
Middle Oregon Agency. *See* Warm Springs Agency				
Middle Park Agency, 1862-69	1862-69	Colorado	197-200	46
Milk River Agency, 1870-74	1870-74	Montana	490-500	99
Minnesota Superintendency, 1849-56	1849-56	Minnesota	428	97
Mission Agency, 1865-71, 1873-80	1865-80	California	40-52	19

241

JURISDICTION AND YEARS OF OPERATION	YEARS OF FILING	FILE HEADING	REEL NO.	PAGE
Montana Superintendency, 1864-73	1864-80	Montana	488-518	99
Moqui Pueblo Agency, 1869-80	1869-80	Arizona	3-23	11

N

JURISDICTION AND YEARS OF OPERATION	YEARS OF FILING	FILE HEADING	REEL NO.	PAGE
Navajo Agency, 1852-80	1852-80	New Mexico	546-582	110
Neah Bay Agency, 1861-80	1861-80	Washington	907-920	193
Nebraska Agencies, 1876-80	1876-80	Nebraska	519-529	103
Neosho Agency, 1837-74	1831-75	Neosho	530-537	106
Nevada Agency, 1861-80	1861-80	Nevada	583-597	108
Nevada Superintendency, 1861-80	1861-80	Nevada	538-545	108
New Mexico Superintendency, 1850-74	1849-80	New Mexico	546-582	110
New York Agency, 1835-80	1829-80	New York	538-545	117
Nez Percé Agency, 1861-80	1861	Oregon	612	123
	1861-63	Washington	907-908	193
	1863-80	Idaho	337-353	74
Nome Lackee Agency, 1854-60	1854-60	California	33-37	19
Northeastern Oregon Agency. *See* Warm Springs Agency				
Northern Agency, 1834-37	1834-37	Fort Leavenworth	300-301	64
Northern District (California), 1860-64	1860-64	California	37-39	19
Northern Superintendency, 1851-76	1851-76	Northern	598-600	118

O

JURISDICTION AND YEARS OF OPERATION	YEARS OF FILING	FILE HEADING	REEL NO.	PAGE
Ohio Agency, 1831-43	1831-43	Ohio	601-603	120
Omaha Agency, 1856-79	1856-76	Omaha	604-606	122
	1876-79	Nebraska	519-527	103
Omaha and Winnebago Agency, 1879-80	1879-80	Nebraska	525-529	103
Oregon Superintendency, 1848-73	1842-80	Oregon	607-630	123
Oregon and Washington Superintendency. *See* Oregon Superintendency				
Osage Agency, 1807-51, 1874-80	1824-53	Osage	631-633	130
	1874-80	Osage	633-641	130
Osage River Agency, 1837-71	1824-71	Osage River	642-651	132
Otoe Agency, 1856-80	1856-76	Otoe	652-655	133
	1876-80	Nebraska	519-529	103
Otoe and Missouri Agency. *See* Otoe Agency				
Ottawa Agency (Kansas), 1863-67	1863-73	Ottawa	656-658	134
Ottawa of Maumee Subagency (Ohio), ca. 1827-36	1827-36	Saginaw	745	154
	1827-36	Michigan	419-422	94

JURISDICTION AND YEARS OF OPERATION	YEARS OF FILING	FILE HEADING	REEL NO.	PAGE
Ottawa, Shawnee and other Indians, Subagency for, 1834-35	1834-35	Fort Leavenworth	300	64

P

Papago Agency, 1864-65	1871-76	Arizona	4-17	11
Pawnee Agency, 1859-80	1859-80	Pawnee	659-669	136
Peoria Subagency, 1821-32	1824-32	Chicago	132	37
Pima Agency, 1859-60	1859-61	Pima	669	137
1875-80	1875-80	Arizona	13-28	11
Pima, Papago and Maricopa Agency. See Pima Agency, Gila River Agency				
Pine Ridge Agency. See Red Cloud Agency				
Piqua Agency, 1812-30	1824-30	Piqua	669	138
Pi-Ute Agency. See South East Nevada Agency				
Ponca Agency, 1859-80	1859-80	Ponca	670-677	139
Port Orford Agency, 1854, 1856	1854-56	Oregon	608-609	123
Potawatomi Agency, 1851-80	1851-80	Potawatomi	678-695	140
Pottawatomie Subagency, 1847-48	1847-48	Fort Leavenworth	302	64
Prairie du Chien Agency, 1807-40	1824-42	Prairie du Chien	696-702	142
Provo Agency, 1855-61	1855-61	Utah	897-900	190
Pueblo Agency, 1854-80	1854-80	New Mexico	547-582	110
Puget Sound District Agency, 1851-62	1851-53	Oregon	607-608	123
	1853-57	Washington	907	193
	1857-61	Oregon	610-612	123
	1861-62	Washington	907	193
Puyallup Agency, 1856-80	1856-57	Washington	907	193
	1857-61	Oregon	610-612	123
	1861-80	Washington	907-920	193
Pyramid Lake Agency, 1871	1871	Nevada	539	108

Q

Quapaw Agency, 1871-80	1871-80	Quapaw	703-713	145
Quinaielt Agency, 1861-80	1861-80	Washington	907-920	193

R

Raccoon River Agency, 1843-45	1843-45	Raccoon River	714	147
Red Cloud Agency, 1871-80	1871-80	Red Cloud	715-726	147
Red Lake Agency, 1873-79	1873-79	Chippewa	160-167	41
Red River Agency, 1821-30	1824-30	Red River	727	149
	1830-42	Caddo	31	18
Rio Verde Agency, 1872-75	1872-75	Arizona	5-15	11
Rock Island Agency. See Sac and Fox Agency				
Rock River Subagency, 1831-34	1831-34	Prairie du Chien	696-697	142

JURISDICTION AND YEARS OF OPERATION	YEARS OF FILING	FILE HEADING	REEL NO.	PAGE
Southeastern District Agency (Oregon), 1854-56	1854-56	Oregon	608-609	123
Southern Agency. *See* Choctaw Agency				
Southern Apache Agency, 1852-77	1852-77	New Mexico	546-572	110
Southern District (California), 1860-64	1860-64	California	37-39	19
Southern District Agency (Oregon). *See* Rogue River Agency				
Southern District Agency (Washington). *See* Columbia River District Agency				
Southern Superintendency, 1851-70	1851-71	Southern	933-939	174
Southern Ute Agency, 1877-80	1877-80	Colorado	207-214	46
Southwestern District Agency (Oregon). *See* Rogue River Agency				
Spanish Fork Agency, 1859-65	1859-65	Utah	899-901	190
Spotted Tail Agency, 1875-80	1875-80	Spotted Tail Agency	840-845	176
Standing Rock Agency, 1875-80	1875-80	Standing Rock	846-852	177
Stray Winnebago and Pota-watomi Indians in Wisconsin, Special Agency for, 1864-70	1864-70	Winnebago	937-942	205

T

JURISDICTION AND YEARS OF OPERATION	YEARS OF FILING	FILE HEADING	REEL NO.	PAGE
Tejon Agency, 1855-60	1855-60	California	34-37	19
Texas Agency, 1847-59	1847-59	Texas	858-861	179
Texas Superintendency, 1859	1859	Texas	861	179
Tucson Agency, 1857-61	1857-61	New Mexico	548-550	110
Tulalip Agency, 1861-80	1861-80	Washington	907-920	193
Tule River Agency, 1864-80	1864-80	California	39-52	19
Turkey River Subagency, 1840-48	1840-42	Prairie du Chien	700-702	142
	1842	Winnebago	931	205
	1842-46	Turkey River	862-864	180
	1846-48	Winnebago	931-932	205

U

JURISDICTION AND YEARS OF OPERATION	YEARS OF FILING	FILE HEADING	REEL NO.	PAGE
Uintah Valley Agency, 1865-80	1865-80	Utah	901-906	190
Umatilla Agency, 1861-80	1861-62	Washington	907	193
	1862-80	Oregon	613-630	123
Union Agency, 1874-78	1875-80	Union	865-887	181
Upper Arkansas Agency, 1855-74	1855-74	Upper Arkansas	878-882	182
Upper Missouri Agency, 1819-74	1824-74	Upper Missouri	883-888	184
Upper Platte Agency, 1846-69	1846-70	Upper Platte	889-896	188
Upper Sioux Agency. *See* St. Peters Agency				

JURISDICTION AND YEARS OF OPERATION	YEARS OF FILING	FILE HEADING	REEL NO.	PAGE
Upper (Ute) Agency. *See* White River Agency (Colorado)				
Utah Agency, 1853-62	1853-62	New Mexico	546-551	110
Utah Superintendency, 1850-70	1849-80	Utah	897-906	190
Utilla Agency. *See* Warm Springs Agency				

W

JURISDICTION AND YEARS OF OPERATION	YEARS OF FILING	FILE HEADING	REEL NO.	PAGE
Walker River Agency, 1871	1871	Nevada	539	108
Warm Springs Agency, 1851-80	1851-80	Oregon	607-630	123
Washington East of the Cascades Agency, 1857-61	1857-61	Oregon	610-612	123
Washington Superintendency, 1853-57, 1861-74	1853-57	Washington	907	193
	1857-61	Oregon	610-612	123
	1861-74	Washington	907-913	193
Western Shoshone Agency, 1878-80	1878-80	Nevada	543-545	108
Western Superintendency, 1834-51	1832-51	Western	921-924	201
Whetstone Agency, 1869-74	1869-70	Upper Platte	894-896	188
	1871-74	Whetstone	925-927	202
White Earth Agency. *See* Chippewa Agency				
White River Agency (Colorado) 1869-79	1869-79	Colorado	200-212	46
White River Agency (Dakota). *See* Lower Brulé Agency				
Wichita Agency, 1857-78	1857-78	Wichita	928-930	203
Winnebago Agency, 1848-79	1826-76	Winnebago	931-947	205
	1876-80	Nebraska	519-529	103
Wisconsin Superintendency, 1836-48	1836-48	Wisconsin	948-949	208
Wyandot Subagency (Ohio), 1832-42. *See* Ohio Agency				
Wyandot Subagency (Kansas River), 1843-51	1839-63	Wyandot	950-952	210
	1870-72	Wyandot	951	210
Wyoming Superintendency, 1869-70	1869-80	Wyoming	953-958	211

Y

JURISDICTION AND YEARS OF OPERATION	YEARS OF FILING	FILE HEADING	REEL NO.	PAGE
Yakima Agency, 1859-80	1859-61	Oregon	611-612	123
	1861-80	Washington	907-920	193
Yankton Agency, 1859-80	1859-76	Yankton	959-962	213
	1876-80	Dakota	256-273	57